PUBLIC SPACE IN METROPOLITAN BARCELONA

INTERVENTIONS AND CONVERSATIONS

2018-2022

We are pleased to present PUBLIC SPACE IN METROPOLITAN BARCELONA: INTERVENTIONS AND CONVERSATIONS, 2018-2022, the sixth book in the collection published regularly by the Barcelona Metropolitan Area (AMB). It includes a selection of public space projects carried out in the metropolitan area over the past five years. These projects were built to move the city forward in line with new perspectives, but they follow the same principles that have brought us to where we are today.

After more than 35 years of working, steadfastly and persistently, towards a high-quality public space that is both the place where social conflicts are revealed, and the place where we can implement the tools for organising, uniting and democratising the territory and for tackling the consequences of climate change, we stand firm in our desire to make the right to the city a reality.

The approval by the EU of the New European Bauhaus initiative highlights the future challenges facing architecture and cities in the 21st century, following years of intense change and situations of acute social need: an economic crisis, a pandemic, and a war that, accompanied by an energy crisis, demands we make a determined commitment to renewable energies, so we can turn adversity into opportunity.

We must maintain our commitment to designing and building a liveable metropolis, taking advantage of this opportunity to make it more sustainable, comfortable and equitable: a city of cities where every neighbourhood has quality facilities, infrastructures and services.

The AMB is a benchmark in the construction of metropolitan public space as a result of its accumulated experience, which will be key to the success of finalising the urban model derived from the new Metropolitan Urban Master Plan – the plan that will make the metropolis of Barcelona more equitable, more socially just and more environmentally sustainable.

We invite you to explore and enjoy this book.

ADA COLAU
President of the Barcelona Metropolitan Area

ANTONIO BALMÓN
Executive Vice-President of the Barcelona Metropolitan Area

PUBLIC SPACE IN METROPOLITAN BARCELONA: INTERVENTIONS AND CONVERSATIONS, 2018-2022 is the sixth book in the "Metropolitan Spaces" collection. We published the first one, the red one, in 1999 and it spanned the previous 10 years. Since then, at a rate of one every four years (give or take a year) the green, grey, black and silver volumes have appeared.

As is to be expected, the collection has seen changes over time: the categories and the number of projects are different; the theoretical contextualisation and even the target audience have shifted. While at first it was directed at specialists, in the latest instalments we have tried to attract any readers who have an interest in public space. It has always been a book for an international audience, which is why from the beginning the texts have been published in several languages and, since the previous edition, there have been versions in Catalan, Spanish and English.

Despite the collection's evolution, over 33 years its essence has remained the same: the books are architecture catalogues that compile the public space projects developed by the AMB that are considered to be most emblematic of each period, for one reason or another.

After the silver book, which marked a turning point in the collection, it was tempting to take a different direction, breaking with the idea of a catalogue, but we believe that the value of the collection goes beyond purely architectural aspects: the projects offer a portrayal of the inhabitants of the metropolis, and they reveal the aspirations of the technical teams who design the spaces where we all interact.

The white book, therefore, maintains that same spirit. It follows the same structure as the previous ones and groups the works by type of space: park space, which encompasses green infrastructure interventions; water space, which groups together projects carried out both along the coast and on riverbanks; covered space, which includes facilities, and which we have divided into two parts to highlight the growing importance of building rehabilitation; urban space, which includes large-scale transformations and small interventions that make life easier for people, and mobility space, which refers to projects in which sustainable mobility is the driver (or the core).

Despite this continuity, the book incorporates three fundamental innovations with respect to the previous edition. The first is the aim of showing a larger number of projects withing the same number of pages, by reducing the information to the essentials.

The second is the incorporation of additional information for some of the projects: the black boxes scattered across some of the pages, which we call a "zoom" view, let us approach certain projects from a different perspective, connecting them with other AMB projects or studies that affect the territory. Because we believe that a cross-cutting vision, so difficult to achieve in practice, provides a change of perspective and a shift in scale, and that "embracing everything" (from drafting the Metropolitan Urban Master Plan to publishing this book) is what gives meaning to our work – which is none other than working with the metropolis we have to create the metropolis we dream of.

Also, within the framework of that cross-cutting perspective and given the context of the projects that are published here, we aimed to collect three broader points of view: the global vision of the metropolitan territory, by Ramon M. Torra; the framework for the development of the new Metropolitan Urban Master Plan, by Xavier Mariño; and the future challenges when it comes to continuing to build public space, by Albert Gassull.

The third new aspect involved turning the introductory texts for each of the six chapters into conversations, a more enjoyable format for readers to help our message reaches the widest possible audience. Each chapter begins with two interviews: with a professional from the AMB who participates in carrying out projects; and with a professional who analyses the same questions from a different point of view, based on experience in other public administrations or in professional practice. These conversations were made possible by the invaluable participation of Anatxu Zabalbeascoa, a journalist and art historian who writes and reflects on architecture and design.

Given a series of defined and structured contents, the team at Actar, led by Ricardo Devesa, Marta Bugés and Ramon Prat, has helped us put together an attractive and interesting book that reflects the public space projects carried out by the AMB during the period 2018-2022.

Finally, we would like to express our thanks for all the help, suggestions, comments and adaptations that accompanied us throughout the preparation of this book. For our part, we have tried to ensure that the contents are as rigorous, concise and attractive as possible, that the images and blueprints reflect the intention of the works, and that the project reports construct narratives and highlight the fundamental values of each project.

Our work ends here and the book now belongs to its readers, who will give it its fair value by reading it, leafing through it, scanning the QR codes and keeping it on their shelves with the other volumes in the collection.

NOEMÍ MARTÍNEZ
LUISA SOLSONA
Design, Communication
and Documentation Section

ISABEL CLOS
Editorial Management Office

INDEX

Presentation   3
Ada Colau, Antonio Balmón

Editorial Note   4
Noemí Martínez,
Luisa Solsona, Isabel Clos

Public Space in   10
Metropolitan Barcelona
Ramon M. Torra

Public Space Projects   14
and PDUM Plan

Towards the Metropolitan   16
Area of the Future
Xavier Mariño

Overview of the Period   290
2018-2022

Challenges   292
Albert Gassull

Metropolitan Spaces   296
Collection 1989-2022

Organisation Chart   298

Technical Team   300

Credits   302

PARK SPACE   22

Conversation with Imma Jansana   23
Anatxu Zabalbeascoa

Green Infrastructure, PDUM   28

Conversation with Cati Montserrat   30
Anatxu Zabalbeascoa

Alps Avenue and Rosa Sensat Park   34
Cornellà de Llobregat
   Cornellà Natura

Can Bada Park   40
Badalona
   Sustainability Protocol

Tortuguer Stream   44
Ripollet
   Network of Metropolitan Parks (XPM)

Classroom K   48
Santa Coloma de Gramenet

Playground in Les Planes Park   50
L'Hospitalet de Llobregat

La Costeta Park   52
Begues

Bosc de Can Gorgs Park   57
Barberà del Vallès
   Improvements in Biodiversity

Can Solei and Ca l'Arnús Park   60
Badalona

WATER SPACE   64

Conversation with Iñaki Alday   65
and Margarita Jover
Anatxu Zabalbeascoa

Water Spaces, PDUM   70

Conversation with Antoni Farrero   72
Anatxu Zabalbeascoa

Riera d'en Font Park   77
Montgat

Dunes   81
Metropolitan beaches
   Learning in the Network

TIV_AMB   84
Metropolitan beaches

AMB Shade Pergola   86
Metropolitan beaches
   Beach Furniture Catalogue

Signage   88
Metropolitan beaches

Hanging Footbridge over the Ripoll River   91
Barberà del Vallès

Footbridge over Comerç Stream   94
Sant Feliu de Llobregat
   Llobregat River Park

Floodable Ford on the Ripoll River   96
Ripollet

Floodable Ford on the Llobregat River   98
Various municipalities

Regeneration of the Riverside   100
Molins de Rei

Access to the Beaches   102
Viladecans

Regeneration of the River Environment   104
Sant Andreu de la Barca

RENOVATED SPACE — 106

Conversation with David Chipperfield — 107
Anatxu Zabalbeascoa

Cultural Heritage, PDUM — 112

Conversation with Carlos Llinás — 114
Anatxu Zabalbeascoa

Palmira Domènech Civic Centre — 118
El Prat de Llobregat

El Molí Library — 124
Molins de Rei
SBAU

Roser Cabanas Music School — 132
Cornellà de Llobregat

Ca l'Altisent and Font del Rector Gardens — 135
Sant Climent de Llobregat

Unió de Cooperadors — 140
Gavà

Sant Andreu Market — 143
Barcelona
Facilities Finder

La Nau Youth and Arts Centre — 148
Barberà del Vallès

COVERED SPACE — 150

Conversation with Josep Ferrando — 151
Anatxu Zabalbeascoa

Level of provisions for urban fabrics, PDUM — 156

Conversation with Oriol Ribera — 158
Anatxu Zabalbeascoa

Virgínia Amposta Cultural and Civic Centre — 164
Sant Vicenç dels Horts

La Guàrdia Civic Centre — 169
Sant Vicenç dels Horts

Ricard Ginebreda Sports Area — 173
Molins de Rei

Teresa Pàmies Library — 180
Cornellà de Llobregat
Signage

Clara Campoamor Library — 186
Cornellà de Llobregat
Signage

Can Xarau Sports Complex — 192
Cerdanyola del Vallès

Sports Courts — 194
Pallejà

Marcel·lí Moragas Sports Pitch — 198
Gavà

URBAN SPACE — 200

Conversation with Beth Galí — 201
Anatxu Zabalbeascoa

Centres in the Metropolitan Area, PDUM — 206

Conversation with Claudi Aguiló Riu
and Eva Pagés — 208
Anatxu Zabalbeascoa

Salzereda Avenue — 212
Santa Coloma de Gramenet
Pinta Verda Plan

Streets of the Historic Centre — 218
Castellbisbal

Església Square — 222
El Papiol

Matas Street — 225
Tiana

Environs of Torre Balldovina Museum — 228
Santa Coloma de Gramenet

Cerdanyola Avenue — 232
Sant Cugat del Vallès

Green Space on Claverol Street — 234
Sant Vicenç dels Horts

Access to the Railway Station — 236
Barberà del Vallès

Joan Salvat-Papasseit Gardens — 238
El Prat de Llobregat

Andalusia Street — 241
Castelldefels
A Model for Open Spaces

Azorín Street and Square — 244
Badalona

Francesc Macià Square — 246
Sant Feliu de Llobregat

MOBILITY SPACE — 248

Conversation with Paul Lecroart — 249
Anatxu Zabalbeascoa

Active Mobility Network, PDUM — 254

Conversation with Javier Ortigosa — 256
Anatxu Zabalbeascoa

Pere IV Street — 260
Barcelona

Cycling Connection — 266
Various municipalities
Metropolis of Avenues

Llorenç Serra Boulevard — 272
Santa Coloma de Gramenet
Bicivia

Access to Bètica Street — 275
Badia del Vallès
Metropolitan Passages

Connectivity in Mas Rampinyo Neighbourhood — 279
Montcada i Reixac
MiR Urban Planning Model

Access to Ciutat Cooperativa — 282
Sant Boi de Llobregat

Access to Central Park — 284
Sant Andreu de la Barca

La Clota Street under the Highway — 286
Cerdanyola del Vallès

Car Park in the Cemetery Area — 288
Santa Coloma de Cervelló

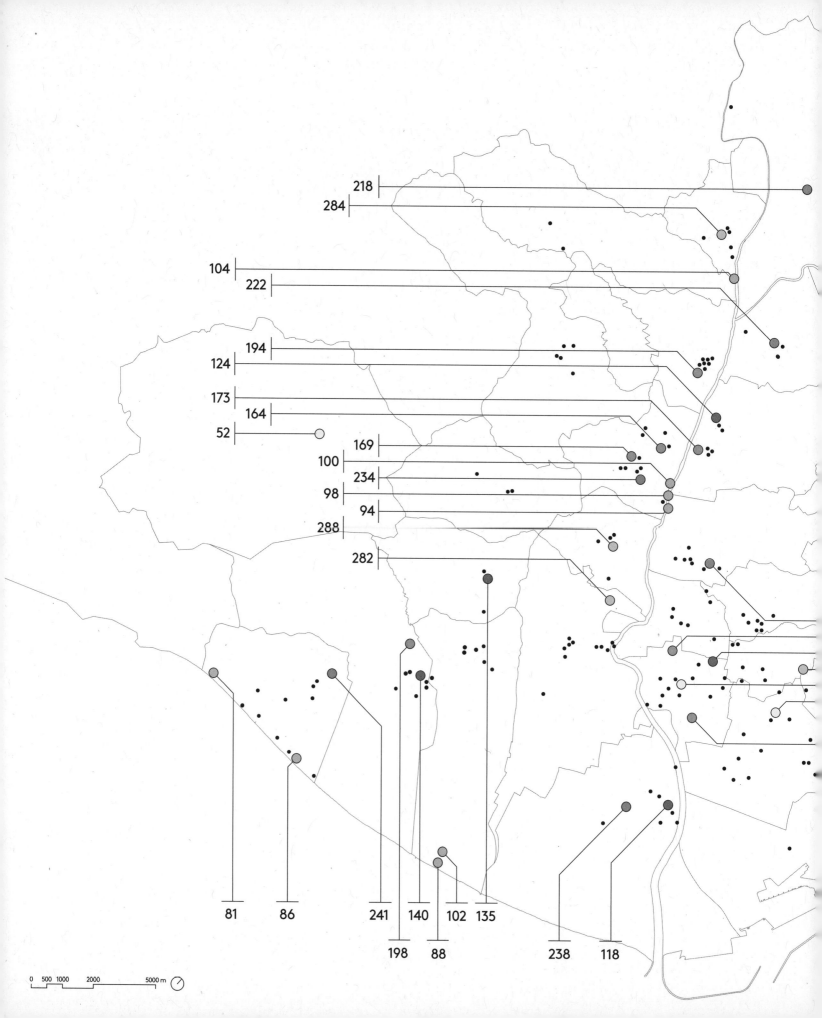

218
284
104
222
194
124
173
164
52
169
100
234
98
94
288
282

81   86   241 140 102 135

198   88   238 118

0 500 1000   2000   5000 m

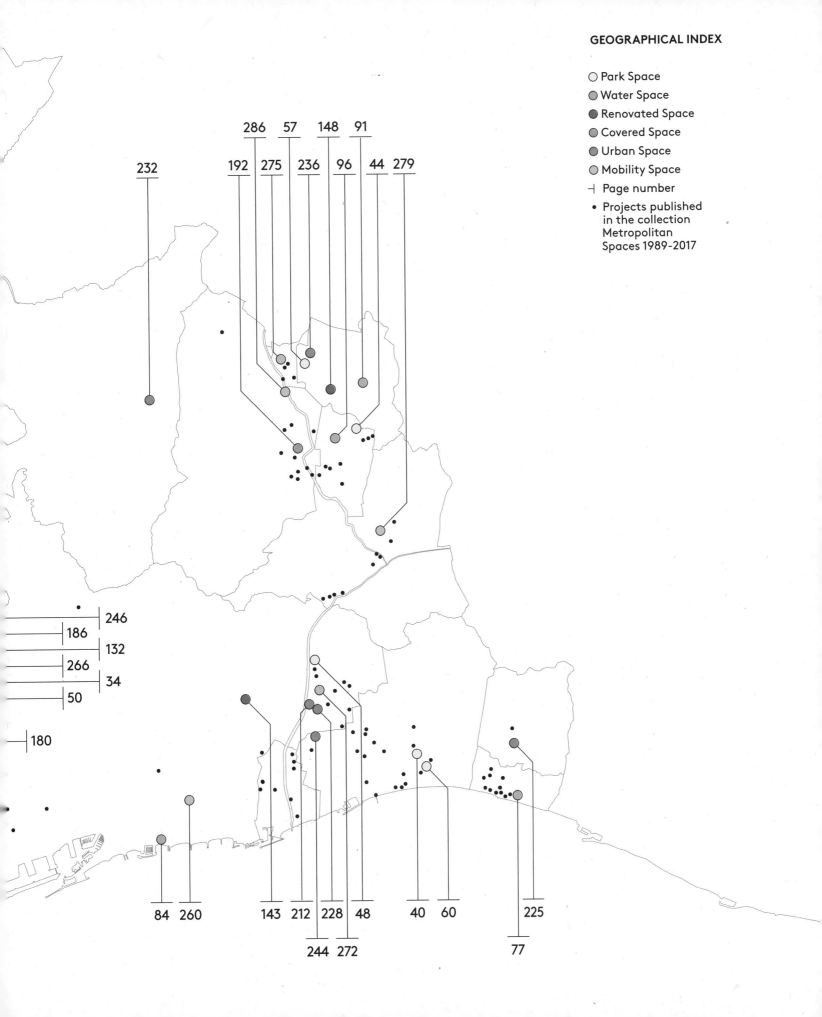

GEOGRAPHICAL INDEX

○ Park Space
◐ Water Space
● Renovated Space
◑ Covered Space
◒ Urban Space
◔ Mobility Space
⊣ Page number
• Projects published
in the collection
Metropolitan
Spaces 1989-2017

232

286 57 148 91

192 275 236 96 44 279

246
186
132
266
34
50

180

84 260 143 212 228 48 40 60 225

244 272 77

In a world where more than half of the population is currently urban, there can be no doubt that the future of the planet depends on the transformative capacity of cities. In these complex entities, public space, which belongs to everyone, is the quintessential democratic space. It defines and identifies collectivity and is a meeting point for citizens; it is a space that promotes social cohesion and coexistence. In the development of contemporary cities, public space is therefore the element that provides structure and internal consistency. It helps alleviate social inequalities and contributes to extending the same urban quality to every part of the metropolis, however large or small, central or peripheral.

In the first quarter of the 21st century, every aspect of society has become increasingly complex, especially in recent years. The health crisis caused by the COVID-19 pandemic has been compounded by the energy crisis resulting from the war in Ukraine, which has contributed to further exacerbating the climate crisis and has led society to re-evaluate many aspects of our behaviour. To address the new challenges facing urban environments, European institutions have launched several initiatives, such as the European Green Deal, pursuing climate neutrality for Europe by 2050, and the New Leipzig Charter, associated with the European Urban Agenda 2030, which highlights the transformative power of cities.

Within this framework of initiatives to complement and drive the growth of cities, the New European Bauhaus (NEB) aims to add a tangible, cultural dimension to the European Green Deal. Taking inspiration from the spirit of the 20th-century Bauhaus, it seeks to improve the lives of the population through actions in different fields that are broadly visible – in buildings, public space, fashion and furniture – while promoting a new lifestyle that combines good design with innovative and sustainable solutions to contribute to decarbonisation while remaining inclusive and affordable.

This European initiative is aimed very directly at all the actors in the territory – professionals, economic agents and public administrations – so that they can promote architecture and public space design rooted in sustainability, aesthetics and social inclusion. In addition to creating a space for reflection to imagine a more sustainable and inclusive way of life in Europe, the NEB supports change by providing access to various financing instruments made available to public administrations by the European Union. The FEDER funds and the Next Generation EU funds offer financial support for projects committed to the ecological transition and the digital transformation of society.

Given that all these challenges have a major effect on the territory, the field of architecture and construction is also spearheading a shift in their objectives and methods to help control, mitigate and redirect some of the most negative consequences of climate change. Aware of construction's role in water and energy consumption and in the emission of greenhouse gases, a commitment is being made to the decarbonisation of materials and construction processes. Other goals include a focus on circularity and bioclimatic strategies which, together with more efficient building services systems, make it possible to reduce the energy and water demand from buildings and public spaces.

Public Space in Metropolitan Barcelona

Ramon M. Torra

Architect. General Manager, AMB

[1] Law 9/2022, dated 14 June, on the quality of architecture, approved by the Spanish Parliament; and Law 12/2017, dated 6 July, on architecture, approved by the Catalan Parliament.

In the context of a society with an increasing interest in participating in public space design processes to ensure they are sustainable and equitable, aside from the NEB and the new energy efficiency directive for buildings being debated in the European Parliament, individual laws[1] have been passed in Spain and Catalonia to preserve and promote the quality of architecture, to regulate contracts involving a jury, and to promote communication to make the public more aware of architecture and its values.

In keeping with the evolution and challenges in the European context, metropolitan Barcelona today is a complex and diverse reality that includes 36 municipalities with their own identity. The area is home to more than 3.3 million people, in a natural environment defined and bounded by two rivers (the Llobregat and the Besòs), the coastal mountain system (the Coastal Range, the Marina range and the Garraf Massif), and more than 40 kilometres of Mediterranean coastline. As a contemporary metropolis, the city is not just its highly dense built environment: it also includes the natural spaces and territorial open spaces, which are an important economic asset and which cover more than half of the region. In that sense, the city can be understood based on its green infrastructure, with the promotion of a new paradigm for naturalising urban spaces – rather than renaturalising, since natural growth is often promoted in deeply urbanised places, where vegetation has long since disappeared or has a very residual importance.

One of the global challenges that is directly affecting the metropolitan area of Barcelona is how to address some of the consequences of climate change – rising sea levels, an increase in the frequency of storms, more prolonged periods of drought, increasingly extreme temperatures, etc. – while making the city more resilient and adaptable. And here open spaces play a key role: they are the most severely affected by the consequences of climate change, but they also house the most potential for the urban ecosystem to adapt to the new circumstances. They are part of the green infrastructure that can be transformed to build a new urban model. This model aims to develop a city that is more permeable in several ways: by incrementing the area of land that is not asphalted or paved, so rainwater can infiltrate more easily; and by creating natural spaces both within buildings (courtyards, green roofs, etc.) and in the spaces between them (streets, squares, etc.).

With the aim of adapting to and mitigating the negative effects of climate change that occur in the territory under its purview, the Barcelona Metropolitan Area (AMB) works transversally within all its areas and services to guarantee a more liveable and ecologically connected city, where sustainability and equity are the common thread – a city where green spaces contribute to reducing the heat island effect and also to improving air quality and, therefore, quality of life for the population.

Stabilising the coastline, restoring the ecology and landscape of riparian spaces, managing woodlands sustainably, and managing the water cycle are just some of the lines of intervention intended to restore and enhance our green infrastructure. No doubt, the metropolitan coast is where the devastation caused by climate change is most evident. The coastline has receded in several places due to erosive processes resulting from episodes of heavy rain and wind. The loss of sand on our beaches is also evident – to the point that some have actually disappeared – and it is absolutely necessary to stabilise them both with interventions on the seabed and by promoting the natural regeneration of dunes.[2]

[2] In 2022, the project to improve and protect the dune systems on the metropolitan beaches south of Barcelona won the New European Bauhaus Prize in the category "Reconnecting with Nature".

On the beds of rivers and streams, ecological and landscape restoration is essential to prevent and overcome the damage caused by climate change. On the one hand, nature-based solutions are implemented, which contribute to the management and maintenance of these water-related open spaces. On the other, the relationship of public spaces on both sides of the riverbed is promoted through the construction of low-water crossings that support the mobility of people without affecting the ecological connectivity and the natural evolution of the river courses.

In open spaces, extreme temperatures, a lack of rain and the consequent depletion of water in aquifers endangers biodiversity and the sustainability of ecosystems, while increasing the risk of fire in forested areas. Here, as in the built city, the comprehensive management of the water cycle is taking on increasing relevance: we need to harness the entire volume of precipitation by channelling it into aquifers or retaining it and reusing it for irrigation, as opposed to letting it flow out into the sea.

In the public spaces of the built city, the consequences of climate change are twofold. On the one hand, the spaces must be planned so that they can withstand periods of drought: they must guarantee the infiltration and collection of rainwater so that irrigation systems can be supplied without the need to connect to the network of drinking water. On the other, it is necessary to provide the population, especially the most vulnerable sectors, with a network of climate shelters to protect them from the thermal stress caused by high temperatures. These shelters can be located both in public facilities – with climate control or cross ventilation to ensure comfortable temperatures – or in outdoor spaces, where comfort conditions can be generated using abundant vegetation and other natural methods to help regulate temperatures.

Since the late 1980s, the AMB has been consolidating a "way of building public space" based on experience and tenacity in the application of a series of criteria and principles. The method begins with a respect for the place and for the needs of the specific environment (in both natural and social terms), and it is founded on the understanding that public works must serve as a model, contributing to social and territorial cohesion not only through theory but through practice. The criteria that might previously have drawn on intuition and exploration have now, within the framework of a new global reality, been consolidated and cemented into fundamental tools for designing the different elements that make up public space.

One of those tools is the *Sustainability Protocol* implemented by the AMB in the works it designs and builds.[3] In this way, it can generate a more direct impact on enhancing the built environment and preserving its heritage by giving it a second life while, at the same time, promoting strategies to mitigate the effects of climate change: improving resource management, reducing the demand for water and energy, and promoting biodiversity, sustainable mobility, renewable energies and urban renaturalisation.

[3] *AMB. Sustainability Protocol Environmental Criteria for Projects and Works (2021).*

Along the same line of change and adaptation to the new reality, the Metropolitan Urban Master Plan (PDUM), which has just received initial approval, lays the groundwork for defining the metropolitan city of the future, this city of cities that is much more than the sum of 36 municipalities. The new plan endorses a paradigm shift that is derived, among other things, from the implementation of the United Nations' sustainable development goals and the application of international urban agendas. This new paradigm begins from the territory's capacities to find solutions to the population's demands and mitigate the consequences of climate change, a plan in which "redoing" is more important than "doing".

The public space of metropolitan Barcelona – parks, coast, river spaces, facilities (both new and renovated buildings), and urban leisure spaces (squares, pedestrian streets), spaces for sustainable mobility, and spaces for commerce and other economic activities – is increasingly being designed to be flexible and adaptable to changes in society and in the natural environment, with major lessons learned during the COVID-19 health crisis and the growing issues derived from the climate emergency.

Working on all the different scales – from territorial planning and the landscape to the design and construction of furniture for a library or a corner in a park – with strategies and projects that overlap and complement one another, the AMB aims to continue building a metropolitan city that can adapt to the changing needs of society and with our sights set on the future. Projects must be designed to respond to citizens' demands, they must be high quality and beautiful to contribute to the well-being of society as a whole, they must be proportionate to public financial resources that need to be managed rationally and efficiently, and they must be devised from the outset accounting for their management and maintenance so they will be sustainable throughout their useful life.

CONNECTION BETWEEN PUBLIC SPACE PROJECTS AND THE CONCEPTS FROM THE METROPOLITAN URBAN MASTER PLAN

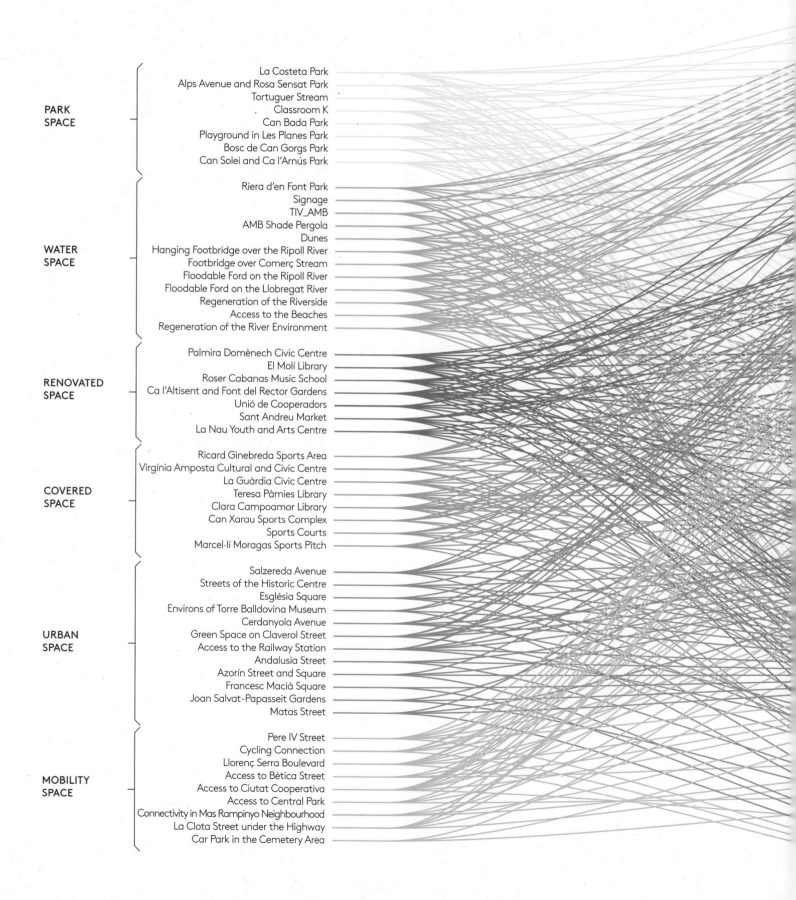

PARK SPACE
- La Costeta Park
- Alps Avenue and Rosa Sensat Park
- Tortuguer Stream
- Classroom K
- Can Bada Park
- Playground in Les Planes Park
- Bosc de Can Gorgs Park
- Can Solei and Ca l'Arnús Park

WATER SPACE
- Riera d'en Font Park
- Signage
- TIV_AMB
- AMB Shade Pergola
- Dunes
- Hanging Footbridge over the Ripoll River
- Footbridge over Comerç Stream
- Floodable Ford on the Ripoll River
- Floodable Ford on the Llobregat River
- Regeneration of the Riverside
- Access to the Beaches
- Regeneration of the River Environment

RENOVATED SPACE
- Palmira Domènech Civic Centre
- El Molí Library
- Roser Cabanas Music School
- Ca l'Altisent and Font del Rector Gardens
- Unió de Cooperadors
- Sant Andreu Market
- La Nau Youth and Arts Centre

COVERED SPACE
- Ricard Ginebreda Sports Area
- Virgínia Amposta Cultural and Civic Centre
- La Guàrdia Civic Centre
- Teresa Pàmies Library
- Clara Campoamor Library
- Can Xarau Sports Complex
- Sports Courts
- Marcel·lí Moragas Sports Pitch

URBAN SPACE
- Salzereda Avenue
- Streets of the Historic Centre
- Església Square
- Environs of Torre Balldovina Museum
- Cerdanyola Avenue
- Green Space on Claverol Street
- Access to the Railway Station
- Andalusia Street
- Azorín Street and Square
- Francesc Macià Square
- Joan Salvat-Papasseit Gardens
- Matas Street

MOBILITY SPACE
- Pere IV Street
- Cycling Connection
- Llorenç Serra Boulevard
- Access to Bètica Street
- Access to Ciutat Cooperativa
- Access to Central Park
- Connectivity in Mas Rampinyo Neighbourhood
- La Clota Street under the Highway
- Car Park in the Cemetery Area

16	Blue structure		Metropolitan green infrastructure
5	Core areas	Large open spaces	
6	Agricultural plain		
5	Agroforestry mosaic		
19	Structuring parks	Urban green structure	
18	Green axes		
11	Paths	Metropolitan roads	Urban and social infrastructure
5	Metropolitan avenues		
	Streets		
	Connectors		
14	Structuring facilities		
7	Decompressing		
20	Intensifying		
21	Diversifying		
21	Renaturalising		
28	Providing facilities		Urban strategies
26	Providing open spaces		
10	Restoring		
32	Renovating		
12	Self-sufficiency		
11	Vallès		
13	Vall Baixa and Ordal		
12	Delta		Functional areas
22	Continuous city		

The metropolitan city of Barcelona enjoys great prestige internationally, the result of multiple factors that make it a modern and cosmopolitan city: its unique territorial surroundings, its historical and artistic heritage, its urban quality, its first-class facilities, its innovation and productive fabric, and its cultural offering, among others. But we have to be on the alert because, in a global world that is changing at breakneck speed, there is a lot of competition between cities. If we hope to continue as a benchmark metropolis on a global scale, we have to evolve and adapt to respond to all kinds of challenges and opportunities, both present and future, while also preserving and enhancing the existing values of our Mediterranean city, which set it apart and make it unique.

With a peculiar orography that is both a feature and a determining factor, the metropolis of Barcelona is made up of 36 heterogeneous municipalities, all with strong local identities. It has an enviable geographical location that makes it the southern door to Europe, in an area that is strategic for the continent's economic development – the Mediterranean corridor – which gives it a great potential for networking with the main capitals of the world.

It is a complex and highly consolidated metropolis that must respond to global challenges, which also have strong local implications, in turn: mitigation of and adaptation to climate change, the energy transition, technological disruption and the new demands of society. It is a metropolis formed by cities that have to look beyond their own borders to understand that the value of the whole is more than the sum of the parts. And we need to foster a collective awareness to guarantee and reinforce the metropolitan vision without sacrificing the diversity that characterises it and sets it apart.

With the approval of Law 31/2010, establishing the Barcelona Metropolitan Area, a metropolitan administration was created that recovered urban planning powers – a power that had not existed since the dissolution of the Barcelona Metropolitan Corporation in 1987. The drafting of the Metropolitan Urban Master Plan (PDUM) and the Metropolitan Urban Development Plan (POUMet) are the most evident examples of this recovered competency. These two instruments are meant to organise the metropolitan territory in the coming decades, replacing – after more than 45 years and more than 1,200 modifications – the General Metropolitan Plan of 1976, a plan that was a fundamental element in the construction of the current metropolitan area, a benchmark in the field of urban planning that has left an unquestionable legacy, but which, today, shows clear signs of having run its course.

The 10 Major Objectives of the PDUM

We are currently involved in drafting the PDUM, the plan that will define the model for metropolitan urban development and will incorporate the diversity of the territory into a shared project. The plan will be ecologically sustainable, socially inclusive and cohesive, and economically efficient, with a clear principle to shape it: responding to the needs of the population based on what the territory can offer, on its capabilities. We are proposing a paradigm shift: it is a plan based on supply, as opposed to demand;

Towards the Metropolitan Area of the Future

Xavier Mariño

Director of the AMB Area for the Development of Urban Planning Policies

a plan based on adaptation, that is not an attempt to start from scratch, and that will make advances possible. The plan includes 10 major strategic objectives, aligned with the Sustainable Development Goals (SDGs) and urban agendas:

— Reinforcing metropolitan solidarity, addressing challenges and opportunities on a scale that reaches beyond the local perspective, and doing so with the cooperation of all the relevant city councils.

— Enhancing the metropolitan capital status, turning the metropolis of Barcelona into a hub that articulates the metropolitan region and the strengthens its position as capital of Catalonia, so that it can relate to and compete with the global system of cities drawing on its intrinsic qualities.

— Naturalising the territory by fostering the values of the biophysical matrix, rebuilding the green and blue metropolitan infrastructures to guarantee their continuity, while incorporating all those spaces that have environmental value and thus reinforcing their ecosystemic functions.

— Improving the efficiency of the urban metabolism and minimising environmental impact, reducing dependence on external resources and pursuing the containment of demand, circularity and the maximisation of local resources.

— Articulating the territory based on a polycentric structure intended to decongest the city centre and redistribute opportunities throughout the rest of the territory, blurring the boundaries between the centre and the periphery.

— Promoting sustainable mobility that rethinks transport infrastructures, guarantees the right to accessibility, makes a commitment to public transport and active mobility, ensures territorial continuity and the integration of infrastructures and recovers space for people and their social interaction.

— Promoting social cohesion through access to housing – especially affordable housing, to nearby, quality open spaces or green spaces, and to basic services and facilities.

— Restoring and recycling the urban fabrics, since land is a scarce resource and, therefore, priority must be given to actions within the consolidated fabric, while preserving its heritage and identity values.

— Increasing urban complexity and liveability and making a commitment to a vibrant, intense, inclusive and healthy city, where all daily needs can be met close at hand: in short, what is referred to as the "15-minute city".

— Promoting the competitiveness and sustainability of the metropolitan economy, providing the physical and infrastructural conditions for the development of a diverse and adaptable economic activity over time, with urban and social environments that allow for harnessing synergies and fostering processes of innovation.

The Plan addresses the various metropolitan realities from a general perspective, but with a cross-cutting logic – in which spatial, temporal and scale dimensions are fundamental – and it emphasises the intermediate scale characteristic of a supra-municipal interest, a scale that reinforces both local values and their relationship with the larger region.

In a dynamic and changeable metropolis that is constantly evolving, it can be difficult to identify and define the specific elements and areas where action must be taken. No doubt, it makes more sense to focus on the variable geometries that arise in response to the problem addressed or the specific goal being pursued. By focusing on the plan's proposals, and turning our attention towards the elements that are most emblematic of the process of rebuilding the metropolis, we can identify many that fall within the sequential logic of planning – design – execution – maintenance and monitoring, and other more specific, yet equally necessary, ones that respond to a logic of execution or even opportunity cost, and that are more independent and have a certain autonomy without detracting from the coherence of the whole.

In the process of defining the Plan, we begin with the metropolitan green infrastructure, one of the fundamental components in the configuration of the metropolitan area of the future, and we advance towards defining the characteristics of each space, and, finally, improving the environmental conditions of the urban fabric, moving sequentially through large open spaces, edge spaces, green structure, and the urban and social structures.

From Green Infrastructure to Large Open Spaces

The metropolitan green infrastructure includes those elements intended to guarantee the ecological functions of the territory's biophysical matrix and its adaptation to the effects of climate change. It includes all spaces with environmental value, regardless of their nature and origin, from large metropolitan open spaces (that include blue structure) to metropolitan green structure, that takes into account private urban green spaces, running through the edge spaces between the built city and natural spaces. This infrastructure combines a high level of biodiversity with the contribution of: environmental values, which maximise the contribution of ecosystem services; social values, through citizen empowerment rooted in education and enjoyment; and productive values, with a commitment to agricultural activity.

To fulfill them and maximise their functionality, the proposals contained in the PDUM aim to guarantee ecological continuity and promote diversity, enhancing all the uses and activities that galvanise the agroforestry mosaic, facilitating its management and maintenance and the prevention of natural risks, and identifying specific interventions necessary for its restoration.

The metropolitan open spaces that are not part of the blue structure – in other words, the large forests and agricultural spaces (Marina mountains, Collserola, Garraf-Ordal and the Baix Llobregat Agricultural Park), can be divided into four main categories: *core areas*, spaces that are removed from human pressures, with high biodiversity and internal connectivity, with the ability to spread these characteristics to their surroundings; *connectors*, strategic spaces that can help ensure the ecological connectivity of the whole; *agricultural flatlands*, areas that are home to professional agricultural and livestock activities of great strategic value, and the *agroforestry mosaic*, deteriorated or semi-abandoned areas, usually located in areas of contact with the urban fabric, where agricultural activity should be recovered.

The blue structure – which must guarantee the continuity of the territory's natural and productive cycles related to water, while ensuring connectivity throughout – is made up of the two large fluvial areas of the Llobregat and Besòs rivers, in addition to the streams, canals, wetlands and coastal areas, but also those areas that are strategic for the natural water cycle: the surfaces for runoff, for recharging groundwater, and for regulating large floods.

Projects and actions such as the adaptation of access to the beaches of La Pineda and La Murtra, in Viladecans, help to implement social values – such as the need to be able to reach the beach on foot, by bicycle or by public transport – without losing sight of the priority of preserving and enhancing the ecological values of the Llobregat delta.

From Large Open Spaces to Urban Edges

Given the highly consolidated territorial context, where the green infrastructure is threatened by strong human-derived pressures generated by the fragmentation of large open spaces and disturbances derived from certain urban activities, the urban edges are one of the strategic focuses of the PDUM. These are areas where action and planning must be prioritised to break with the current dynamics and trends.

These transitional, hinge spaces, with their richness and nuances, cannot be addressed using only a rigid and inflexible urban planning tool like land use regulation. It takes imagination and a bold approach to re-envision them. They must be incorporated into shared projects, without sacrificing the best parts of both sides or the underlying systemic vision; the places with true environmental values must be preserved and protected from urban pressures, and social uses should be concentrated where the conditions of accessibility and connectivity to metropolitan networks and the physical and territorial conditions allow it. With the idea of holding back latent speculative expectations definitively.

La Costeta Park is a good example of a project that contributes to defining edge spaces: it transforms a wooded area on the urban limits into a metropolitan park, while respecting its natural character, and it blurs the dichotomy between city and nature by ensuring the ecological continuity between the Garraf park and the urban fabric of Begues.

From Urban Edges to the Urban Green Structure

Urban edges are closely linked to the metropolitan green structure; and they guarantee continuity, the integrated transition between large open spaces and the consolidated city. They are points for where the intensity of use and enjoyment on the part of citizens can be concentrated, which relieves the pressure on other spaces.

The green structure is made up of structuring parks and green axes. Structuring parks are urban green spaces that have an ecosystemic and strategic function in the territory as a whole because of their environmental characteristics, size or urban significance. Green axes are green routes within the network of active mobility. Passing through the structuring parks, they articulate the urban fabrics and city centres and relate them, via the edge spaces, to the metropolitan large open spaces. Together with the metropolitan roads, they help to consolidate extended metropolitan itineraries connecting different areas that are of value in terms of landscape and heritage.

The main function of the green structure is to ensure all citizens have easy access to ecosystem services and environmental values. This can help improve quality of life in the urban environment and support its resilience to the effects of climate change, promoting conservation and ensuring the continuity of the metropolitan green infrastructure in urban areas, especially in connecting the mountainous zones with the seafront.

A series of projects and actions are helping to gradually build up his network, which combines parks and green axes in a single metropolitan structure. The Rosa Sensat Park, remodelled following the criteria of ecological and environmental sustainability, is connected to the rest of Cornellà's urban green spaces and to the nearby natural spaces through Alps Avenue, transformed into one of the eight municipal green axes that promote active mobility.

The new Can Bada Park in Badalona provides continuity for the green axis running from the mountains to the sea that begins in the metropolitan park of Torrent de la Font and Turó de l'Enric and runs all the way to the historical park of Can Solei and Ca l'Arnús.

The green structure complements, and even merges with, the metropolitan road structure and the two share many of their aims and functions. Together with the structuring facilities, they make up the urban and social structure of the PDUM, a hierarchical structure intended to support efficiency in daily life for the metropolitan population. The aim is to consolidate and reinforce the polycentric metropolitan system: structuring the territory, with a foundation on sustainable mobility and ensuring that people are the focus of the proposal; establishing interdependencies between all the elements; and connecting the different metropolitan centres.

The metropolitan roads are the axes that structure the metropolis; they articulate the urban fabric, define public space, make mobility possible, and encourage activity and social interaction. They are the main support channels for active mobility and public transport, and they should facilitate modal exchanges and foster intermodal spaces to promote a gradual reduction in the presence of private vehicles.

We can divide them into four types. *Metropolitan avenues* are the main axes in this structure and connect almost all the municipalities (many are historic roads); they play a key role in the generation of urban development surrounding them, based on an intensification of their sphere of influence (for example, a metropolitan Gran Via connecting Castelldefels with Montgat, passing through the centre of Barcelona). *Structuring streets* form the backbone of the urban fabric around them and connect with the superstructure of avenues. *Structuring connectors* have a double character: distributing the flows of the segregated infrastructures and connecting isolated municipalities. Finally, the *structuring paths*, often defined following historic routes, are understood as paths for active mobility that provide alternatives to urban roads, and they connect the urban fabrics with large natural spaces, taking over from the green structure.

As we stated above, the other component of the urban and social structure are the metropolitan facilities. On the one hand, there are *structuring facilities* with a clear metropolitan scope, located in the different areas of centrality and connected to metropolitan arterial roads and major transport infrastructures. They play a key role in supporting capitality and relevance to the outside world, and they foster economic activity in their surroundings. On the other hand, there are the *essential facilities*, which guarantee citizen welfare in terms of education, health, and social services, among others. These facilities provide local services, associated fundamentally with the green infrastructure and active mobility, but also with metropolitan roads in general; they make up for the shortcomings in the urban fabrics and respond to people's day-to-day needs. Both types of facilities are spaces that can contribute to adaptation in the face of climate change, and they can form part of a resilient network of climate shelters.

This metropolitan imaginary takes shape in projects such as the remodelling of Llorenç Serra Boulevard in Santa Coloma de Gramenet, one of the sections of a future metropolitan avenue, which contributes to reinforcing this paradigm shift: the pavements are widened, more space is given to public transport and a bicycle path incorporated as part of the Bicivia network. In addition, upon reaching the Besòs River, and before the old bridge, this metropolitan avenue intersects with Salzereda Avenue, a structuring street for the metropolis that runs parallel to the river and combines spaces for active mobility with natural spaces that enhance biodiversity.

From the Urban and Social Structure to the Liveability of the Urban Fabric

The intensity of traffic and the density of urban greenery are different in the different urban centres of the metropolis, and that fact has important effects on citizens' quality of life. The vast majority of the proposals presented in this book have a direct effect on the improvement of the physical and environmental qualities of the urban fabric. They invigorate the conditions of empty spaces, of urban spaces, and are consistent with the urban strategies proposed by the Plan. They complement and reinforce the Plan's strategies, especially those related to improving habitability and living conditions for the population at large.

The projects renovate public space and outfit it with green areas that offer environmental and social quality: they focus on the presence of greenery and the permeability of the soil to minimise the impacts on the immediate environment (air quality, excessive noise, heat island effect, etc.) and they aim to design leisure spaces that encourage social interaction. In addition, they contribute to refurbishing an increasingly aging built fabric (more than 50% of the built stock in the metropolitan area is over 50 years old): they encourage and promote the renovation and remodel of public space and the existing building stock; they attribute value to the historical and cultural heritage and, consequently, to the residents' sense of belonging.

Projects and actions like the El Molí library, in Molins de Rei, or the renovation of Ca l'Altisent, in Sant Climent de Llobregat, are clear examples of this desire to foster the transformation and preservation of metropolitan heritage. In the case of the construction of the El Molí library, which was initially planned to be located in a new building, the decision was made to recover and adapt an old textile factory. The Ca l'Altisent project represents the recovery of a heritage building which, with the opening of its gardens, has contributed to improving the liveability of public space by adding a new green space to the city.

Intervening in such a highly complex and dense territory, and with so many overlapping interests and friction derived from its operations, makes leadership like that of the AMB – drawing on knowledge, ambition and an open and proactive attitude – absolutely necessary. Leadership that is capable of involving not only the public administrations (both local and regional) but all the agents across the territory, promoting spaces for participation and consensus and combining local needs with general systemic functions.

In this sense, the AMB is developing the planning instruments to carry out this transformation towards the metropolis of the future. The PDUM is one of them, with the capacity for laying out the road map for the urban transformation of Barcelona's metropolitan area and supporting the deployment of the different sectoral plans related to mobility, energy, waste prevention and the water cycle, among others.

In the current context, where demographic forecasts indicate that 70% of the world's population will be concentrated in cities by 2050, we need to address the metropolitan reality around us with responsibility and determination if we want to guarantee sustainable and inclusive development at all levels. So let's take advantage of the opportunity in front of us.

Park
Space

Imma Jansana (Barcelona, 1954) is an architect. And a landscape architect. She became interested in the discipline at a time when the ETSAB curriculum did not yet include analysis of the territory. It was the early years following the Franco regime, and "Barcelona, like almost all Spanish cities, was completely lacking in gathering spaces and services for citizens." When she discovered that caring for the territory was also architecture, she decided to work in that field. "I'm self-taught. I took workshops to learn to understand nature." She taught her professional partner, Conchita de la Villa. For three decades, their work together has consisted of rescuing landscapes, plant life and the memory that builds public spaces.

From escaping into nature, have we come to find it in the city?

Sometimes it can still be hard to find. But we're trying to reintroduce it. We introduce plant life into the city to recreate green corridors that provide the environmental conditions so that the diversity that exists in nature can penetrate into the city. I'm talking about axes that cross the city, connecting areas where nature grows. River walks are very clear: they follow the course of the river. But we try to create a green corridor beyond that, by joining parks together: from the Ciutadella park to Collserola. The idea is to make the greenery continuous. So there is a continuity for walking, playing, enjoying the shade, maintaining biodiversity or lowering temperatures. The city has to become a climate refuge.

How can we do that in the face of global warming?

With nature, planting and caring for it. Trees and greenery can save us. But you have to help them to live. Saving them saves us.

Have parks shifted from being places for recreation to becoming tools for citizens' health?

Absolutely. Although they are still spaces for recreation and well-being, they are places for relating that serve the entire population. In parks, children's playgrounds coexist with places for sitting in the sun, for resting or for adults to gather. Plus, now we're paying attention to biodiversity.

So, what is a park today?

In the 21st century, the concept of a "park" has been expanded. It isn't an enclosure. Today, historic urban parks coexist with a network of parks along the periphery that are intended to stitch the city together, to relate its parts, to fill in the gaps with nature, to care for the city by planting greenery in the interstitial spaces. The aim is unification. There should be no qualitative difference between the city centre and the periphery, and "non-places" should be green spaces with the capacity to develop the ecosystems that correspond to them, but that have been taken from them by misuse. The aim is to promote the existence of living places that forge connections between urban activities and join municipalities together.

The parks you design are often restorations. Can they be regenerated naturally?

They need help. Sick people don't just get better in a natural, spontaneous way. These neglected spaces need an intervention, landscape architecture that can help them to heal and then, little by little, to become more and more autonomous. That care aims to encourage the original ecosystems to re-emerge after having been wiped out. But they need a little a push. You have to create the conditions for that to happen.

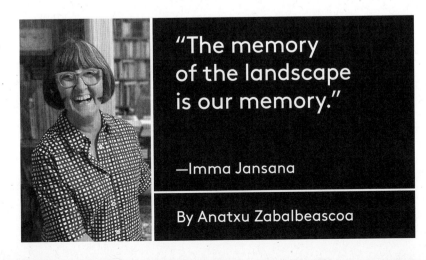

"The memory of the landscape is our memory."

—Imma Jansana

By Anatxu Zabalbeascoa

We've gone from flower beds planted with bulbs to wildflowers.

We're reintroducing the nature that is characteristic of the place.

The nature of the place describes both its vegetation and its characteristics.

Exactly. The nature of a place is what is easiest for a site to be. It also supports native fauna and biodiversity. Also, because it belongs in the place, it's easier to maintain and much cheaper to care for because it's what's natural.

You're describing *The Third Landscape* that Gilles Clément talks about.

Precisely. What used to exist but had been lost. We've worked hard to replanting sites that have been completely degraded and destroyed by polluting industries around the periphery.

Does regenerating those spaces require more sanitation than design?

Definitely. It's an exercise based on clean-up and sanitation. Our parks have always been more sanitation than design. I haven't always had to work on things that are broken, but I like repairing things. I think doing so is part of nature's process of transformation. Urban nature needs to be healed, cared for, and then left alone.

Like a child.

Surely. Give it the conditions it needs to continue growing on its own. In freedom.

Do you have children?

A boy.

Have you let him grow freely?

I did my best. Like everybody. Now that I'm a grandmother, I'm really enjoying my granddaughter. Children are exhausting. But grandchildren are the best. You'll see.

What developed your vision as a landscaper-repairer?

I would say the Gavà Seaside Promenade. More than 30 years ago I was faced with the remains of a pine forest that had been planted several decades earlier and had become a landfill of sorts. There was an uncontrolled picnic area, and at the same time it was a dump site for rubbish and waste.

How did the decision to clean it up come about?

The new coastal plan had been approved, which required increasing setbacks by 100 metres. A developer wanted to build housing in the area. And the dune became apparent. My intervention was to build a light promenade: two strips of pavement that blended in with the dunes of the landscape. The goal was enjoyment of the place.

How is it that we end up destroying what we like most?

I don't know. But it happens in this country.

You designed that project 30 years ago. Any changes in civic behaviour?

No. People still make a huge mess. It's incredible. We destroy what we love.

But there have been improvements: chewing gum on the pavement, sugar packets on the floor in cafés...

That's true. But we still don't know how to respect nature. Maybe it's the wind blowing trash around.

The wind picks it up because it's there.

Of course. It's terrible.

What help developed your perspective in understanding places?

I've always done projects where it looks like you haven't done anything, as though you had tiptoed past, to highlight what's already there, the memory of the place, the vegetation. Sometimes, when I've tried to publish a project in an architecture magazine, the response is: "You can't see anything in these pictures!" But that's just what I want, to not see anything, to make it seem like that landscape has always been there. To work with the landscape, not against it. With the idea of adapting my work to the material conditions and to the conditions of the site.

When you restore a landscape, what do you recover? The place? The use? The vegetation? The memory?

All of it. It depends on the site. For example, when we refurbished the anti-aircraft battery in Turó de la Rovira, in Barcelona, the restoration was based on the memory of the place. That's what was recovered: a heritage site with testimonial (as opposed to cultural) value, as a remnant of the Civil War. The important thing was the memory of the war, evoking the slums that had defined the neighbourhood.

Why is it important to remember the existence of slums?

To recover a memory that had been buried, erased. When the last shacks were evacuated in the 1990s, they left all the rubble on the site so that no one could occupy it. Now the battery has been restored and it houses exhibitions organised by the Barcelona History Museum that explain the struggle of citizens to survive in the city. First surviving the war and then surviving not having a place to live. The remains of flooring are the markers of the traces. There are the floors of whoever lived there and fabulous views over the city.

Is a landscape like a book?

The idea is to rescue the elements that write it. Sometimes they are architectural. Other times, they're plants. A tree can tell you about the past. It has seen it all. The memory of the landscape is our memory. So is the memory of the city. The scars tell us stories about ourselves. In those places, we open up the scars. We clean them up, but we don't erase them. When you're dealing with a project, it's essential to understand that it has written on the city, how it has changed it. Understanding how the site has been transformed is essential to finding out where we're going and what we prioritise.

Can things that have been erased be recovered?

Landscapes, like cities, consist of layers. They are palimpsests where we can read time. The sum of layers is the landscape. And the landscape includes the events, the place, the vegetation and the people.

Does the landscape also tell a story of mistakes? Have trees been planted following the wrong models?

There have been fashions, sure. In Barcelona it would be absurd to plant chestnut trees like the ones in Paris because they would die. But historically, gardeners worked according to trends. Think of the cut cypresses from topiary art, or the monkey-puzzle trees... It isn't a good idea to plant trees in the city with roots that will break up the pavement or trees that need a lot of water. The plane trees are having a hard time. They don't have enough water and their roots aren't getting enough oxygen. Right now, the trees that are thriving in Barcelona are the jacarandas and tipuanas, which are exotic trees. But agronomists know a lot more about that than I do.

Does the vegetation reflect the climate?

Absolutely. And we're getting closer and closer to being a tropical country.

Are urban parks becoming more like forests or cultivated fields?

We're recovering the relationship between the city and agriculture. The countryside and the city should never have been in conflict. The city is a more urban landscape, but it shouldn't interrupt the natural landscape. It isn't easy. You have to design it. Urban vegetable gardens are successful because they are meeting places, points of social connection for people. They have an ecological, recreational and social value. Forests, on the other hand, have a fundamentally biological value because they concentrate the entire range of plant life: from herbaceous plants and shrubs to trees. They make up all the levels of the ecosystem. That's the key. Without all the phases and parts of an ecosystem, sustainability is just a wish.

What kind of vegetation does a dense city need?

It depends on its location. On the climate, on pollution, and even civic behaviour. A street isn't the same as a square.

What is more decisive in terms of decision making, pollution or water shortage?

I would say they're equivalent. Water is essential, and many cities only introduce greenery if there's an automatic irrigation system; otherwise everything dies. That is essential during the first years. Then plants used to be able to survive with just the rain, but there is increasingly less water. One of the last restorations I did was the Costa i Llobera gardens, in Barcelona, which are full of cacti. Even there they have to water from time to time!

How do you construct the identity of a park?

It always has to tie in with its history. It's connected to what was there before, in terms of the territory or plant life. That has to be channelled into the new use that citizens will give to the space.

And how is the current moment reflected then?

Through use. The goal is not to mummify things. A landscape is something changeable, it adapts to the needs of society, which has to understand it and care for it.

Do we need a landscape that makes it easier for us to care for what we destroy?

I don't know if that's possible. Just like every country has the government it deserves, it also has the landscape it deserves. As soon as you cross the French border, you see it: the green disappears and there's the disarray. And yet, there are villages that seem like part of the landscape. That shows a different relationship with the surroundings, one of respect and belonging. Human beings should feel like part of the landscape. When that isn't the case, the landscape gets destroyed. And destruction begets destruction. It's a vicious circle.

Has modernity wreaked havoc?

Human beings should tend to feel like part of the landscape, and that doesn't happen when a place has been destroyed, devastated, squandered. Respecting the landscape is a legacy and an education. When you understand that your parents respected it, you try to maintain it, you feel a sense of belonging. There are many villages in Spain that are part of the landscape. They are often villages that live off the landscape, cultivating citrus fruits or olives. That belongs to the past now.

Isn't all greenery ecological?

Definitely not. Some greenery is entirely artificial. And then there is greenery that is contrived: people who plant palm trees as if they lived in the tropics. And I won't even broach the subject of lawns. Or vertical gardens, which need a lot of water. That's absurd. The roofs could be landscaped instead, for example. There are recent examples. In the Porxos d'en Xifré building, in Barcelona, the residents got together and did it themselves. The more greenery the better, absolutely. But there has to be a balance between what the greenery offers and the resources it consumes. Having a dose of common sense is important in any case.

Is greenery distributed unevenly in cities?

Yes. But it has less to do with wealth than with land management. Newly developed areas have more parks. They can often result from exchanges: construction companies agree to plant a certain area adjacent to their new developments. That way everyone benefits: the new residents and the city as a whole.

The public and private interests come to a consensus?

Exactly. The operative word is consensus. We all live in the city. And it should be built by everyone and, especially, for everyone. Those collaborations are an example of joint efforts.

Is there invisible greenery in cities?

If only. There are very few green roofs, for example. And there should be more, because a green roof offers thermal insulation, it produces oxygen, and it requires very little maintenance – unlike a vertical garden. Terraces could be landscaped. Roofs, assuming they are structurally sound, could be gardens. There is so much room for improvement. But, it's hard to get all the residents of a building to agree on the cost of water, on how to care for the garden, and even what kind of plants to grow.

Are citizens consulted to decide what their parks should be like?

The Barcelona City Council has shown itself to be in favour of citizen participation when it comes to interventions in public space. What I don't know is whether that participation reflects the concerns of all the residents, because only a small number of people actually participate. Many parks in Barcelona are associated with a history of neighbourhood demand. But one thing is demand – like in the case of La Pegaso Park or La Tamarita Gardens – and another thing is citizen participation to decide on specific uses. Demand sets things in motion. And the design is developed with participation from citizens. Today, it's part of the design process.

Does that intervention improve or impede the design process?

It's hard to say. For example, why should the people who have the time to participate be the ones to decide what the parks should offer? The citizens who were mobilised have already gathered signatures to demand more urban benches, or escalators, or better maintenance in parks. You can't force people to participate.

Is the idea of a natural city an oxymoron? Is it city vs. nature?

Not at all. We should put aside the opposition between natural and non-natural spaces. The city is part of the landscape. It is a more urban landscape, but one that can incorporate natural elements. You just have to design it. In dense cities like

Barcelona, it's more difficult. But it's still possible. The superblocks are proof of that. They introduce more nature and better public spaces. I remember Portal de l'Àngel Street without a single tree. It was the first street where tactical urbanism was applied.

What is tactical urbanism?

It's a test, a provisional urbanism intended to see whether education and changes in behaviour are possible. At the time, they brought in railroad ties and laid them on top of the asphalt. And they planted flowers and plants. It was an experiment. To see what would happen. And now it's pedestrianised. No one ever wants their street to be pedestrianised. But they're all happy after the fact.

Are people today paying more attention to greenery than to design?

Yes, but it also depends. It's more important to plant vegetation than to come up with the idea for a tree pit because tree pits don't even need to be designed. Its objective is to let the tree breathe. The best kind is just a big hole. But you can't always have that.

What led you to working on the landscape?

The Portuguese architect Pedro Antonio Janeiro sums it up in one lovely sentence: "Long ago, the shade of a tree was a seed." The shade of a tree is the origin of public space, of the space for coexistence, for relationship, the Roman forum. The phrase talks about time, about the past (the seed), the present (the situation now, the shade) and the future (the growth of the tree).

And what is fundamental in a landscape?

The natural elements – water, earth, plant life – are the driving forces. And they shift along with the landscape. When devising a project we put ourselves at their service. Avoiding imposing on the natural elements is fundamental in design. Devising a landscape has to be an exercise in humility. We have to be aware of our own human time in relation to the Earth's geological time. Respect for what exists, recycling, reusing, rather than trying to leave a mark, should be a landscape architect's goal. You have to be without being noticed because the territory shelters us, it cares for us and feeds us.

Does the city grow by assaulting the landscape?

A serious conflict is taking place between the rural and urban world. The greatest imbalances happen, above all, in those transition areas between the urban and rural spheres, in the peri-urban areas or urban peripheries that are increasingly extensive. That's where we find the highest concentration of unoccupied land, or land that is occupied by activities that have no regard for the environment or the surrounding landscape. Where the city has been growing in a dispersed way, and the territory has been interspersed with the city, giving rise to large terrains vagues.

How should we deal with the landscape of the periphery?

We need to restore, rescue, redirect those large pieces of unoccupied and mistreated land. Work to recover the biological connections in the territory, to restore quarries, landfills, rivers, streams and contaminated spaces. Those are the materials landscape architects use in their projects. We need to take responsibility for the sustainable management of resources. A public space can be designed from the outside, from a bird's eye view, or with the people who will use it in mind. As a landscape designer you have to become a user while you're designing.

To what extent can the countryside and the city mix?

Agricultural space is at the origin of our humanised landscape. It's the most genuine anthropogenic landscape, the first one. A built landscape, architecturalised by humankind for the production of food. It is the first economic exploitation of the land, the world's first writing. And it is also the territory of collective space, a historical and cultural landscape, and a territory that feeds us.

0 500 1000   2000   5000 m

GREEN INFRASTRUCTURE
Diagnostic map. PDUM Proposal

- Fields
- Forest
- Parks
- Beaches
- Rivers, streams and wetlands
- Bare or eroded soil
- Greenery on urban plots
- Greenery on public roads
- Burnt areas
- Interstitial green spaces

Source: AMB. Master Plan
Drafting Service.

An agricultural engineer, Cati Montserrat (Madrid, 1963) comes from a family of botanists. She asserts that she learned "by working hard and by observing people who are more knowledgeable." She studied in Barcelona and in Lleida, "the only places you could study back then". After six years of university, she did a postgraduate degree in landscape architecture, "the first ever to be offered in Barcelona, and it has changed a lot since then." In other countries you could earn an undergraduate degree in landscape architecture. It meant that you studied plants and their requirements. Here, landscape architecture is more associated with architecture and design. She offers the counterpoint.

What are the consequences of that?

That landscape architects always need someone who knows about plants. They make an effort, but the central focus is formal. That's why I think there should be more studies on the needs of plants in the city. We're hobbled in terms of research. That's just my personal opinion.

Landscape projects are designed by architects.

Exactly. There are many species available, and you need to have knowledge of them. The time of expression is delayed in trees. It isn't something immediate. There's more information on trees from Atlantic climates than from Mediterranean ones.

You never know how a landscape is going to work.

It's difficult. Because it also depends on the use. I work above all in public space, and in projects that involve people it's hard to foresee and regulate uses in advance. Now, for example, we're putting flower beds everywhere.

Sometimes they're raised.

So that the dogs don't get into them and, above all, so that they don't get filled with rubbish. The rain washes in bits of paper, and cleaning between the plants can destroy them if it's done carelessly.

Why do cities need greenery?

It has been shown to have health benefits for people. Beyond cleaner air and climate regulation (shade from trees in summer), it has psychological effects. We're biophiles; it feels good to look at nature. For years now there have been studies that relate healing speed in hospitals with proximity to nature. And it isn't just respiratory effects: watching the changing seasons generates health. Plants have a healing effect.

You've been working to naturalise cities for more than 30 years.

And we've gone from being ornamental, that is, expendable, to being generators of health.

From progress associated with asphalt to addressing the consequences of asphalt.

It isn't easy to introduce sustainable greenery in dense cities like Barcelona or L'Hospitalet.

How can it be done?

It isn't a technical problem: today we can make plants live wherever we want. So long as there are resources – water, soil and drainage – anything can be revegetated: from roofs to landfills. Historically, parks were in the worst places: with steep slopes, debris... because the market economy had no interest in building there. As a result, the conditions for plants to thrive have to be built, a balance between resources,

"We still have a long way to go in learning how to live with trees."

—Cati Montserrat

By Anatxu Zabalbeascoa

maintenance and results. Once that is achieved, then you can move on to uses: people, dogs, paths and rubbish that will need to be cleaned up. And how do you keep it clean without destroying the plants?

Don't we know how to coexist with nature?

In cities, you have to plant trees of a certain size, so they don't get broken. And when it comes flower beds, use will prevail: a flower garden next to a school will never be able to grow. No matter how many times you replant it.

Is coexistence with nature a question of education?

And awareness. Greenery in the city generates a space that is as artificial as the city is within the landscape. It is just as important for us to create hardy spaces as it is for citizens to understand how much they need greenery in the city.

Would consulting with citizens help to improve maintenance?

We try to engage in education; the gardens are a reflection of people's respect. There are meagre environments that have been transformed. As such, they are cared for because citizens think of them as their own. Public space belongs to everyone. It's paid for by our taxes and that's why we can all use it, but we should also all take care of it.

In Barcelona there are many parks that originated with citizen initiatives, demanded by the neighbourhoods.

There is a need for greenery and for public space. Green spaces are spaces for leisure, gathering, tranquillity, walking and sport, but also for union and coexistence. They are shared spaces.

Should nature no longer be the opposite of the city?

It's unavoidable. The pandemic has made it very clear. An ISG Global study has shown that a large number of deaths can be prevented by bringing greenery into the city. It can be measured by the WHO standards (green spaces of at least half a hectare at a distance of no more than 300 metres) or by using the 3, 30, 300 formula: every house should have a view of 3 trees; 30% tree cover in every neighbourhood; and a park less than 300 metres away.

Where does the greenery of the metropolitan area of Barcelona fall on that scale?

It depends on how you measure it, whether or not you include Collserola. We're lucky to have Montjuïc and the Parc Agrari, but the city needs to be less dense.

Historically, the city was the polar opposite of nature.

Many of the large parks in cities are a legacy of monarchies.

El Retiro was a royal hunting ground.

In Barcelona, a city encircled by walls, that didn't exist. The advent of democracy uncovered the need for the city to incorporate more green space.

What is an urban park today?

There's a broad spectrum. A real urban park needs to have a certain size. But, at the same time, squares can serve as parks. They should let citizens connect with nature, but they should also be a place to pass the time, meet with others, relax, feel good. In recent years, the AMB has done a fantastic job with outreach, bringing citizens into parks for educational experiences.

A park in an urban area can be the reason a senior citizen will leave the house. But what's the point of planting greenery if its surrounded by cars? Is it possible to design vegetation for a city without taking mobility into account?

Our job is to revegetate, not to design. I can't determine the width of a street. I can point out things like the fact that trees, in general, need much more space than the tree pits they're allocated. A tree planted in proper conditions in open space will grow much more than in an urban setting. At the same time, proximity creates a tree cover that offers many benefits. That has led us to rethink our strategy and switch out smaller trees – that would avoid problems – for species that grow more and can generate more benefits, accepting that they may entail more work. In the city, you usually look for deciduous trees that provide shade in the summer and let the sun through in winter. That's a problem because, in our mild Mediterranean climate, most of the native species are evergreens – holm oaks, pines or tree-shaped shrubs, like mastic trees – because our most difficult moment comes in the summer, when there is a lack of water, and those species are sclerophylls so they can survive with little water. In our environment, deciduous trees grow in humid areas: poplars, alders...

You defend revegetating the city with non-native plants.

Yes, with adaptable plants. Every city has its characteristic tree. Lindens in Paris, or elms in Amsterdam, where, when they drop their white seeds in the spring, instead of looking at it as a nuisance, people flip the script and celebrate the "spring snow". Here, people complain because there are so many tipuanas that have yellow flowers. We still have a long way to go in learning how to live with the trees. People are always asking for the trees to be pruned back. But to achieve tree cover that will help cleanse the air and generate shade, you can't prune as much. Excessive pruning ends up killing the tree, depleting its reserves. People want parks, but not bugs.

What would you propose?

Taking care of the trees, pruning existing delicate ones. And choosing the right species: the semi-persistent species that come from South America will adapt much better to the Mediterranean climate than deciduous trees. And letting recently planted trees grow with ample space without touching them hardly at all. It's the best way and the cheapest. The trees reach a point of stability. They grow because growing is their way of life, but there's a point where they reach stability.

Why are they pruned so often?

Because of political pressure, motivated by pressure from residents. If you don't prune, it looks like you aren't taking care of the plants. But that isn't true. Every time you prune, you're hindering CO_2 capture. There's a lot of ignorance, although luckily there are a growing number of people who understand that trees shouldn't be topped. The citizen demand for pruning coexists with the defence of poorly positioned trees that don't generate benefits. And sacralising the life of the trees isn't the solution either, they need to be managed.

What's an example of a poorly placed tree?

A poplar stuck in a tree pit. And there are a lot of them. That's coming to an end though because they have higher water needs than cities can provide.

Does urban vegetation cost more in trees or tree pits?

Generally in tree pits. Trees are cheap. It isn't a money problem, it's a problem of space and maintenance. It is difficult to make pavements that are compatible with vegetation. Streets are highly contested spaces. They're full of utilities. They keep piling up; the obsolete installations aren't removed. How can you make it possible for trees to thrive with so many other needs?

How?

Surprisingly, the trees adapt. The construction causes soil compaction and drainage problems that have to be resolved. The key is balance. It's a question of putting in the effort. But we need more studies on improving the life of trees in Mediterranean cities.

Do you plant seedlings or sow seeds?

Both. We sow meadows and wild flowers. Greenery requires waiting.

It is cause for optimism that no one picks those wildflowers?

We've made a lot of progress, yes. Now we're sowing seeds in tree pits to support biodiversity in the insect population, among other things. As a result, we have fewer pests in the rest of the greenery.

Had urban greenery seen a big reduction?

Everything evolves. There are citizens who find flower beds beautiful, but not wild species. When we started planting grasses, a council member asked us to get rid of "those weeds". People have a very simple vision of what a garden is: lawns and trees. It would be great for us to open our minds to the coexistence of real nature with the city.

What are the dangers of regreening cities?

Earlier, when people used to think that because the lindens and horse chestnut trees in Paris were so beautiful that we should have them here. Now, failing to maintain the greenery. If we're planting more greenery, we need to increase the time and budget dedicated to its maintenance.

What is an exemplary intervention?

Can Rigal, between Barcelona and L'Hospitalet, is a benchmark for me. It was the first time that we used a wide variety of shrub species. We worked extensively on the drainage of the subsoil, which made it possible for all kinds of species to grow — a section of pines and holm oaks and another more formal area with rows of different species that outline the paths. We also recovered water from a mine that was running directly into the sewers so it could be used for irrigation. The trees have grown a lot and the public response has been good, following a phase in which an area was destroyed by dogs. The idea is to extend the project.

How can it be possible for dogs to use parks without destroying them?

I don't know. But there are an increasing number of dogs. We have to learn to live together. Because actions aimed at prevention — creating raising beds or fencing them in – lead to a loss of water infiltration or affect the aesthetics of the gardens.

It's encouraging that only few owners leave behind dog droppings.

That's true. Education and raising awareness are the way forward.

Is the design of urban green a reflection of us?

All of us. Now it's a shared effort. Architects aren't the only ones doing the drawing; agronomists are also consulted. We've gone from looking for a red tree to collaborating in teams. Vegetation is diametrically opposed of civil engineering. Architects need to compact the earth so the pavements won't sink, and we need soil, drainage and water. We have to move forward at the same time.

What contributes to the identity of a park?

The vegetation, the design and the memory of the place. The Torrent d'en Tortuguer, in Ripollet, was built in a ravine that had been filled in and converted into a car park. There was already a very interesting park there, Pinetons, which had been recovering rainwater for a few decades. We created an artificial wetland to promote biodiversity. The stream couldn't be recovered, but we reinterpreted it, generating biodiversity spaces. In a year, the frogs and toads had recovered. Compare that to a paved square.

Speaking of paved squares. Were they a mistake?

They responded to a series of needs. It's much easier to maintain a paved square than one that's unpaved. It remains to be seen how we'll maintain what we're planting and sowing. It should be done, but only if we can maintain it. We're heading toward a scenario where there will be less and less water. And each new garden requires a lot of labour. Especially when it comes to repairing what has been spoiled or damaged. That's a growth area. We need to achieve robust solutions. And people need to learn not to destroy their surroundings.

What constraints have you learned to work with?

Some very necessary ones: limiting the consumption of potable water. In the parks managed by the AMB, 78% of the surface area is not irrigated. There's a control of the water they can accumulate. Today, we ask each new design to include actions to increase or improve biodiversity. And a protocol that limits CO_2 consumption. There is a clear effort to achieve more sustainable cities.

Is urban farming a tool for social cohesion? .

Urban productive gardens are an educational tool. An activity for seniors and even a meeting place. Population groups of all origins are users of the parks because it's free and they're pleasant places. And having people living peacefully together is good for society. But also for each of us individually. In the best green spaces, people, flora and fauna coexist. And everything helps.

Goats are cropping the grass in the Tuileries garden.

That's the highest level. Batlle and Roig tried to do something similar in the restoration of the Garraf landfill, but it adds complexity. The herds eat the vegetation that has been planted... I wish we could do it in natural spaces. The coexistence between livestock, agriculture, vegetation, recreation and urban life would teach us so much. All of us.

We've sought out more shade than sun. But a lot of kids these days are dealing with a lack of sun exposure.

We've pursued pleasant bioclimatic shelters that provide cooler temperatures. But the lack of sun exposure may have more to do with lifestyle factors, and screens, than with the existence of the parks. In the wake of the pandemic, parks are being used en masse. They are places for gathering and leisure. But also for sport. They are spaces of hope. A different city can grow there.

Alps Avenue and Rosa Sensat Park

Cornellà
de Llobregat

**CLAUDI AGUILÓ ARAN
ALBERT DOMINGO
(DATAAE)**

XAVIER VENDRELL

2016–2018
19,309 m²
€2,056,167

COLLABORATORS
Brufau Cusó
Calderon-Folch Studio
Ecivil Enginyeria

Eulalia Aran
Roser Vives

DEVELOPERS
AMB
Cornellà de Llobregat
Town Council

CONTRACTOR
Eurocatalana

PHOTOGRAPHER
Adrià Goula

AWARDS
Finalist, Spanish
Architecture and
Urbanism Biennial 2021
Shortlisted,
Barcelona Architecture
Exhibition 2019

The remodel of Alps Avenue and Rosa Sensat Park is part of the Cornellà Natura project, which promotes renaturalisation, sustainable mobility and the energy transition. Specifically, it is part of the green axis that connects Can Mercader Park with Canal de la Infanta Park.

To transform the avenue into a new green axis, the number of traffic lanes is reduced by half, the width of the pavements is expanded, a two-way cycling lane is added, and more greenery is planted along the street.

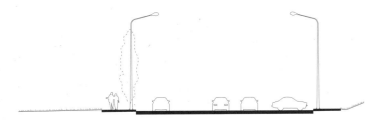

1/400   PREVIOUS STATE   CURRENT STATE

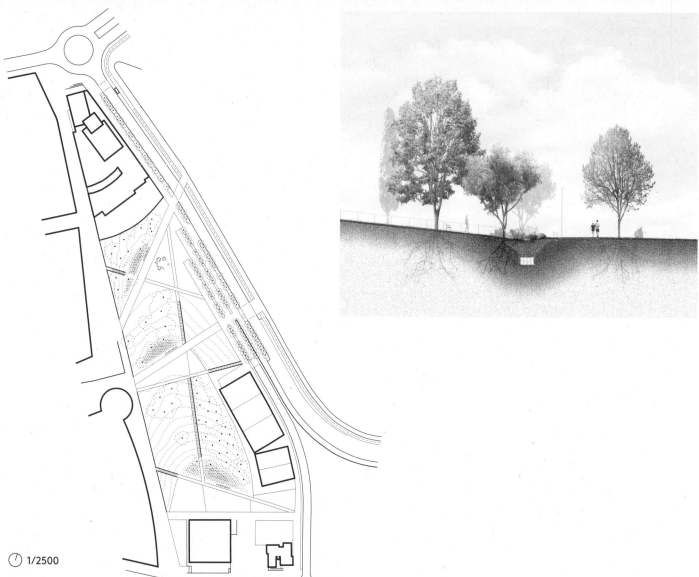

1/2500

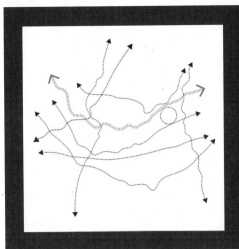

CORNELLÀ NATURA

Transform the city to naturalise it: that is the goal of Cornellà Natura, a locally focused project that connects the green spaces of the municipality along axes that stretch beyond the limits of the municipality. It is a strategic local project that fits into the framework of the metropolitan logic but with a personality all its own, with the aim of contributing to the consolidation of green infrastructure.

In the park, there are three main types of interventions. Pedestrian permeability is improved through three new paths stretching from one side of the park to the other, thus improving the continuity of the city without modifying the existing topography.

The self-sufficiency of the vegetation in terms of irrigation is increased through spaces for rainwater retention and infiltration; more grass is planted, and new areas are designed with shrub species of different colours as well as lines of trees to enhance the new layouts in the park.

Finally, the park installations are updated: all existing urban elements are reused, the photovoltaic structures are maintained, and the amount of children's play equipment and seating areas is incremented. This promotes improvement in habitability and ensures the park can be used by everyone, with new spaces for sitting, walking and playing.

Can Bada Park

Badalona

ENRIC BATLLE
JOAN ROIG
IVÁN SÁNCHEZ
JOAN BATLLE
(Batlleiroig)

2018-2020
8,185 m²
€736,072

AMB TEAM
David Aguilar

BATLLEIROIG TEAM
Yago Cavaller
Mercè Lorente

COLLABORATORS
SBS Simón i Blanco

DEVELOPERS
AMB
Badalona
City Council

CONTRACTOR
UTE Drim - Talio

PHOTOGRAPHER
Jordi Surroca

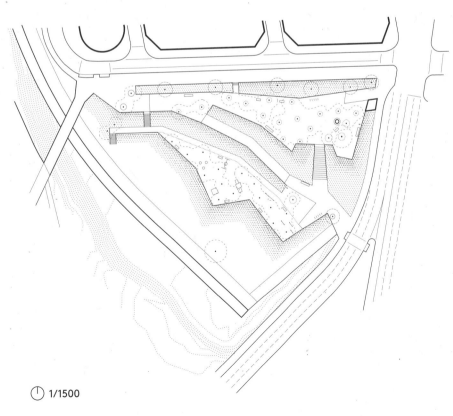

◔ 1/1500

SUSTAINABILITY PROTOCOL

Providing tools to assess the environmental impact of the decisions that are taken in the design and execution of projects for the AMB and IMPSOL: this is the main goal of the sustainability protocol. The guide lays out a series of specific values and three timespans, and it incorporates 19 criteria grouped into 6 categories: transversal analysis, energy, water, materials, comfort, and sustainability of the site.

Site sustainability

Water

Materials

Comfort and health

Energy

Cross-cutting follow-up and analysis

Located in an old plant nursery on the edge of the Torrent de la Font and Turó de l'Enric Park, the site takes advantage of the existing agricultural terraces and gives them specific uses: a large sitting area under the shade of the trees on the upper terrace; children's play areas and sports courts on the second terrace; and a large wildflower meadow adjacent to the streambed on the lower terrace.

As a positive counterpoint to the neighbourhood that surrounds it, almost all the surfaces of the park are soft and natural, and thus the park serves as a new green lung for Badalona, connected to the green axis of the Torrent de la Font.

A sustainable drainage system has been built to manage rainwater. It is collected in ditches filled with gravel or planted with vegetation; from there, it seeps into the ground or is retained in the biotopes. Thanks to this system, which avoids dumping water into the municipal sewer network, and through the renovation of the old well in the plant nursery, the park supplies its own water for irrigation. The species planted are native or adapted to the climate conditions in Badalona to ensure they will take root and will not need much watering.

Can Bada Park is a 21st-century urban park, designed to combat the climate emergency from within the city.

Tortuguer Stream

Ripollet

CLAUDI AGUILÓ RIU
EVA PAGÉS
(AMB)

2017-2020
13,600 m²
€906,979

SITE MANAGEMENT
Proido
Eva Blanco

AMB TEAM
Francesc Germà
Ainhoa Martínez
Mireia Monràs
Cati Montserrat
Maria Sánchez

DEVELOPERS
AMB
Ripollet Town Council

CONTRACTOR
Voltes Connecta

PHOTOGRAPHER
Jeroen Van Mieghem

The recovery of the Tortuguer Stream serves to extend the Pinetons Park, connecting it with the Casa Natura environmental education facility. In a space occupied until recently by a parking lot, the goal is to recover the conditions typical of a former seasonal Mediterranean stream, with a flow of water that varies throughout the year.

In the 1980s, the canalisation of the streambed and the spread of impervious surfaces in the area led to an increase in runoff, which caused flooding and damage to the lower part of the basin. Now, the aim is to reverse this situation in order to improve the resilience of the urban areas to the effects of climate change.

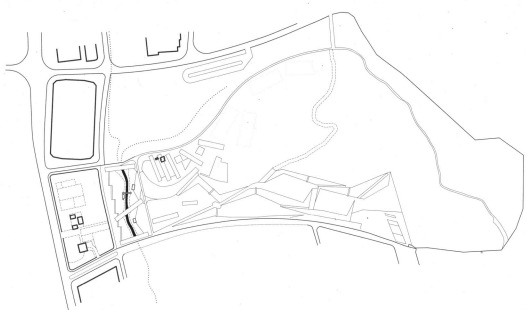

⊕ 1/7500

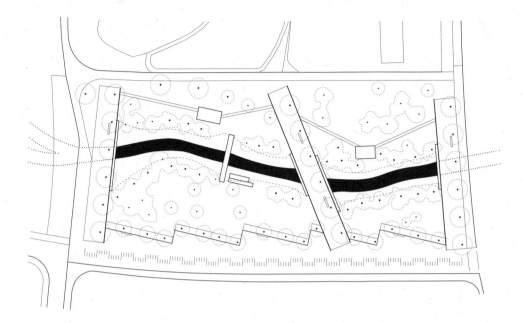

1/1500

Through the movement of earth within the project site, the topography is modified to create a depression: the centre is excavated, and the edges are built up; three platforms are erected atop rows of prefabricated gabions, crossing the streambed and acting as small dams, creating temporary flood spaces to restore the stream bank conditions and recreate wetland habitats.

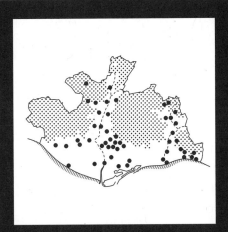

NETWORK OF METROPOLITAN PARKS (XPM)

The metropolitan parks that form the XPM act as transitional spaces between small urban squares, which play a more social role, and large open spaces with a more natural character. With surface areas ranging from less than one hectare to over 25, they contribute to consolidating the green infrastructure of metropolitan Barcelona and raising awareness among citizens through educational activities.

The planting of the vegetation expresses the gradient in water requirements. The chosen species include trees that already grow in the park, herbaceous plants and shrubs for the wetlands adapted to the environment and with ornamental qualities, and grasses and legumes to provide contrast, such that, in the unmown basin, the mix of species will provide an ornamental bloom and accentuate the expression of moisture. The arrangement of all the lighting elements and the choice of solutions and materials reinforces the continuity with the Pinetons Park.

The recovery of the Tortuguer Stream ultimately aims to restore a forgotten landscape, a space that was part of the city's natural heritage.

Classroom K
Santa Coloma de Gramenet

DAVID BAENA
ANTONI CASAMOR
MANEL PERIBÁÑEZ
MARIA TALTAVULL
(Baena Casamor
Arquitectes BCQ)

2016-2018
110 m²
58 m² (urban
development)
€179,519

**EXECUTIVE
MANAGEMENT**
Paco Sánchez (AMB)

AMB TEAM
Marta Juanola

BCQ TEAM
Petra Boulescu
Vanessa Díaz

DEVELOPERS
AMB
Santa Coloma
de Gramenet
City Council

COLLABORATORS
AIA Instal·lacions
 Arquitectòniques
Fustes Borniquel

CONTRACTOR
Calaf Constructora

PHOTOGRAPHER
Marcela Grassi

AWARDS
Shortlisted,
Barcelona Architecture
Exhibition 2019

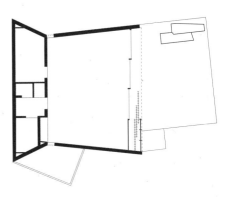

1/300

This pavilion, designed using a modular prefabricated construction method, is the prototype for the environmental education classrooms to be installed in different locations within the AMB's network of metropolitan parks. It is designed as a space that opens onto the park, flexible and with multiple possible uses, to support learning and discovery of the environmental aspects of the park and its surroundings. At the same time, it is also intended to serve as the habitat for animal species: insects, invertebrates, birds, etc.

The building results from combining three uses (services, classroom and pergola), and its construction based on industrialised systems makes it possible to optimise costs and the time required for installation.

The prototype was built of wood, largely offsite. The inverted roofs make it possible to install solar panels and to capture and use rainwater, which is channelled and returned to the ground.

Playground in Les Planes Park

L'Hospitalet de Llobregat

JONA GARCÍA MONTSE GARCIA (AMB)

2017-2019
3,000 m²
€968,494

AMB TEAM
Sara Arguedas
Jaume Fornés
Jordi Martínez
Paco Sánchez
Miquel Àngel
Soriano-Montagut

SITE MANAGEMENT
Eulàlia Codina
(AMB)

DEVELOPERS
AMB
L'Hospitalet
de Llobregat
City Council

CONTRACTOR
HPSA

PHOTOGRAPHER
Joan Guillamat

The new children's play area aims to contribute to socialisation in Les Planes Park, encouraging residents to visit and enjoy it.

At the foot of the chimney from the former brickyard kiln, an inclusive children's play area is designed to be open to everyone. The location in the centre of the park, in an area where the main walking paths converge, takes advantage of the existing uneven terrain as part of the project.

Most of the play equipment is located on the lower esplanade, near the chimney and a large plane tree, adjacent to seating and leisure areas under new deciduous trees that provide shade in the summer. The original slope is transformed into another play area, with climbing equipment and slalom elements, and slides of different sizes and types, turning the upper platform into a lookout point over the whole.

The design encourages inclusiveness by removing architectural barriers and through the choice of play equipment and the forms and colours used for the pavement. It also takes into account aspects of sustainability, such as minimising earthworks in the construction process and ensuring the infiltration of rainwater through two large drainage strips.

La Costeta Park

Begues

MONTSERRAT PERIEL
SARA FERRER
JOAN CASTELLVÍ
(AMB)

2016-2019
7,890 m²
€1,210,886

SITE MANAGEMENT
Natalia Castaños
(AMB)

AMB TEAM
Sara Arguedas
Jordi Bardolet
Cristina Magallón
Álvaro Sainz

COLLABORATORS
Bosch&Ventayol
Pi Enginyeria Civil i
Urbanisme

CONTRACTOR
Rogasa

DEVELOPERS
AMB
Begues Town Council

PHOTOGRAPHER
Santiago Periel

Located in Begues, between the neighbourhoods of La Costeta and La Parellada, this park is set on a 30-metre high hill in a Mediterranean woodland. As part of a comprehensive project that begins with the preservation of the site's nature, this phase places priority on generating new entrances and accessible paths as well as adding functional lighting along the main path. At the same time, specific areas of interest along these paths and elements in the park are marked and highlighted, defining new areas for leisure and recreation, and the need to alter certain slopes along the park's perimeter is studied.

In all the interventions, native species of trees, such as the holm oak or the stone pine, and understory species like kermes oak, rosemary or prickly juniper are prioritised and protected.

The paths through the park run along linear routes – which adapt to contours, are paved with decomposed granite, and are given a transverse slope so that they drain into the ground, where there is a gravel curb with infiltration wells – and connecting paths that create shorter routes perpendicular to the slope, linking the linear routes by way of earth-coloured precast concrete stairs.

◷ 1/3000

Corten steel is used in the different elements of the design to generate a unified identity and integrate the elements into the environment: shaping the paths and entrances, containing the earth along the perimeter of the park, and for the urban furniture and lamp posts. The steel plate outlining the paths rises and folds over at the park's edges, creating a play of irregular shadows that evokes a rocky perimeter.

Recreational activities also offer ways of moving through the park. The slides that drop down through the forest adapt to the topography like a small streambed. The climbing forest, made from oak logs and ropes, is located on an esplanade of scrubland with few trees; a cushioning pavement of pink sandstone is installed around it.

In short, the intervention aims to create a new way of occupying and enjoying a forested space while, at the same time, improving connectivity between the surrounding neighbourhoods and the centre of Begues.

Bosc de Can Gorgs Park

Barberà del Vallès

**JONA GARCÍA
MONTSE GARCIA**
(AMB)

2019-2022
2,250 m²
€469,303

SITE MANAGEMENT
Eulàlia Codina
(AMB)

AMB TEAM
Sara Arguedas
Jaume Fornés
Jordi Martínez
Miquel Àngel
Soriano-Montagut

DEVELOPERS
AMB
Barberà del Vallès
Town Council

CONTRACTOR
Eurocatalana

PHOTOGRAPHER
Gemma Miralda

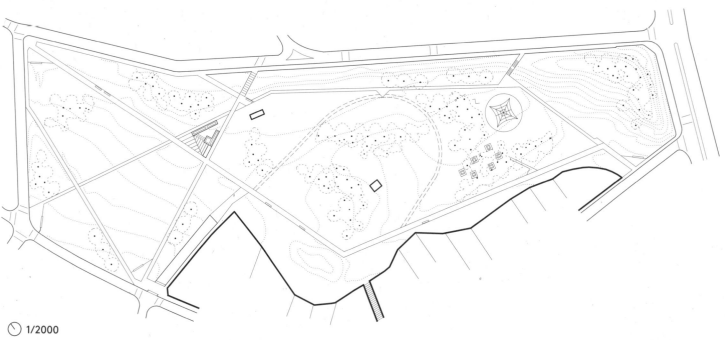

⊘ 1/2000

IMPROVEMENTS IN BIODIVERSITY

Enriching the biodiversity and educational potential of metropolitan parks and beaches is one of the AMB's main objectives as part of its Biodiversity Improvement Plan. With an emphasis on citizen participation, some of the proposed actions include the installation of nest boxes and the construction of butterfly gardens and insect hotels, as well as the study of the primary habitats in parks and beaches, along with measures to enhance biodiversity.

More than 20 years after its being designated a public park, the lighting and accessibility are improved in this wooded area in the middle of the city. New streetlamps are is installed along all the paths and leisure areas: children's play area, picnic area, fitness area and butterfly garden.

The creation of a paved path makes it possible to set up a new access to the west side of the park and it solves the maintenance problems arising from the lack of definition and the steep slopes in the previous layout. This new gateway to the park is combined with the improvement of the other entrances: an expansion of the access points with areas paved in acid-washed concrete, where the furniture and park signage are located; a ramp next to the stairs at the northern entrance, and a new staircase that connects with the path. Shrubs are planted to create a visual reinforcement of certain routes and areas of the park.

Can Solei and Ca l'Arnús Park

Badalona

JONA GARCÍA
(AMB)

2018-2021
11,600 m²
€639,922

SITE MANAGEMENT
Paco Sánchez (AMB)

AMB TEAM
Sara Arguedas
Julieta Duran
Jaume Fornés
Jordi Martínez

DEVELOPERS
AMB
Badalona
City Council
UE – FEDER

CONTRACTOR
Ambitec Servicios
Ambientales

PHOTOGRAPHER
María José Reyes

Following various efforts at refurbishment and improvement over the course of more than 30 years, several micro-interventions are required to help tidy up the paths and public use spaces in Can Solei and Ca l'Arnús Park.

The same type of acid-washed concrete is used to pave the new access from Navarra Avenue, which serves the residents of the northern part of the city, and several paths to access the environmental education classroom and the children's play area on Sant Bru Street and to connect the two levels of the park around the Lola Anglada school.

Near the Ca l'Arnús building, the esplanade is outfitted with large flowerbeds full of meadow grasses and fruit trees that define decomposed granite paths and leisure areas, while recalling the vegetable gardens from the park's agricultural past; in the enclosed garden, new flower beds are laid out and heritage elements such as the drinking trough are restored, and the tile roof of the Clock Tower is repaired.

The lighting is improved along the plane tree alley: low beacon-style lamps and light posts are situated at key points along the promenade, where there are intersections with other paths and leisure spaces. The aim across all the interventions is to use standardised materials and solutions to provide a unified image across all areas of the park.

Ultimately, this metropolitan green space is improved and made ready for use by everyone through small interventions that address problems caused by the passage of time.

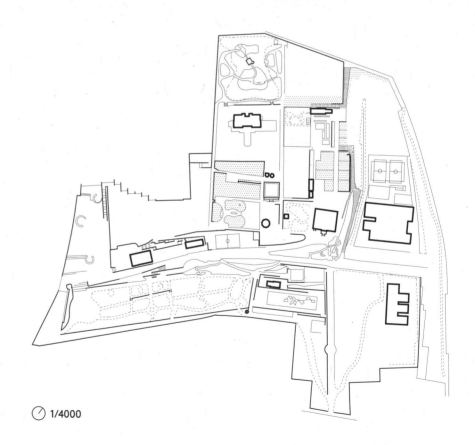

⊘ 1/4000

Water
Space

Pioneers in the recovery of riverbanks as flexible public parks capable of absorbing rises in the water levels and functioning as places for urban leisure the rest of the time, the architects Margarita Jover (Paris, 1969) and Iñaki Alday (Zaragoza, 1965) are full professors at Tulane University in the United States. Alday is dean of the Tulane School of Architecture in New Orleans, specialised in the relationship between water and the city. Jover was awarded her position by an anonymous jury due to her defence of systemic thinking that relates water, landscape and architecture.

Prominent designers of projects to recover riverbanks, such as the Water Park in Zaragoza (2008) and Aranzadi Park in Pamplona (2013), they advocate the social, biological and climate-related value of understanding the changing nature of the landscape. This interview began in person in Barcelona and Madrid and ended virtually from both sides of the Atlantic.

We have gone from escaping into nature to finding it in the city. What is a metropolitan, urban park today?

Iñaki Alday: Like all good public spaces, it is first and foremost a space of equalisation. A place where all citizens can share shade, clean air, benches or play spaces equally, regardless of their economic means. A city with abundant good parks is a more egalitarian city, with more possibilities for democratic quality based on the habit of sharing and coexisting. "Getting out in nature" requires resources; bringing nature into the city, and into every neighbourhood, makes the city a fairer place. Investing in parks means investing in the foundations of social justice.

Today, a park is an ecological infrastructure that can manage water (our most precious and scarce commodity) – storing it, minimising the effects of flooding, recharging groundwater, cleaning the air and absorbing carbon, reducing ambient temperatures in summer, promoting biodiversity and providing a home for flora and fauna. A place to cultivate the spirit, to enjoy life and beauty, and to improve our health and happiness.

Margarita Jover: A metropolitan park is a nature preserve, typically along a river, in mountainous areas that are hard to build on, or in former royal hunting reserves that were transformed into public parks with the advent of democracy. Due to their large scale, metropolitan parks can play a major role in climate regulation. But, at present, we need to go further than metropolitan and urban parks. Cities need to be reforested to prepare them for climate change. We need more trees, but since that is not always possible where the land has been occupied by residential buildings or facilities, we can reforest open spaces, from streets and squares to rooftops. We need to transition towards a city designed as a hybrid ecosystem: half forest, half city. To that end, there have to be more pedestrian areas, permeable soil and more trees.

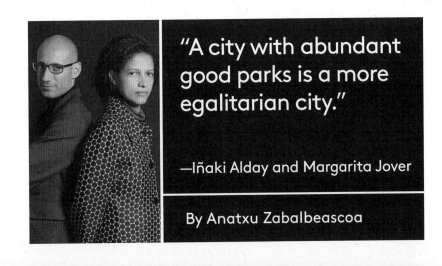

"A city with abundant good parks is a more egalitarian city."

—Iñaki Alday and Margarita Jover

By Anatxu Zabalbeascoa

Pedestrianisation reduces emissions and energy consumption; permeability helps to recharge the groundwater table that will feed the trees, which in turn will temper the urban microclimate. The trees should be understood like a forest – in other words, multispecies, with different sizes, ages and genders (yes, trees have a gender!). Caring for them would be the purview of a hypothetical Ministry of the Urban Ecosystem, which would be responsible for the microclimate (temperature, pollution, ventilation, pruning, irrigation, etc.). If cities could be more like the forest while maintaining their urban functions, people wouldn't need to run away from them every weekend. That would save energy.

To what extent does water conservation determine the type of vegetation in a place?

M.J.: There can be no vegetation without water and soil. The amount of water available must always determine the type of vegetation in each region. That's an inevitable basic principle. In our parks, the main strategy is based on recovering floodable land so that the water can support the new riparian forests. This simple, powerful strategy involves removing certain protection dikes, and you'll find it in some of our projects in Spain, like the river park in Zuera (2001), the Water Park in Zaragoza (2008), and Aranzadi Park in Pamplona (2013). As a result, cities can recover large, wooded areas at no cost because the river maintains them.

Outside the riverbed, the classic ecological criteria aren't sufficient anymore when it comes to choosing species; you have to take into account the particularly harsh urban conditions (pollution, solar radiation, etc.) and climate change. In Spain, in the future, that will mean planting trees that are native to more southerly latitudes.

Isn't all greenery ecological?

I.A.: No, of course not. A lawn that is artificially irrigated and maintained has little value or may even be anti-ecological. The kind of greenery that represents an ecosystem with native or adapted vegetation and that sustains various layers of life – insects, birds, and other animals – is ecological. A series of lavender bushes that feed bees and butterflies are ecological, whereas flowerbeds that have been protected by insecticides are a small-scale attack on nature.

M.J.: But everything doesn't need to be ecological in cities. Just like we invest in sewers and water pipes, we will also need to invest in green infrastructure to make cities more liveable for everyone.

How can we democratise access to the sun?

M.J.: Modernity advanced a long way in urban planning toward bringing sunlight into cities and homes because those cities were designed during a tuberculosis pandemic. The current planning regulations have to be respected, always, and in all neighbourhoods alike. That should be enough.

I.A.: But most of the territory is occupied by private constructions that use and sometimes misuse assets that are essentially public: air, sun, water, energy and nature. More public space is tantamount to more health and more equity in the city.

What responsibility lies with an increasingly demanding citizenry?

I.A.: It's a delicate balance, where experts (architects, landscape architects or engineers) are not designing for themselves but for citizens and nature. That's what makes a good park or a good building; all the rest is just spectacle. The experts work for citizens, who, in turn, inform the experts; it's an essential partnership. For example, if I had a heart problem, I wouldn't want my operation or my treatment decided by an assembly. I'd want it decided by a good doctor, whom I trust and whose ultimate aim is to protect my health.

M.J.: Cities aren't designed by neighbourhood assemblies. That's what experts are there for. What is worth discussing on a social level are the values promoted by the city model. Isotropy entails an equal amount of resources for life across the city, regardless of neighbourhoods and household incomes.

Have the urban productive gardens that you've designed promoted social integration?

I.A.: The vegetable gardens in the Water Park in Zaragoza and the Aranzadi Park in Pamplona have a wide variety of users and functions. There are gardens for research and dissemination, family gardens, gardens that supply a farm shop in Zaragoza, and gardens for the social integration of people with special needs in Pamplona.

The riverbanks have gone from being disregarded to being valued. What has that process been like?

M.J.: There are many examples of riverbanks being recovered in post-industrial cities. When pollution and attacks on the topography of the riverbed cease, it begins to transform and both the landscape and citizens' interest in it begin to recover. However, those cases are still a minority. Cities with large migrations from the countryside to the city often end up with self-built homes in dry riverbeds, although construction there has been prohibited by law. The only way it will be possible to prepare the city for climate change, which we're already seeing, is through housing provision policies and large investments in green infrastructure to reforest riverbeds and mountainsides.

How do we foster shared spaces for sport, recreation, gathering and floodwaters, for different speeds and age groups?

I.A.: Today, we're designing for very different users. The key is to avoid allocating portions, chopping up a park into specialised spaces. A river needs to have room to flood (which helps with irrigation, sowing seeds, fertilising the soil, and minimising overflows upstream or downstream). It's only logical during those periods for citizens to relinquish preference of use and appreciate the spectacle of nature. The rest of the year, the spaces can be used for outings, sport, events, or play.

We understand public space like a chessboard, which can be used for very different games – as opposed to a specialised board, like pachisi for example.

M.J.: *Cohabitation* means that the 20th-century model, characterised by a relationship of power, domination and control in human beings' attitude towards nature, is transformed in the 21st century into a relationship characterised by collaboration.

Is it more dangerous today with the new flooding?

I.A.: Between the Zaragoza Water Park and the Aranzadi Park in Pamplona, in 12 years we have already seen four 25-year floods and one 100-year flood. And we also know we'll never succeed if we're only trying to protect ourselves. The more protection there is, the greater the catastrophe on the day it fails. That's why we need to change our mindset and understand that we have to live with floods, which are part of the natural cycle of rivers – and even more so with climate change. Strategies for coexistence need to be designed and we need to learn to interact with an entity, the river, that has a life of its own and doesn't want to remain confined to a canal. We need to prevent what we build from conflicting with the life of the river, so it won't be damaged when the river rises, and so that, when the river recedes, it will have helped us to maintain and ecologically enrich that space of coexistence.

Is a river nature or a construction?

M.J.: A river is a vast space for the movement of water and nutrients, a characteristic that makes it attractive for the emergence of biodiversity in both fauna and flora. Humans need to learn to listen, to let rivers be and to negotiate seasonal spaces – as opposed to trying to impose a tidy visual order on nature by using pesticides and high levels of maintenance.

In other places and cultures, rivers are gods. In pre-industrial times, most cultures understood rivers as key agents for their survival. People were able to coexist with them. If we manage to stop thinking of rivers as drains or sewers and start seeing them as providers of life, fertility, vegetation and beauty, it would be a first step toward preparing for climate change.

The rivers in Spain have their peculiarities. The Ebro and the Guadalquivir are large rivers that carry water year round, and they may need less attention than the more invisible ones, which are just as important – or even more so.

What has made the changes to the riverbanks possible?

I.A.: Farmers growing their crops organically. Environmental activists fighting for rivers, for their flora and fauna. Citizens wanting the old river back, like it used to be when they were children and they could swim in it. Engineers understanding that rivers are more than just drainage channels to get as much water as possible out of the way as quickly as they can. Designers being concerned with processes and not just forms. And, of course, a growing ecological awareness on the part of society as a whole. Also, the knowledge that if we don't change the way we treat the planet, we won't last much longer on it...

Has that change come from citizen use, from care, from planning?

I.A.: There can't be systemic change if all the agents aren't involved.

M.J.: In our part of the world, this change in the riverbanks has been possible as a result of a vacating of industrial land due to the shift in part of the economy towards the service sector. A classic example is the transformation of the mouth of the Besòs River and its banks from industrial use to civic use for the 1992 Barcelona Olympics and the 2004 Universal Forum of Cultures.

What builds the memory of a river?

M.J.: Rivers move in a bed that is larger than what we can see. They are also under the surface and between old and future water ways. From people's point of view, the overarching narrative is always how high it rose in one place or another and how far it spread into a neighbourhood or certain fields. But the river builds its memory by modelling the terrain and leaving traces of old channels. We like to think of our designs not as oil paintings but as watercolours, where we have to add a few layers, with a lot of transparency, on top of a painting that already has many layers and to which more will be applied.

How do you approach a river?

M.J.: To approach a river you have to give it space with seasonal floodplains. And to take care of it, citizens need to have an affection for it. That can be promoted through a good landscape design that includes cultural and recreational elements. There are criteria, but no recipes. For example, instead of giving space to the Arga River by expanding the riverbed, in the Aranzadi Park we found a possible parallel bed for it through the lowlands, which farmers call the interior river, because that was where water tended to accumulate during flooding.

There are underground rivers in Spain and rivers with reconstructed riverbeds. What should we do with them?

I.A.: In the Mediterranean, dry washes are extremely important and they are the most mistreated and misunderstood of waterways. With the pressure of urbanisation, they have become marginal spaces, considered dirty, dangerous and useless. When people talk about doing something in a wash they tend to say, "Clean it up". That's a big mistake! Washes are our safety valves for managing storms, but they are also very delicate ecological and water management systems. When we channel them through pipes, we limit their capacity and ensure flooding when the size of the pipe becomes insufficient. We prevent groundwater from recharging in areas where it is most needed and where water is a scarce commodity. And of course, we wipe out an entire ecological system, one of the richest in the Mediterranean forest. We are working to reopen the Sant Just stream, near Barcelona at the foot of Collserola. The current project foresees extending the piping, but fortunately that mentality is changing. In a few years, we hope to reverse the poor decisions that were made when people still believed that concrete, pipes and hard engineering could solve all our problems.

M.J.: Underground rivers need to be given their space. Even though we can't see them, they are alive and they support specific ecosystems. We need to understand them and restore them. Their health can contribute to preventing desertification and tempering the climate.

Barcelona is defined by two rivers.

I.A.: Ildefons Cerdà's project for Barcelona's Eixample included a large peri-urban, metropolitan park along the Besòs River. The rivers of Barcelona play a role in how traffic is organised ("toward the Besòs" or "toward the Llobregat") and their recovery for citizens is coming a century and a half after Cerdà's plan, but without contributing any additional green lungs for the city, which is full of dense construction. Barcelona was founded on Mount Tàber facing a small Roman port. It spread out toward the rivers like an oil stain, expanding without much intention, except for the initial (and rapidly dismissed) idea of Cerdà's park, which, at the time, must have been considered an eccentricity.

What inspired you in the design of your proposals that foster a coexistence between civic life and rivers?

I.A.: During a site visit when we were beginning the design for the Zuera bullring (how the recovery of the banks of the Gállego began), we found that "there was no site": the river had overflowed its banks. We were familiar with Pascale Hannetel's designs for exquisite retention ponds in a small stream – just a trickle of water in a channel – called the Petite Gironde. That project for the Gironde helped us imagine rethinking the bullring that we had been commissioned beside the river, without trying to "protect" it from flooding, but designing it to make it compatible with a new park and the river. When we finished construction in 2001, we didn't know if we had made a great discovery or if it was trivial or irrelevant; there was simply no precedent. The closest thing conceptually would be the *ghats*, the stepped banks at certain points along rivers in India that provide access to the water both when the water is low and when it rises during the monsoon. The bullring in Zuera lets water in through the bullfighters' door and lets it out through the bulls' door. Thus, the sporadic flooding doesn't harm it, and the views from the amphitheatre take in the river water and the vegetation on the riverbank.

0 500 1000   2000   5000 m

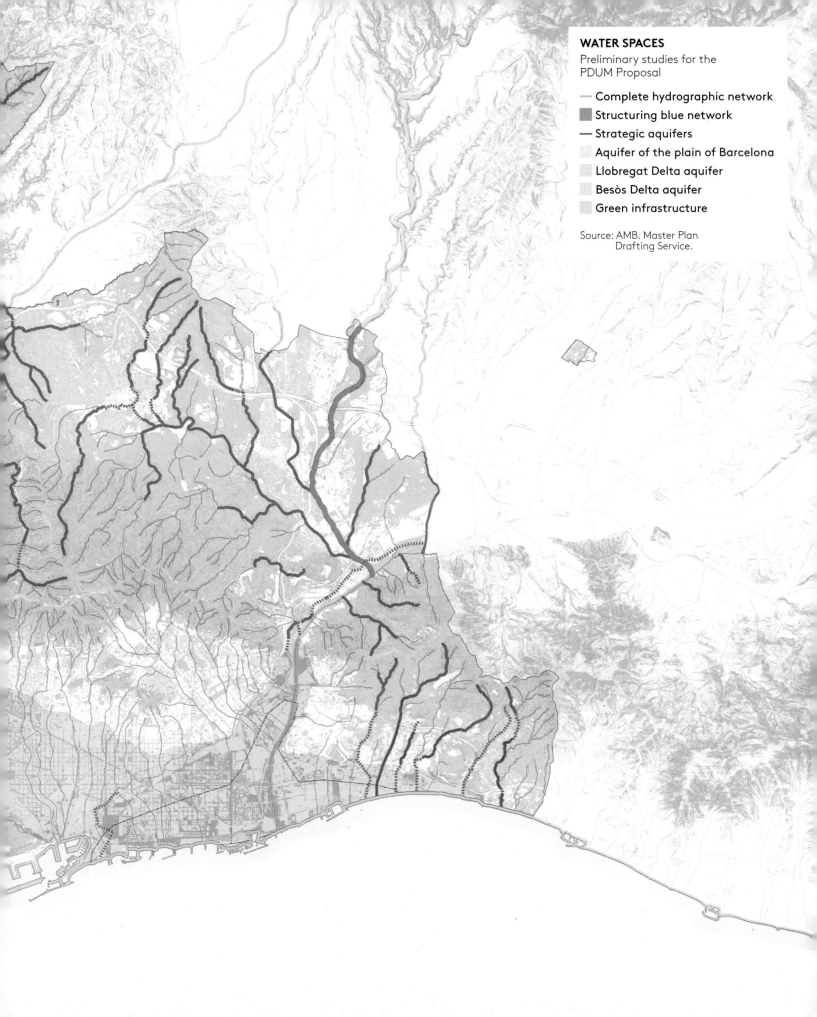

Antoni Farrero (La Seu d'Urgell, 1957) is a forestry engineer who knows plenty about the relationship between nature and the city. Specialising in public spaces, he studied at the School of Forestry in Madrid "because in the 1970s, that kind of training didn't exist in Barcelona". He says that, at that time, knowledge of the natural environment was very much spread over the different disciplines. At the School of Forestry there was a chair of Planning and Projects "directed by Professor Ramos: he trained in the United States because, at that time, nobody talked about landscape". Farrero began collaborating with Ramos when he was a student. Ramos oversaw Farrero's thesis on the planning of open spaces in metropolitan environments. And this is what he continues to work on today in the Barcelona Metropolitan Area. Landscaping was an eye-opener, allowing him to get to know the city. But his journey to the Metropolitan Area was a long one. His first job was director of the Montseny Natural Park.

And what does the director of Montseny Park do?

Well, they try to manage the challenges faced by the park – such as its very intensive use for social purposes – as well as possible with the resources available. Some 70 or 80% of the area of Montseny is privately owned. Some of these landowners make their living from the woodlands, from forest harvesting. The area has a longstanding tourist tradition, yet it is also a fragile territory located very close to several infrastructures and impacted by the exploitation of both wood and water. The park's director must try to keep these elements in order, working with the above conditions. In 1975, the Special Plan for the Montseny Natural Park was a pioneer initiative in Spain. It establishes rules that you have to interpret. And if you detect any shortcomings, you need to push for changes. Nature's requirements overlap with urban planning issues. You are always navigating between two sets of regulations.

What was it like to go from this post to being in charge of managing the riverside spaces of the Barcelona Metropolitan Area?

It has been a long road. I was involved in the management of the Collserola area, dealing with fire issues and reforestation. Then I entered the private sector in the execution of works related to public spaces, restoration and maintenance.

Have you always combined nature with civil works?

Yes, from squares to river areas. In the Metropolitan Area I was responsible for the conservation of parks and beaches; later, I coordinated the management of green infrastructures.

Will the recovery of riverbanks turn them into major inter-urban green lungs?

Riverbanks have a great deal of interest.

But they haven't always been seen that way. For years, people lived with their backs turned to them.

Well, they didn't just appear out of nowhere. But their interest lies in the fact that they are lines. In some cases they act as borders and in others as connectors. They can also be areas of great wealth because they connect different territories.

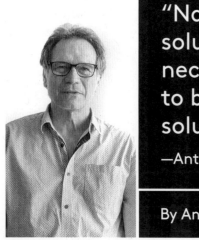

"Nature-based solutions don't necessarily have to be natural solutions."

—Antoni Farrero

By Anatxu Zabalbeascoa

So what determines whether they are connecting or dividing lines?

Basically this is down to the territorial role they have in each case. For example, the Llobregat and the Besòs riverbanks are elements that connect different territories, from the point of view of green infrastructure, so their role is a connector. However, once a territory is developed, river courses tend to mark the limits of that territory. They are geographical elements. One idea that we defended in the Collserola Special Plan is that of making such limits less solid, seeking to make spaces more permeable so that they blend into one another. Instead of a policy of islands, we wanted to create something more porous, so that greenery is introduced into the cities.

The representation of riverbeds as dividing or uniting, does it have more to do with the places themselves or with our perception of them?

It has to do with our degree of knowledge and how we value landscapes and environments: whether what we need to do is to delimit them or make the most of these border spaces, creating places where there is a mix. The most primitive action is to create a divide between the natural and the artificial.

That ties in with the usual jokes about engineers.

Indeed.

You are an engineer who advocates organic lines that echo topography and geography.

That's right. This makes the territory richer, more diverse. We need to position ourselves more on the side of nature. We need to be more geographical than political. Nature-based solutions do not necessarily have to be natural solutions. A territory is something complex, permeable, biodiverse, and what we have to do is to live with this complexity instead of trying to simplify it.

Do you mean for us to undertake an exercise in humility as planners and as a society?

You can read it like that, but urban planning has also evolved. In earlier times, people would build a city based around a main street, like what we see in Western movies. When you think a little bit about growth, you have to give it a bit more structure. In today's landscape we have to negotiate with complexity.

Riverbanks have become a valued civic space. Why have people returned to the rivers? What has been done to make this happen?

Rivers, which were once the backroom of cities, have now become urban parks. They used to be where sewage or industrial waste went. They were always dark spaces – even in literature. Today they are living spaces.

Where has the transformation occurred, in the rivers themselves or in people's minds?

The banks of the Llobregat are a success because they have gone from being a highly polluted area with very high salinity levels that practically wiped out the fish to being a high-quality public space.

Everything ended up in the rivers. They were the cities' sewers. They were not pleasant spaces. No one considered using them for social purposes.

They were dangerous spaces.

Marginalised, murky, remote, abandoned and flood-prone. The floods were unpredictable. They still are. So a first phase of the story involved eliminating the risk of flooding. The next step was to channel rivers to protect the cities from flooding.

It meant that the riverbank was lost.

We went from having a river to having a canal. In many places we are still in that phase. But there are more and more projects working to ease this situation, which also involves understanding the nature of the river.

We've gone from managing water to managing urban leisure.

Partly yes. We started out with water management, ignoring the rest of the life around the riverside space. This was a reaction to the floods suffered – in particular by the Llobregat – in the 1960s, but it also applies to the rest of our rivers.

How were rivers treated in the past?

They had meandering courses that were accompanied by natural vegetation. They were more scenically pleasing, but they were also more dangerous. They were subject to patterns of flooding that endangered the population and infrastructures such as roads. However, when they were taken under control they were no longer attractive for social use.

We had turned the rivers into sewers.

At the same time, they had become a natural passage for infrastructure, roads and railway lines.

Precisely because the connection was already made.

That's right. You're not going to travel through the mountains using tunnels or viaducts if you can move through the valleys. However, with the revival of landscape and ecological awareness, society turned its attention back to rivers.

This is also a cultural issue.

Yes. A quest to recover lost values and places. In the case of the Llobregat, under the Delta Plan the final section of the river was diverted, the port and airport were enlarged, and the high speed railway and the A-2 motorway were built. In parallel with the construction of these infrastructures, it was decided to enter into an agreement with the relevant ministry to restore the natural systems. As a result of this agreement, we began to recover the Llobregat riverbank, from the Pont del Diable bridge to Sant Boi and from Sant Boi to the sea. We restored old paths and eliminated illegal farmland and even small dumping grounds.

Did people protest?

There was a big debate. But once they saw that a space had been recovered for social use and understood the environmental value, they sided with us. They understood what had motivated the change.

What needs to be done first: manage the land or clean up the river?

The first thing to do is clean up the river. This happened when the large wastewater treatment plant was built at the mouth of the Llobregat. One option would have been to place several small plants along the course of the river, and another was to channel the water and take it to the treatment plant at the end. All the water is piped through a collector. Once it reaches the treatment plant, there are several options and the reclaimed water is pumped upstream for agricultural irrigation or sent to deposits that inject water into the aquifer to prevent saltwater intrusion. In other words, a nature-based solution is applied to create a completely artificial water cycle that has an ecological function.

Once the water has been sanitised, you can begin to manage the land.

The initial action taken aimed to cover more than 20 km straight. The second aims to connect the two riverbanks by means of fords. Fords are a more economical solution, but above all it they are much more respectful of the river and its landscape.

So it's about how to go from channelling the river to making the banks permeable?

The channel isn't broken but enabled: it is treated above and below the embankments. Then, a certain landscape is reconstructed. We don't work with rivers by thinking only about high waters. We also have to keep low waters and recreational areas in mind.

Which is how the river is most of the time: not overflowing but flowing.

That's right. Flooding is the exception, although when it happens it is catastrophic. That is why we have to work on both: the possibility of flooding and periods of low and medium flows.

How do you strike a balance?

Through good design.

And with knowledge of vegetation and woodland.

Of course. Some people think it's possible to return to the river landscape of the 19th century. That's clearly impossible because the environmental conditions have changed.

What was the Mediterranean river landscape of the 19th century like?

There was less water use throughout the basin, so the water in the river was more abundant. Aquifers were fuller. And there was riverside vegetation with poplars, willows and wetlands. After doing a lot of "mischief" to the river, adjusting the erosion-sedimentation patterns and engaging in damming, deforestation and urbanisation, it is now impossible to turn back the clock. What we have to look for is a new landscape, which will be "new" because the conditions of the environment have changed: there is less water, aquifers are at low levels... We've ruined it, to put it simply.

Irredeemably?

Is it all going to become a moonscape? No. We can recover a certain ecological functionality, albeit with different methods: regenerating water, recovering a certain river flow and finding ways for the river to relate to the surrounding landscape. It's about ensuring that while the landscape may be different, it is still ecologically functional.

How do you decide on the type of vegetation that should be present in a new landscape?

The vegetation will be compatible with the current ecological characteristics and the intended functionality. For example, tamarinds withstand salinity very well. Poplars and willows will be used to create shade...

What you're describing sounds quite similar to that of the 19th century...

No. It's totally different, even if visually they may be similar. We're in a different situation. Many plant and animal species have been lost along the way. Wetlands have disappeared.

How can we promote the recovery of riverbank biodiversity?

The key is not to do too much. It's easier to restore than to start from scratch. The idea is to help and encourage spontaneous vegetation if it promotes what we are looking for. That's why it is protected. It is more about being attentive and directing spontaneous growth than engaging in substantial intervention. Sometimes you see developments that have been built where a stream used to run: these developments change the topography and then they have to landscape the area. They do everything over again. They raze everything to the ground and then build a walkway, a square... Wouldn't it have been easier to recover the stream? To focus on a simple solution?

Will a regular flow of visitors to the riverbanks affect them?

A thousand times less than they were affected by industries or infrastructure. Social use is very positive: it is a source of knowledge and a way to raise awareness about looking after the environment. This is what justifies the initiative. Nature for humans and humans for nature.

When did we start to realise that riverbanks were public spaces?

When we started to prepare them with a little vegetation and a minimum of signage and care.

How are riverbanks treated? Are they a public space, a natural space, a space for mobility?

The term *public space* encapsulates all of this. It is difficult to define what is natural today. An extensive linear park is close to a natural model.

Will any new floods be bigger?

Absolutely.

Are you preparing the riverbanks for that?

In general, yes, because all the recovery plans have been created with very significant safety margins. But climate change has made it clear: droughts and floods are going to be more extreme and more frequent. I am not as concerned about this issue now as I am about the stability of the coasts.

Why not?

Because we are running out of beaches due to storms and diminishing sediments. There's practically no sand left in Montgat. And the same is true of many beaches south of Barcelona. Storms coming from the east punish the whole sandy area. The rivers are not transporting as much sediment because there are dams and revegetation of catchments. All together, this makes the beach disappear. That's why we're working to form dunes, which are a sand reserve. That is one option; another is to regenerate the beaches with sand from elsewhere.

How do you deal with that?

In the Barcelona Metropolitan Area we have developed a project to recover the beaches in the area called "Hybrid Dunes", recovering the dune morphology. The project won a New European Bauhaus Prize in 2022.

What constitutes the memory of a river?

I think it's more about history than what was there in the first place. What happened there as opposed to what existed there. Josep Pla wrote: "The landscape is years and years of history poured into the territory." For example, Collserola has had many different aspects. It has been bare, and it has been a jungle. It has been burnt and it has been built on. History has had much more of an influence than what was originally there. There are landscapes once lush that are now deserts. Humans have enormous means to act on the landscape. That's why the river's memory is the memory of the people who use it.

This riverside space is for sport, leisure, contemplation, circulation... How do you define its use?

This is often undecided. The agricultural space next to a river arises from certain conditions. The Baix Llobregat Agricultural Park covers more than 3,000 hectares and is one of the most fertile areas to be found in Catalonia. They grow artichokes which are very well known and much prized – the El Prat artichoke – as well as peach trees, onions, garlic, leeks, beans and other horticultural products.

Do you advocate small kitchen gardens or are you in favour of concentrating farming?

Plantations should be large and few in number for economic reasons: to be able to mechanise and recover investment. Even if you have "zero-kilometre" products, you have to look for ways to make your product competitive in the market. A very small plot won't be competitive. It's a romantic concept that can only be applied to products with high added value. But that's for the owners to decide, not us.

What interventions on riverbanks would you highlight from recent years?

The Salzereda Avenue in the Besòs River, by Eva Pagés and Claudi Aguiló Riu. It offers the city and the river. The dialogue between the two when the river is highly artificialised, like in the case of the Besòs, calls for the imposition of order on the border between them with shady trees and riverside vegetation.

Poplars and willows again.

They're chosen according to the conditions of the site and the function you want it to serve. If you only chose trees that are native to the site *strictu sensu*, you wouldn't be able to play with areas of shade or colour.

And is colour important alongside rivers?

Rivers have their own colour. What we need to do is to understand how to capture it and enhance it. I don't think colour schemes should be strident.

Is this colour of the river changeable?

It's totally changeable and that's the fun of it. Spring is different; so is autumn. Every day is different because the river never stops moving.

How can rivers be better cared for?

They must be identified as an asset to the cities through which they pass. Even if they only pass through the suburbs. It is essential to seek a dialogue between the river and the city. This can be done by working on routes from the city to the river or by cycling and light vehicle travel. One thing that would safeguard their future and their care would be to identify them as pathways, as something that unites.

Does the big revolution on the riverbanks lie in the small details?

Yes. It lies in this concept of the pathway. In seeking proximity to people and their lives, their movements and their leisure. Their sport, their walks. Anything goes: the Turia had its course changed, a river was covered over in Zaragoza. In our case, we try to take care of what we have, and it's important to do little and do it well. We're on an upward trend in terms of the quality of projects. Quality is no longer measured by design alone. Greener solutions are given more importance. But the territory is also better understood now. There is experience of maintaining these spaces. Projects have improved greatly in recent decades. Notwithstanding, investment is still scarce.

The idea of nature as untouchable no longer dictates design.

Spontaneous nature – as opposed to "natural" nature – sometimes leads to formations that aren't exactly desirable. Today, the alternatives used are more realistic and give better results. I am talking about forest mosaic landscapes, with agriculture and forests that are much less vulnerable to fire, flood or pests. We must re-naturalise the riverbanks, but when doing so we must also support them by using our knowledge and technology.

Riera d'en Font Park

Montgat

JOSÉ ALONSO
(AMB)

2018-2020
4,338 m²
€449,334

SITE MANAGEMENT
Albert Puigdellívol
(AMB)

AMB TEAM
Montserrat Arbiol
Eloi Artau
Roberto Martínez
Álvaro Sainz

COLLABORATORS
BAC

DEVELOPERS
AMB
Montgat Town Council
UE – FEDER

CONTRACTOR
Eurocatalana

PHOTOGRAPHER
Joan Guillamat

The recovery of the final section of the Font Stream (Riera d'en Font), just before it flows into the sea, begins with intervening along the edges of the park. The redesign of the boundary adjoining the left bank of the stream – replacing a wall with a mound of earth that is the continuation of an existing hillock further upstream – creates a more pleasant, open relationship with the city and the beach. The planting of aspens, chaste trees, and willows on the rolling terrain of the riverbank introduces the conditions typical of the riparian ecosystem and, at the same time, it improves the hydraulic capacity during episodes of rain.

On the other side of the park, the existing slope is reinforced with shallow ponds dug into the ground that ensure runoff is harnessed and rainwater is retained, reducing the salinity of the soil. The new greenery, a mixture of shrub species and trees, is concentrated there to take advantage of the presence of water. With the same aim of increasing the permeability, a paved area has been replaced by a dry meadow, which fulfils a double function: to serve as a leisure space and to provide variety in the landscape throughout the year.

⊘ 1/1250

Inside the park, the incorporation of an old obsolete sports pitch made it possible to provide the park with a large multi-purpose esplanade, surrounded by vegetation and with a small area of stands. In the central part, away from traffic and protected by another hill, there is a children's play area that integrates some of the play elements into the slope, in the shade of a line of poplars.

The result of the intervention is a flexible space that has recovered the fluvial character of the riverbank, with new recreational uses and an obvious focus on natural elements: the palette of materials and colours is reduced to a minimum to give pre-eminence to the changing textures of nature.

Dunes
Metropolitan beaches

**JORDI BORDANOVE
DANIEL PALACIOS
ALBA BARRERA
ESTELA GUÀRDIA
AIDA GIRONA
NURIA MACHUCA
(AMB)**

From 2012
17 km, 580,000 m²
Budget included in
beaches management

DEVELOPER
AMB

CONTRACTORS
Innovia Coptalia
FCC

PHOTOGRAPHER
Robert Ramos

AWARDS
Winner, New
European Bauhaus
Prizes 2022

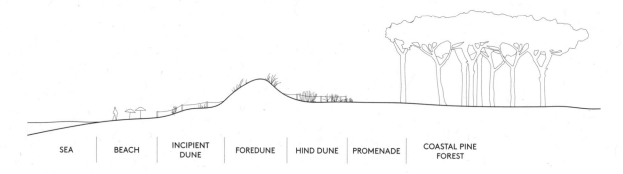

| SEA | BEACH | INCIPIENT DUNE | FOREDUNE | HIND DUNE | PROMENADE | COASTAL PINE FOREST |

The dune areas are reservoirs of beach sand, hubs of biodiversity, and shock absorbers for storm energy. The construction and management of dunes is meant to guarantee the continued existence of the metropolitan beaches, so they don't disappear due to the effects of water and erosion.

To support the natural construction of a dune, the wind needs to be strong enough to transport sand and there needs to be beachgrass (*Ammophila arenaria*), the plant species that helps retain the sand. On the coast of Barcelona's metropolitan area, the wind stopped adding to the dunes naturally more than 30 years ago, although it can still contribute to destroying the existing dunes.

The first step toward dune regeneration on the metropolitan beaches involves protecting the dune areas with pole-and-rope enclosures; then the existing dune fronts need to be reinforced with movements of sand and action on the vegetation, removing invasive plants and planting native species.

1/3500

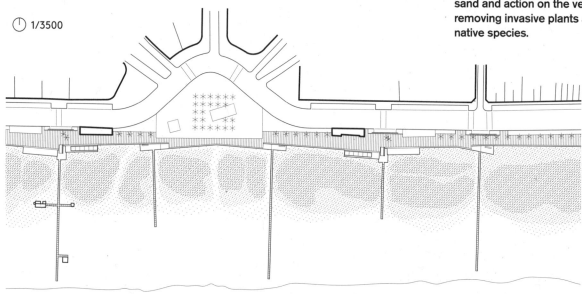

In the spaces where the dunes have completely disappeared, the foundations for new dunes need to be built and their continuing growth as a natural system must be fostered. Since dunes built parallel to the wind have a greater chance of thriving because they are subject to less wind erosion, the beach is divided into different sectors depending on the direction of the wind. Once the position of the dunes has been determined, irregular non-rectilinear piles of sand are formed to let the wind define the final shape. Once the sand has settled, beachgrass is planted – buried to prevent it from being pulled out and to make sure it has access to the necessary moisture – and it is protected with reed screens to give it time to build up the dunes.

Dune regeneration is a nature-based solution that reinforces natural systems so they can stand up to extreme weather events like strong storms.

TIV_AMB

Metropolitan beaches

MOISÉS MARTÍNEZ-LAPEÑA
CARLES ESPAÑOL
(AMB)

2017-2018
7 m²
€49,888

COLLABORATORS
BBG Estructures
Eprototips

DEVELOPER
AMB

CONTRACTOR
Olprim

PHOTOGRAPHER
Adrià Goula

The new prototype for the lifeguard tower, the TIV_AMB, is an evolution of the lifeguard chairs on metropolitan beaches. It rises more than a metre above the sand and is accessed by a ramp or stairs that can be folded up when the facility is not being used.

The main element is the cabin, open to the sea and the swimming area, although it can be closed off with transparent movable panels to protect the lifeguards from inclement weather, without restricting visibility. Inside, all the materials are permeable to prevent the accumulation of water or sand. The roof is waterproof and insulated, and it has a large sun shade that protects the lifeguards from direct sunlight. The tower also serves as the support for a flagpole that displays the status of the service.

The structure of the TIV_AMB is made of steel, anchored at a single point for easy removal in case of strong storms and at the end of the swimming season.

AMB Shade Pergola

Metropolitan beaches

MOISÉS MARTÍNEZ-
LAPEÑA
CARLES ESPAÑOL
(AMB)

2020-2021
25 m²
€23,974

COLLABORATORS
BAC

CONTRACTOR
Pont de Querós

DEVELOPER
AMB

PHOTOGRAPHER
Stela Salinas

BEACH FURNITURE CATALOGUE

With the aim of unifying the image of the metropolitan coastline and defining a brand that evokes a feeling of belonging, the AMB has designed the service elements installed on the beaches with criteria of quality, functionality, durability, aesthetics and adaptation to the surroundings. The Catalogue includes all the elements to help make sure beaches are comfortable, safe and accessible.

To provide better service to users who need assistance in reaching the water, shaded spaces are built next to the wooden walkways using 5 x 5 metres modules that can be grouped on each beach in response to specific needs. The modules must be easy to disassemble so they can be moved to a storage warehouse at the end of the swimming season.

Each module is a structure of lacquered, galvanized steel tubes that are bolted together, with a wooden floor at the level of the sand and an element that provides sun protection at the top. The floor is made from pine wood slats treated with an autoclave machine to extend the walkways to access the beaches and to ensure water will drain through the spaces between the slats. The modules are connected to one another and to the structure to guarantee a flat and horizontal surface, without differences in height, to support movement for users with reduced mobility.

The element that protects bathers from the sun is a handmade natural wicker panel treated with an autoclave machine, which provides a deep, cool shade.

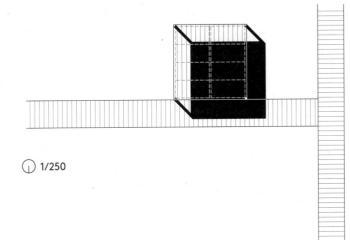

◯ 1/250

Signage
Metropolitan beaches

CLASE
SALVA FÀBREGAS

2016-2018
€380,000

AMB TEAM
Jona García
Estela Guàrdia

DEVELOPER
AMB

CONTRACTOR
Dilart

PHOTOGRAPHER
Adrià Goula

The new signage for the metropolitan beaches is an evolution of the design of the signs for the parks; it creates a shared identity for all the public space managed by the AMB. The predominant colour is blue, in a clear reference to the sea.

The homogeneity of the criteria in the signs conveys to users the idea that they are in a continuous space under common management, regardless of which beach they're visiting. The information is concise and easy to understand, the signage elements are placed strategically according to the type and characteristics of the sign, and graphic symbols take precedence over text.

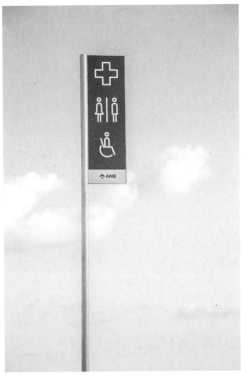

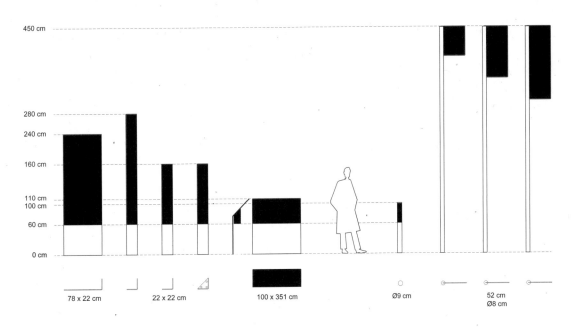

450 cm

280 cm
240 cm
160 cm
110 cm
100 cm
60 cm
0 cm

78 x 22 cm   22 x 22 cm   100 x 351 cm   Ø9 cm   52 cm
                                                                                        Ø8 cm

There are four types of signs: beach access, directions, information, and signs for marking sand dunes. The access signs and directional signs are built from a piece of aluminium sheet, folded into an L-shape, to which a vinyl decal is attached with the relevant information. For the informational signs, an aluminium tube is used to hold up a banner of different sizes at more than four metres above the ground. For information related to the dunes, the signs are installed on the posts that hold the ropes surrounding the dune areas; they are built from a slightly curved anodized aluminium sheet, to which a vinyl decal is attached. In the case of some beaches, the same communication codes are used for the installation of an observation table.

Hanging Footbridge over the Ripoll River

Barberà del Vallès

INFRAESTRUCTURES DE MUNTANYA

ÁLVARO SAINZ (AMB)

2021-2022
2,848 m²
€488,695

AMB TEAM
José Alonso
Adriana Rodríguez

COLLABORATORS
BAC
JBP Enginyeria
Otherstructures
UTE CSS Espai Públic

DEVELOPERS
AMB
Barberà del Vallès
Town Council
UE – FEDER

CONTRACTOR
Infraestructures
de Muntanya

PHOTOGRAPHER
Simón García

The construction of a hanging footbridge over the Ripoll River is part of the efforts to improve and regenerate an area of Barberà del Vallès that was quite run-down. From the right bank of the river, near the Molí Vermell wetlands and the urban core, to the route that leads to Barberà Castle and the green ring on the left bank, this new path, exclusively for pedestrians and bicycles, connects two parts of the municipality that were previously kept separate by the river.

The metal walkway is held up by two nine-metre pillars that support two steel cables (catenaries). It covers a span of 84 metres and the deck is two metres wide; in some places it hangs almost five metres above the level of the river. Several cables running crosswise under the deck serve to reinforce the structure, increasing resilience in the face of extreme weather such as strong winds or storms and reducing possible vibrations.

Care was taken with the materials used to integrate the footbridge into the river's natural environment: trees and shrubs were planted at the entrances to the footbridge and along the river path, and a green gutter was built to channel rainwater, prevent erosion of the path, and support the adaptation of the species that were planted there.

1/1000

Footbridge over Comerç Stream

Sant Feliu de Llobregat

AIDA MUNSÓ FRANCISCO JAVIER NAVARRO (AMB)

2015–2018
1,725 m²
€238,207

AMB TEAM
Montserrat Arbiol
Sara Arguedas
Eloi Artau

COLLABORATORS
CTP 1999

DEVELOPERS
AMB
Sant Feliu
de Llobregat
Town Council
UE – FEDER

CONTRACTOR
Freyssinet

PHOTOGRAPHER
Adrià Goula

LLOBREGAT RIVER PARK

The metropolitan stretch of the Llobregat River is an intensely humanised space, but it also stands out as a green corridor and waterway that connects the Collserola range with the coast. For years, the AMB and the municipalities along the river have been working to improve the environment and the landscape on its banks, seeking to strike a balance between environmental values of the river and its social use.

As part of the global strategy to restore the landscape and promote the social use of the Llobregat River environment, a footbridge was built over the overflow channel of the Comerç Stream to provide continuity to the pedestrian and bicycle traffic along the river, while also fostering the recovery of the natural surroundings.

The footbridge avoids a long meander in the path and is situated upstream of the mouth of the channel, creating a small detour with respect to the existing path, which runs parallel to the stream bed. The route is redrawn to form a curve, which minimizes the slope of the road and guarantees access to the footbridge, located 70 cm above the level of the current path.

Thus, building the footbridge is another step in improving connectivity for pedestrians and cyclists through the network of paths in the Llobregat River Park.

Floodable Ford on the Ripoll River

Ripollet

MIREIA MONRÀS (AMB)

2018-2020
4,470 m²
€355,848

AMB TEAM
Montserrat Arbiol
Yéssica Ramajo
Albert Puigdellívol
Álvaro Sainz

COLLABORATORS
ABM Consulting
Naturalea

DEVELOPERS
AMB
Ripollet Town Council
UE – FEDER

CONTRACTOR
Izer

PHOTOGRAPHERS
Joan Guillamat
Víctor Bello
Xuan Yin

A U-shaped path descends into the riverbed and crosses it with a floodable ford to connect the two paths on the right and left banks of the Ripoll River. The connection is exclusively for pedestrians and bicycles and takes the form of a 4-metre-wide concrete path.

The crossing is on a stretch of the river where the riverbed was irregularly occupied with productive gardens and agricultural constructions, fences, a self-built irrigation system and a type of vegetation that was unsuited to a riparian woodland. To regenerate the fluvial ecosystem, the proposal entails removing all unsuitable elements and incorporating nature-based solutions. Earthworks are used to form a topography that will facilitate water retention in strategic points, where vegetation is planted to take up the surplus water from the irrigation channel. Water from the industrial estate is now treated through phytopurification, and a structure of fascines is built to protect against erosion. The landscaping is always centred on native species and adapted to the riverside environment.

Floodable Ford on the Llobregat River

Various municipalities

AIDA MUNSÓ FRANCISCO JAVIER NAVARRO (AMB)

2016-2018
14,600 m²
€642,259

AMB TEAM
Montserrat Arbiol
Sara Arguedas
Eloi Artau

COLLABORATORS
CTP 1999

DEVELOPERS
AMB
Sant Feliu de Llobregat Town C.
Molins de Rei Town Council
Sant Vicenç dels Horts Town C.
UE – FEDER

CONTRACTOR
Moix

PHOTOGRAPHER
Adrià Goula

The construction of a new river crossing over the Llobregat River is part of the global strategy for environmental recovery and promotion of the social use of the river. In this particular case, the ford is located in a stretch of river that guarantees connectivity between Molins de Rei and Sant Feliu de Llobregat (on the left bank) and Sant Vicenç dels Horts (on the right bank).

The floodable structure crosses the river at a point where the riverbed is relatively narrow, upstream of where it meets the Torrelles Stream; it provides a crossing for foot and bicycle traffic, as well as for service

vehicles, as long as the rising waters don't make it impassable. From the two gravel paths on the banks, the difference in height, of five or six metres, is resolved with concrete ramps that run down into the riverbed.

In the entire area of the intervention, both on the newly created slopes and along the gravel paths, the aim is to plant species of trees and shrubs that can grow without needing to be watered. The intervention strengthens the metropolitan green infrastructure and joins the existing network of river paths.

Regeneration
of the Riverside

Molins de Rei

JOSÉ ALONSO
MIREIA MONRÀS
(AMB)

2015-2020
38,757 m²
€381,440

AMB TEAM
Montserrat Arbiol
Eloi Artau
Albert Puigdellívol

DEVELOPERS
AMB
Molins de Rei
Town Council
UE – FEDER

CONTRACTOR
Talio
Voracys

PHOTOGRAPHER
Judith Casas

As a continuation of previous interventions, the path along bank of the Llobregat River is improved where it runs through Molins de Rei. A 3-metre-wide path made of decomposed granite and aggregate is designed to run the length of three kilometres. It slopes crosswise towards the river and the profile lengthwise adapts to the existing path to minimise earthworks.

The resulting topography facilitates the accumulation and retention of water at the lowest points (ditches and ponds) and takes advantage of the higher ground for planting trees. Thanks to the resulting different degrees of humidity, the necessary environmental conditions can be created for the optimum growth and maintenance of the vegetation – made up of native species characteristic of riparian zones, thus restoring the fluvial ecosystem.

In short, the new path improves accessibility to the river, strengthens the relationship between the city and the river, promotes the recovery of the river ecosystem, and favours its biodiversity.

Access to the Beaches
Viladecans

LOLA SIMÓN
MARIA BLANCO
(SBS Simón i Blanco)

2018-2021
13,095 m²
€581,786

SITE MANAGEMENT
Mireia Monràs (AMB)

COLLABORATORS
Proido Consultors

DEVELOPERS
AMB
Viladecans
Town Council
UE – FEDER

CONTRACTOR
Hercal Diggers

PHOTOGRAPHER
Robert Ramos

The beaches of La Pineda and La Murtra, in Viladecans, are areas of great ecological value in the Llobregat delta, and the paths to access them needed to be improved: regulating the different types of traffic; updating signage and urban furniture; and improving the quality of the surrounding landscape.

Foot and bicycle traffic is encouraged, as well as the use of public transport; the spaces for private vehicles are outlined, and paths for active mobility are designed in keeping with the characteristics of each section and the available widths of the roadway.

The edges of the paths are naturalised through the planting of native species, and green gutters, ponds and wells are built using recycled gravel for a more sustainable management of rainwater.

Thanks to the new road signs, furniture and improved landscape, mobility for beachgoers is safer and more pleasant.

Regeneration of the River Environment

Sant Andreu
de la Barca

JOSÉ ALONSO
(AMB)

2018-2020
67,675 m²
€740,700

AMB TEAM
Montserrat Arbiol
Eloi Artau
Roberto Martínez
Albert Puigdellívol
Álvaro Sainz

COLLABORATORS
AYESA
Nuno Paiva de Almeida

DEVELOPERS
AMB
Sant Andreu
de la Barca
Town Council
UE – FEDER

CONTRACTOR
UTE Drim - Talio

PHOTOGRAPHER
Judith Casas

Several interventions are meant to improve the green infrastructure in Sant Andreu de la Barca, along the banks of the Llobregat River from the Corbera Stream to the Palau Stream. Existing paths are consolidated, new sections of footpaths and cycling paths are created, along with small areas for rest and leisure, planted with trees and native vegetation.

The construction of a pedestrian access and a new cycle path around the industrial estate makes it possible to cross this area in a safer, more comfortable way and helps to better connect the urban centre with the river area. The river is reached from a path parallel to the AP-2 highway, where the pavement is improved, and through three underpasses, which are adapted and where daytime LED lights are installed.

In short, the project consolidates the socio-environmental and landscape recovery of one more section of the network of river paths being built along the Llobregat River.

Reno-
vated
Space

It is difficult to think of an architect who has approached architectural restoration and remodelling buildings from so many points of view. He has done it based on an absolute respect for the work: the Neue Nationalgalerie in Berlin; and based on an intent to depict each layer of history: the Neues Museum, also in Berlin. For the latter, he received the Mies van der Rohe Prize for making it possible to talk about the past, the present and destruction all at once, through new construction. He has also done it based on repair, in the Procuratie Vecchie in Piazza San Marco in Venice, and based on dialogue and contrast, in the Saint Louis Art Museum. In this interview, via Zoom, Chipperfield (London, 1953) talks about his work and his love for his adoptive home, Galicia, where he believes he has found his very own Arcadia.

How should we deal with the built environment?

Working with existing buildings is a very broad field. We might be talking about a 16th-century Baroque cathedral in southern Italy, or an office building in Berlin from 1965. It could also be a building from the 1990s that was left empty.

Exactly. And you have dealt with it in all its versions.

In the past, restoration was concentrated on historic buildings. We protected buildings that constituted a cultural legacy. Heritage was restored. Today things have changed a lot. In today's restoration, both the heritage value and the environmental value have a weight.

Have we put artistic legacy and environmental legacy on the same level?

It has been shown that knocking down a building, however bad it may be, creates a pollution footprint, to which we must add the energy costs of putting up a new building, which the world can no longer afford.

Heritage is no longer the criterion.

It isn't the only one. From this plural point of view, from this new perspective, it may be more appropriate to tear down a small heritage building – not a masterpiece – than a larger nondescript building.

You've done all kinds of restorations. From the recovery of the last building by Mies van der Rohe, the Neue Nationalgalerie in Berlin, to the reconstruction of the Neues Museum with all its layers of history, including its destruction.

Indeed. We've been working in Berlin for 20 years, a city where heritage can be difficult to identify. History has been so complicated there that everything has patrimonial importance now. A crude modification of an existing building from 1978 may have heritage value, but not because it's artistic: the value is political, it's what it signified. It helps to tell the story of history.

Where do you take your cues, then?

Our experience in Berlin has been one of continuous discussion and argument. I've spent years arguing, more than designing.

And what have you learned?

That in matters of heritage everything blends together because what's at stake is our relationship with the past and its interpretation. Let me give you an example.

"In today's restoration, both the heritage value and the environmental value carry weight."
—David Chipperfield

By Anatxu Zabalbeascoa

A church burns down, and the foundations of a Greek temple are found inside. What do we restore then, the church or the temple?

You tell me.

It's a very difficult question. In Italy, for example, they have had to choose. And all the recovery, restoration or remodelling is focused, fundamentally, on the Renaissance, the 15th and 16th centuries.

Who decides what to restore?

That's the question. Between a cathedral and a Greek temple, the bishop will always want to recover his own building. These are intellectual debates. You learn by listening to arguments, but they don't have a mathematical solution. In Italy, for example, the debates aren't just about art or emotions; they're political. And economic, of course. In Germany, intellectual discussion dominates in politics. At least in our experience.

In Berlin, you've done restorations in very different ways. Letting the past speak for itself and rebuilding from the present, and being rigorously faithful to the original design.

What do you do when you're tasked with repairing a Mies van der Rohe building? Who corrects the mistakes of an architect like him?

What kinds of mistakes?

Significant mistakes in terms of insulation: the lack of thermal insulation. You find things such as: the most beautiful windows don't work as an insulating element. They're innocent, ideological. But they've contributed to the beauty of the building. What should restorers do in those circumstances?

What should they do?

Do you update and modify an icon by sanitising it, or do you persuade the government to uphold the mistake to protect something that is going to cause problems? I've only had such intelligent and articulate discussions in Germany.

And what were the results?

In that case, we had to convince the experts and that politicians that Mies should have the last word in the Nationalgalerie. His voice still had to be heard over and above any modifications. Even if it meant a little thermal disaster. It's a fascinating topic.

How do you decide how to intervene?

One of the fascinating things about working on recovering cities and buildings is that you quickly learn what they don't teach in architecture schools. It isn't about protecting individual creativity; it's about putting collective creativity first: eras, geniuses, icons, the city itself. Restoring and recovering makes you a collaborator. We collaborate to improve the city. And that's a struggle.

An exercise in persuasion?

And rectification. The technical, economic, patrimonial, political and creative parts have to be in agreement. We listen, we design, and we correct or we argue. And, little by little, the agreement is forged. Everything is called into question, not just the form. Why this type of metal? Will there be too much space? Won't there be too much light?

Are the decisions motivated by questions of loyalty, budgeting or technical aspects?

Imagine I've been commissioned the Nationalgalerie, starting over from scratch. The questions might be: Why does it need such a big lobby? Are you sure it will be useful? But when it comes to restoring an iconic building, everyone agrees on one thing: the building should be protected. And then the question is: How can you protect the form without improving the insulation? The hardest part, and the most exciting thing about restoration, is the dialogue it generates.

Doesn't that happen in any architectural design?

With a new design, you spend half the time persuading based on an idea and a form. When you're restoring Mies van der Rohe, you can bypass that debate: everyone agrees on saving the building. That's clear. The question, then, focuses on the how. Does everyone also agree on how to restore it? Not necessarily. They agree on the goal and on finding a way to achieve it while being as loyal as possible.

What is the biggest difference between restoring and starting from scratch?

There are many. But a crucial one is that common goal. In architecture it's never clear that the goal is common. For two reasons. Architects aren't usually pursuing a common goal. They're looking to build their design, and that interest comes first. Their ambition comes ahead of the common goal. And it's also very difficult for trades to compete with the speed and economy of industrial solutions. When it comes to restoration, there is usually a common goal. Although, given the energy-related and environmental issues, the debate is becoming more and more complex. Even so, a restoration that incorporates all those different points of view will undoubtedly be one that puts common growth first. There is strength in unity, but you have to dedicate time to it. The good thing about the crisis in the European Union is that it has given certain architects the opportunity to take stock of their careers.

What do you mean?

It has been a time to reflect on the personal reasons that lead you to defend a design and the decision to be honest and serve the common good. I may sound romantic or idealistic, but that's how I see it.

In the Neues Museum you opted for a coexistence between the ruins of the original building, the traces of destruction during the Second World War, and the imprint of the present.

I had the enormous privilege of working on that project. But I should also say that we worked for that privilege.

How is that?

When I won the competition, my wife said to me: Why do you want to spend the next 20 years rebuilding a ruin? A lot of people thought the same thing. It could have been a nightmare. We knew all about the original building. We had the plans and elevations. Society expected a restitution of what had been destroyed.

Why did you choose a different solution?

It would have involved 10 years of boring work. We decided that we preferred 10 years of intellectual stimulation. Could we protect the parts that had survived? Could we make them functional? Could we take smart decisions instead of simplistic ones? The achievement of the Neues Museum is not the result but the process.

The result is what validates the process.

Exactly. But without the process, the result wouldn't exist.

That's exactly what you perceive upon entering the building: the remnants of the past, the traces of pain, the attempts at healing.

Right. I agree.

It's unusual for so many layers of history to speak at the same time in a building, with the same strength.

It's something you see more often in cities, that's true. But that's why what is patent in that museum, at least as I see it, is the dialogue surrounding its recovery. We had to persuade a lot of people. We struggled with getting the permits to do what we did. All the decisions had to be agreed upon by the technical, political, operational, economic, and patrimonial consultants... There were more than a million decisions because the project's focus was not just restoring a ruin, the recovery had to function as a 21st-century museum.

How did you do it?

By militarising the collaborations. It was the only way. We agreed with all the teams to be part of this exercise in military precision. People say it's so beautiful, there's so much sensitivity... but the building isn't the fruit of an architect's genius. What I think is an extraordinary achievement was the agreement that we reached. The consensus among so many parties participating in the process.

What did the process involve?

Including everyone. Talking with people who didn't agree with you, convincing them with arguments. Every party had their well-argued reasons and presented them for the sake of improving the project. There was a shared goal: the best design. No one was looking to come out on top or show off. The aim was to build the best museum possible, the most dignified, logical and just. And that is essential for good architecture. That building demonstrates that a building is decided by many voices. I spent many more hours in conversation than on design work. I'm not a formalist architect. I don't think things can be resolved with formalisms.

You place a lot of importance on form.	It's very important. It isn't that I'm not interested in the way things are. But what comes first, the idea or the form? That's the key. The form should be derived from the idea. As I see it, design is a tool for doing things, including improving society.
Have you always thought that way?	Yes. We architects are living in an ascending cycle, like the top half of a circle: it goes up and comes down again at the end. But I've lived the bottom half, a downward cycle that rises again in the end.
What do you mean?	After World War II, European architects designed based on idealism, with the aim of creating a better and fairer world and making it visible. They were looking to build a world with decent schools, streets, buildings and housing. My teachers were those kinds of professionals: the kind who wanted to rebuild Europe after the ravages of war. Civic involvement was a priority. Throughout my lifetime, I've witnessed the collapse of that civic ideology. To the point that architects are no longer a part of that civic reserve. They aren't idealists, they're pragmatists. They offer services. They don't want to change the world. They're companies in the service of power. And power today is very uninteresting.
Its objectives aren't directed towards the improvement of societies and cities.	The goal of power today is economic profit. Especially in the Anglo-Saxon world.
You've witnessed the transition from idealism to disenchantment.	And I've been part of that system. Very few architects have escaped putting our skill and talent at the service of making money for other people.
Why have they done it?	Because most architects believe that good buildings improve the world. We may be sinking, but we're always thinking about trying to salvage some part, doing something good on the way down. By doing that, paradoxically, you manage to save yourself and ascend again.
Your upward curve.	Right. We win when we realise that we can't work only in pursuit of economic growth. That's where recovery comes in, with everything that should never be lost: quality construction, decent spaces, skilled trades, proper housing, the right of people to have a home where they feel like sitting down for a cup of coffee in the morning. It's a political and social issue. We can't grow economically if we don't grow as humankind.
Industry has precipitated a fast architecture that will be impossible to restore.	Precisely, we are the victims of our society's priorities. You can't be an architect and say: I'm going to build houses without having a client. But the industry has an immediate, and very harmful, effect on the environment. We can't hide behind excuses anymore.
Are you a resistant architect?	I do what I can. But I don't want to go against my beliefs.
You spend summers in Corrubedo. And your house there updates the local tradition.	What we see in Galicia, and that's the reason we've become so involved in the region, is that Galicia is, still today, a community that is holding out.
What is it holding out against? There are as many bad buildings in A Coruña as in any other city...	The region missed out on progress, but that saved it. It has maintained a sense of community that is hard to find in other parts of the world. We come from the privileged Anglo-Saxon world where, if you have money, you can buy whatever you want. That doesn't happen in Galicia. It doesn't matter how much money you have. There are many things you just can't buy.
Don't you have an idealised vision?	I don't think so. You may come to Galicia with lots of money, but there's a lot that money can't buy. Money can't buy the calm, the well-being, the education your children get when you live there. In Galicia there's so much you get just for being a neighbour... We've been so happy there with those basic aspects of life that, while understanding that we can't negate the global world, we feel compelled to support the local one.
How?	We're convinced that the whole world should be more like Galicia. We know where our tomatoes are grown. We know where our eggs come from. We depend on our neighbours. We've found a community.

You talk about Galicia as if it were all Corrubedo. That's the best version of rural life.

Galicia may be behind the world in lots of things, but it's a leader when it comes to community life. Seven years ago they asked us for help in improving. I took a year to think about it and I came back to them. I told them that the problem wasn't in the architecture but in the urban planning. In the young people who are leaving the villages. What's the point of designing a great façade if it's not going to improve people's lives? I'm an architect. I believe in architecture, but not in an architecture that is disconnected from people's lives. That's why I decided to set up a foundation.

That isn't aimed at restoring, but at maintaining, a place.

I try to expand on architects' traditional mentality. I've tried to find another way of working.

Which consists of?

My office works in the classic way. We get a phone call or participate in a competition and if we win, we work on the project. With the foundation, we make our own projects. We identify challenges, and we put our concern for the environment and unity before politics.

What have you learned?

Fundamentally, to listen. We've been able to use our knowledge as architects to try to improve things.

What kind of things?

There's a highway, the AC-305, that connects Santiago with Finisterre. It's a highway. But in some sections, it's also a street. It runs through many towns. And people live on that street. To preserve the social value of that highway-street, we needed to reduce traffic speeds where the road was passing through the towns. The quality of life in many towns depends on the speed of traffic. It seems like it would be easy to improve, but it isn't. The schools are on one side. Elderly people don't have enough time to cross. What could we do?

What did you do?

We went to speak with the people responsible for the Public Works and Transport departments. They told it wasn't their job to slow down traffic, but to make sure circulation was possible. Now we have a plan. We've managed to reduce the speed limit. From that point, we're working on little, tiny advances, like widening the pavements along the road to expand the area that isn't for vehicles. That also cuts down speeds.

What is your goal with the Ría Foundation?

To solve urban problems by non-formal means.

That seems incredible coming from you.

Of course we are interested in the form, but the quality of the public space needs to determine that form. The biggest problem of our time is the collapse of urban planning. It has led to a degeneration in our relationship with the environment. Little by little we need to recover urbanism, urban planning, and that's difficult. We need to do it in keeping with the criteria that originate in the place. In Santiago, I tell them: "You have such good examples of architecture! In the city, in the streets, in the porticos, in the galleries, in the use of materials..."

What happened?

The 2008 financial crisis. That's what they say. The public administration was responsible for the development of the city. After 2008, there were major cutbacks in the planning department. And the urban planning started coming in from outside. It was no longer aimed at the public good. The market is looking for profit, and it's impossible to control the result.

The market is interested in selling buildings, not building a city.

Exactly. Everything ends up being privatised. And when that happens, the business interests are put first, and the interest in quality disappears. One of our challenges involves recovering party walls, the space between buildings, and working with it. We're working in Santiago, Pontevedra and Vilagarcía de Arousa. We have a serious challenge ahead. And, little by little, that also entails restoring, recovering, rescuing.

You're looking to restore a whole region!

We want to recover Galicia.

CULTURAL HERITAGE
Informative map. PDUM Proposal

HERITAGE CATALOGUE

■ Assets of national interest
■ Assets of local interest
■ Other assets
□ Urban environment
□ Element sphere of protection
□ Archaeological area

HISTORICAL ROADS

— Structuring historical roads
— Secondary historical roads
--- Former historical roads

Font: AMB. Master Plan
Drafting Service.

The architect Carlos Llinás (Barcelona, 1957) has been building for 30 years and rehabilitating for almost as long. He supports working with the bare minimum, recovering anything of value and removing what is unnecessary. He has been working for the AMB for 25 years and is currently an expert in urban renewal, an area that once dealt with the past and now focuses on the future.

Never demolish, always transform. What do you think of Lacaton&Vassal's motto?

I agree with it. I would even add, "Often, do nothing." Weren't they the ones who made a proposal for the renovation of a square in Bordeaux saying that nothing needed to be done? Well, exactly that. That should be our outlook from the start, right? To observe what is there in order to understand what needs to be done. If anything actually needs to be done.

Do you put that into practice at the AMB?

I try to. It's a matter of considering what your proposal will improve and if there's anything it might hurt. I always pay attention to what already exists, partly because I don't ever have brilliant ideas. The buildings I design end up looking like the ones next door.

Is prioritising the context and what others have done, rather than what you yourself could do, a way of understanding the city? A personality trait?

I guess it responds to the desire not to be too ostentatious. Or if you do make that choice, for the intervention to make sense. We were asked to build a civic centre in a warehouse in an area full of industrial warehouses. It was a rehabilitation project, but we couldn't reuse anything except for the structure because it had no windows. In the end, the civic centre is a public building but it's also an industrial warehouse. It doesn't stand out from the other warehouses. Putting the city first is one way of working. There are others.

Is rehabilitation today intended to salvage history, change uses or enhance energy savings?

All of that. The issue of energy is the most important today, and investments are being made in that sense. There's a lot of new architecture that looks like rehabilitation because it uses techniques and materials from the past: compressed earth blocks, wooden structures, etc. Construction systems are being recovered.

Are more construction techniques being recovered, or buildings?

Both. I think it's all connected and all related to sustainability. I've always thought that wood-framed doors and windows were a good option. They were called into question because of insulation and fire hazards, but now they've been improved in technical terms and they're making a comeback. And yet the trades have disappeared. It's paradoxical. Sophistication in building services exists alongside a return to traditional materials and building solutions. There was a time when it didn't seem possible to install windows that could open in buildings. Things had to be increasingly more closed off to protect the climate control. Doing things like that turned their back on traditional cooling methods, like using thick walls, creating shade and airflow. It's good to recover both the buildings and the building traditions that worked.

Did recovery used to be aimed at maintaining heritage?

Yes. And to give it a new use. And now controlling energy is the predominant motivation.

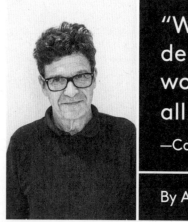

"When you see a demolition you wonder, where is all this going?"
—Carlos Llinás

By Anatxu Zabalbeascoa

Will historic buildings need to be rehabilitated again from the perspective of energy?

Historical-artistic architectural heritage is a world of its own: the conservation (security and safety) of artistic value takes precedence. Those buildings are recovered as works of art, not as highly functional elements. That's why I don't think the demands should be the same since the priorities are different. When you're rehabilitating a church with extraordinary artistic value, you aren't worried about extreme light control. Certain regulations are waived because they often don't identify building's use value. The regulations are the same for everything from a locker room to a house. You spend 15 minutes in a locker room, and it has to have permanent ventilation. That's not the case for houses.

Have the regulations changed since the pandemic because ventilation is even more important?

I've always installed windows that can be opened in my buildings. It's an obsession of mine. And it isn't easy because users open windows that the administration would rather keep closed for safety or temperature control. A window that can be opened in a public building can be used for ventilation, for someone to jump out, or for a thief to climb in. One solution is detachable handles. In other words, the window can be opened or kept shut.

How do you combine the recovery of certain traditions with new technologies?

Through collaboration. It isn't that we can't handle the complexity, but managing it requires collaboration. There is a tendency towards excessive and often unnecessary complexity. Why do you need six different lighting setups in buildings that are only used during the day?

When is it worth rehabilitating a building?

In the buildings with artistic value, the Heritage Department decides. Otherwise, we should always aim to recover buildings that are over 50 years old, as long as it's possible structurally, just because of the material value and the environmental impact. When you see a demolition you wonder, where is all this going?

More has been built in the last 30 years than in our entire history up to that point. What does a building need to have for a change of use to be possible?

It depends on the new use you want to give it. A building with load-bearing walls every four metres will be difficult to transform. If you need large classrooms, for example. I once visited a Koolhaas museum with my children. We were camping in Holland, and I tricked them into going to these places. We went into an event hall and there were pillars in the middle of it! They'd even put one of the chairs behind a pillar. With that in mind, anything is possible.

Doesn't designing in keeping with that goal – with an eye to extreme flexibility and potential changes – result in a loss of identity for the building?

I don't know – because the structure has its own expression. Everything has its expression.

When you recover a historic building, is it possible for each of the layers of the different extensions to have their own voice?

It's possible for the various interventions to express themselves simultaneously through their vestiges, yes. I'm thinking of Pepe Llinás's Metropol Theatre, for example, but that's somewhat difficult to achieve. At the AMB, some of my colleagues have had success with that approach in a simpler way – but we don't deal with buildings with the heritage value of the Metropol. We're working on a site in Sant Feliu de Llobregat. We take our coffee breaks at a market that was renovated by a colleague, Blanca Noguera, using a wooden structure. You can see the layers of the building's history. It's obvious which parts were already there and which parts are new. And it all coexists nicely.

How do you decide what to change and what to keep?

I've worked with extremes: from only changing the paint to only maintaining the structure. The budget plays a key role, of course. But sometimes it's difficult to convince others to change very little or to work with what's already there because there's always someone with ideas about what should be done: a playground, a fountain, what have you. I'm always thinking about trying to improve what's already there when you get there.

Are we living in an era that is more focused on rehabilitation than building?

We're getting there. It's the trend in Europe because space is limited.

To what extent can a building be recovered, and who makes that decision?

I think it depends on the building's nature and its cultural value. When there's a change of use, the new functional programme or the regulations should be adapted so that it doesn't affect that value. In general, the designer alone doesn't make the decisions about how much can be recovered, and the scope of people involved can be very broad. Perhaps an extraordinary case would be the decision to completely rebuild the Barcelona Pavilion.

How do you decide how much to intervene?

In the case of a historic building, you tend to maintain everything you can, regardless of its value or functionality.

How long should a building last?

I have wondered that often myself. And I don't know. Sometimes I think it shouldn't be very long.

In Japan they set the useful life of a building at 30 years, and in the United Kingdom it's 40. And it shows in the buildings: they use prefabricated building materials.

Here, I think we still build without setting an expiration date. I don't know if that makes sense, but it's the goal.

Have you changed the way you build based on the knowledge that, in today's economy, buildings don't last very long?

No. The economy hasn't affected the way we design. But I think maybe we should still consider how long we want a building to last when we're building it. That would be a good start.

A friend once told me that whenever he got in a taxi, he would ask the driver to take certain streets to avoid seeing the passage of time in his buildings. We should build so that we can drive past our buildings in a taxi and not feel ashamed.

Will we see concrete degradation in the future?

There will always be something. I've discovered leaks, and you just feel awful. I imagine it must be similar to what doctors feel when something goes wrong. We're contradictory. We're very strict about building services but our construction still bears a lot of similarity to what the Romans did.

But you advocate building like that!

There are a slew of chemical products that guarantee proper maintenance for building roofs. I'm hesitant every time new material appears. Even if they assure you it's the best, you never know what will happen because it hasn't seen the test of time.

How do you learn?

Trial and error and observation. The buildings in the Eixample, with their Catalan style flat roofs, are still in use.

Not to mention Santa Maria del Mar.

Of course. I'm talking about buildings that have ventilated flat roofs. They can be fixed if they spring a leak. That's a guarantee I'd like to offer with my work. And one that I think citizens should be able to expect.

When did we start building badly?

When business interests, which had always existed, became the main value. When money was prioritised over architecture. Our priorities are apparent in the architecture. I understand that people have to earn money, but...

Does focusing only on the short-term result in greedy cities?

These days, there are people who don't want a salary; they want to earn money, and the more the better. And that also influences the type of architecture that is valued and built, and its lifespan.

How do you decide how to rehabilitate a building?

Everything tends to deteriorate. We're living proof of that [laughs], but some things are more admissible than others. You don't even need to use the same material as the original in a rehabilitation. And the tendency is to intervene very little. The materials are decided based on the budget and the design. But restoring Gaudí's Casa Vicens isn't the same as when you're restoring a relatively recent building.

Should a restoration be evident?

I guess it's inevitable. I appear in some projects, and I disappear in others. Sometimes I disappear so that the new parts look more like the neighbourhood. So they can blend in and be better camouflaged. In Santa Coloma de Gramenet, we were commissioned to build an auditorium at a music school. There was a courtyard and we decided to put the auditorium underground to maintain the courtyard. The better the original building was built, the easier it is to rehabilitate it.

Do we take care of our buildings?

Maintenance is getting better. If tenants feel the building belongs to them, they take care of it. Taking care of public space is more complicated because it has a wider variety of uses, and there may be conflicts among the users.

Is accessibility part of the rehabilitation of buildings?

Yes. It was a pending issue for years, which is why it's included in rehabilitation. But today it is taken into consideration as a basic design requirement. It's a priority. There's awareness of it and it's regulated. I recall working on a school and being concerned about the slope of the ramp. A teacher told me: "Don't worry about it, the slope is just little steeper, and it's also important for kids to help one another."

Kindness over precision in rule-following.

But within reason. It can't be an excuse to sneak in impossible slopes or take independence away from users. No one asks for directions anymore. Instead, we look things up on our mobiles. The internet is an isolating force. It's nice to help someone who's having trouble crossing the road. Instead of assuming they can do it alone.

You've been building for 30 years. And you've had to rehabilitate one of your own buildings.

A sports pavilion in Santa Coloma de Gramenet. We accepted a change in the roof proposed by the construction company. Now, 30 years later, I realise that I shouldn't have accepted it. Fortunately, I've designed many buildings that are holding up well. But when something like that happens to you, you have to admit that you were wrong.

What was the mistake?

Using more lightweight materials that make it difficult to resolve issues with water drainage. In a design, you specify a material, stipulated the model and brand, or its equivalent. They always find the equivalent, but it never actually is equivalent. And you have to be careful.

Which rehabilitations done by the AMB do you think have made the biggest contribution?

The market I mentioned earlier, designed by Blanca Noguera, the CIBA building by Cristina Sáez in Santa Coloma de Gramenet and El Molí library by Antonio Montes in Molins de Rei. All three were properly rehabilitated and the architects got it right on what to keep and what to alter. The result is simultaneously new and old. It belongs to the place and renews it, which is why it breathes new life into the building.

Palmira Domènech Civic Centre

El Prat de Llobregat

CARLOS LLINÁS
(AMB)

2017-2019
3,144 m²
626 m² (urban
development)
€4,731,576
€116,879 (facility)

EXECUTIVE MANAGEMENT
Mònica Mauricio
(AMB)

AMB TEAM
Susana Casino
Tamie Delgadillo
Ferran Roca

COLLABORATORS
Joan Gonzalez Gou
Martí Cabestany i
  Puértolas
PFP, disseny

DEVELOPERS
AMB
El Prat de Llobregat
Town Council

CONTRACTOR
GrupMas

PHOTOGRAPHER
Marcela Grassi

The new facility is located in an industrial area, on the limits of the residential fabric in the northern section of the municipality of El Prat de Llobregat. It is the result of the transformation of an old four-storey warehouse that sits on the north-west corner, with a structure based on a grid of pillars and slabs that is maintained, and which conditions the distribution of the spaces inside.

The building is designed with a foyer, where the main staircase is located. This foyer crosses the building lengthwise, separating the public part of the facility from the area reserved for the municipal archive, the toilets and the elevators. This distribution is repeated across all the floors, making the area intended for public use a square surface that is open on three of its façades, given that the original construction is separated from the neighbouring plots by a space of three metres. Here the functional programme typical of a civic centre is laid out, with multipurpose rooms, meeting spaces and offices for associations, among other uses, with all the rooms receiving natural light and ventilation.

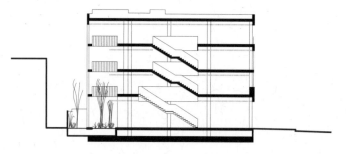

1/500

The internal organisation of the facility is also visible from the outside: the most opaque section corresponds to the archive, and the lobby is like a slice running from top to bottom of the building, an interior passageway that ends in a covered garden patio. The volume, four storeys in total, is carved out at the corner with a large double-height void that also creates a visual relationship between the facility and the immediate urban surroundings.

The exterior envelope is a ventilated façade in corrugated sheet metal, reminiscent of the industrial buildings in the surrounding area, or a curtain wall with aluminium profiles in the glazed sections. As protection on the ground floor facing the street, there is a gate built from vertical slats of larch wood, the same material that is used for the drop ceilings in the lobby and the terraces.

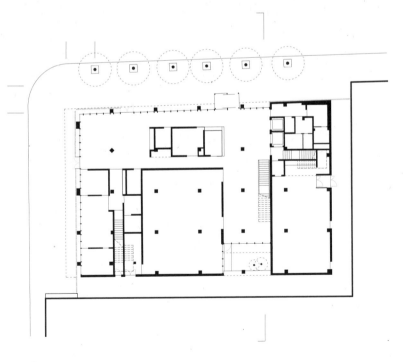

1/500   GF

El Molí Library

Molins de Rei

ANTONIO MONTES (AMB)

2016-2019
2,004 m²
3,537,942 €
€957,222 (structural consolidation)
€560,246 (facility)

EXECUTIVE MANAGEMENT
Mireia Diaz
Maria Sánchez (AMB)

AMB TEAM
Paula Beltrán
Rosa Bertran
Marta Juanola
Irene Puig

COLLABORATORS
Eskubi Turró Arq.
ICA Grupo
Mur Arquitectura
PFP, disseny

CONTRACTORS
Cots i Claret
GrupMas

PHOTOGRAPHER
Jordi Surroca

DEVELOPERS
AMB
Molins de Rei
Town Council

AWARDS
Shortlisted,
Catalonia Construction
Awards 2020
Finalist,
FAD Awards 2020

The strategy for the construction of El Molí Library in the old Ferrer i Mora textile factory, dating from the mid-19th century, was designed in keeping with several conditions: it partially occupies two of the three industrial buildings, which will be rehabilitated in phases, and it is meant to highlight the most attractive areas of the roof, such as the views and the wooden trusses.

The library programme occupies the two upper floors of the main building and the four floors of a smaller annex.

The users' experience of the library begins under the entrance canopy on the ground floor, which gives the building visibility from the adjoining public space. From there, an open vertical communication core connects the different floors and sections with a system of walkways surrounding a staircase suspended from the ceiling. The space is lit from above, and it preserves the traces and textures of the past on the walls where pulleys and belts were once attached, while enhancing the sightlines between the different levels.

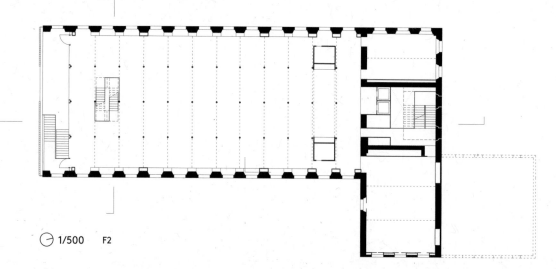

◔ 1/500   F2

← SALA D'ACTES

The second floor holds the largest room of the central bay, for the collections of newspapers, journals and children's books, among others. This wall-less room is also connected to the upper floor through an open double staircase. There is also a large room on the third floor, although it is less wide because the original profile of the roof of the factory has been recovered, and the old terraces are refurbished to be used as spaces for sitting and reading and for enjoying the views over the city.

On the exterior, the materials of the side façades are restored and the south-facing façade, which was nearly windowless, is transformed into a gallery that brings light into the interior, filtered by a screen of ceramic and glass. Given the building's position in relation to the surrounding streets, this facade takes on a new relevance and has become a visual landmark of the former factory.

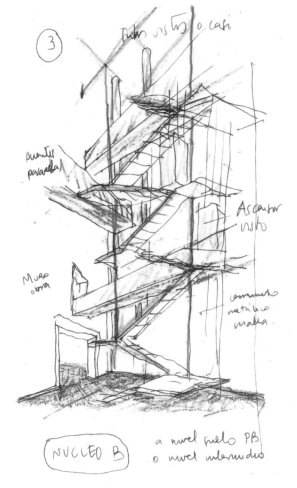

③ Tubo visto o casi

puntal paralelo

Muro obra

Ascensor visto

conmuto metálico malla

NUCLEO B

a nivel suelo PB o nivel intermedio

SBAU

Since 2017, the AMB has participated in the Seoul Biennale of Architecture and Urbanism (SBAU) presenting several projects focused on the concepts of hybrid facilities (2017), city of cities (2019), and digital transformation and the ecological and energy transition (2021). The aim is always to give international projection to the work done to improve public space and metropolitan residents' quality of life.

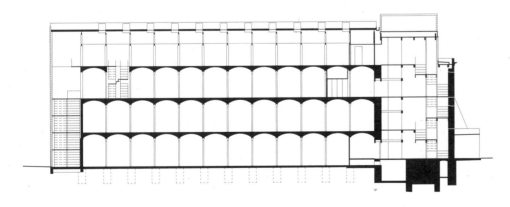

1/500   LONGITUDINAL SECTION

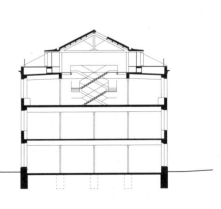

CROSS SECTION

Roser Cabanas Music School

Cornellà de Llobregat

MARINA SALVADOR
(AMB)

2017-2021
1,863 m²
€3,468,355

EXECUTIVE MANAGEMENT
Albert Dalmau (AMB)

AMB TEAM
Marc Alemany
Jordi Bardolet
Verónica Delgado

COLLABORATORS
Arau Acustica
BBG Estructures
Dopec
Ivana Rossell Acústica
Joan Gonzalez Gou

DEVELOPERS
AMB
Cornellà de
Llobregat
Town Council
UE – FEDER

CONTRACTOR
Arcadi Pla

PHOTOGRAPHER
Simón García

The old warehouse from the Can Bagaria textile factory, an example of 20th-century modernist architectural heritage, is being rehabilitated and adapted to house a municipal music school. The original building is a single bay more than 100 metres long, with a gabled tile roof held up by wooden trusses, and a main façade in brick with regular openings. To break up this marked linearity, the different spaces needed for the music school in the interior are grouped together: the foyer with spaces for common use; classrooms of different sizes spread across two floors; and a performance room to be built at a later date.

The access takes place through one of the old bay doors, facing the large entrance to the industrial complex where musical activities can be held outside the classrooms, once it has been urbanised. In addition to the spaces for the school administration, just inside the entrance are the stairs and the elevator, and a gate that will eventually lead to the performance room.

On the ground floor, the smaller classrooms are distributed along a corridor next to the main façade; the top floor holds the larger classrooms and spaces, on both sides of a central corridor. To ensure proper lighting and ventilation, the old windows have been repurposed and several new courtyards have been created that run the full height of the building. They help to lessen the impact of the intervention and reveal the original section and interior volume, leaving the wooden trusses in view.

F1

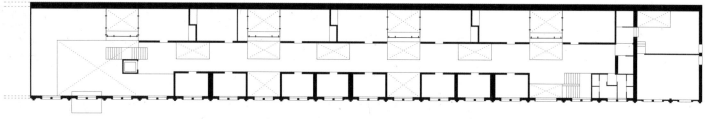

GF

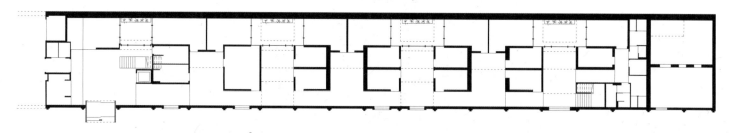

 1/500

Ca l'Altisent and Font del Rector Gardens

Sant Climent de Llobregat

ROBERT BAGÓ
RAMIRO CHIRIOTTI
MÀRIUS QUINTANA
(Col·lectiu Brusi)

2018-2022
893 m² (library)
5,457 m² (gardens)
€1,534,850 (library)
€594,087 (gardens)

EXECUTIVE MANAGEMENT
Mireia Diaz (AMB)
E3 Solinteg (gardens)

AMB TEAM
Álvaro Sainz
Carlos Villasur

CONTRACTOR
Rehacsa
Bigas

COLLABORATORS
Bernuz-Fernandez
 Arquitectes
Naxal Arquitectura
Oriol Vidal
 Enginyeria
Zeb3consulting
Enginyeria Reventós
Anna Zahonero

PHOTOGRAPHER
Adrià Goula

DEVELOPERS
AMB
Sant Climent
de Llobregat
Town Council
UE – FEDER

AWARDS
Shortlisted,
XII Ibero-American
Architecture and
Urbanism Biennial 2021

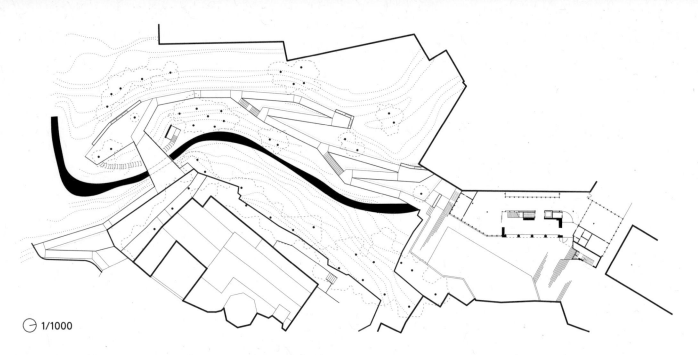

1/1000

The rehabilitation of the Ca l'Altisent building to transform it into a public library means that the garden can be open to the city and access to the Font del Rector source and stream can be possible. The additions built over the years are removed and only the main volume, consisting of two storeys, is preserved along with the tower, which serves as a landmark from a distance.

The façade, which shows the textures of the construction techniques used in the different phases and extensions, is treated with a uniform layer of paint, lending a unified image to the whole and integrating all the original constructive and ornamental elements: mouldings, cornices, cornerstones and railings. The ground floor of the original building is used for receptions and promotions, and around it are gathered the necessary spaces to accommodate the functional programme of a small library. They receive natural light from a courtyard adjacent to the party wall around the perimeter and the glass façade.

The new public square – once occupied by a private garden – is part of a sequence through a relandscaped natural space that follows the contours of the terrain and connects the two banks of the stream with a new platform.

In short, the rehabilitation of Ca l'Altisent has led to a new urban itinerary that connects the Vila and Església squares through the park and the new library square.

Unió de Cooperadors

Gavà

MERITXELL INARAJA
(Meritxell Inaraja
Arquitecta)

2018-2022
524 m²
€1,415,036

**EXECUTIVE
MANAGEMENT**
Mònica Mauricio
(AMB)

AMB TEAM
Oriol Paluzie

M. INARAJA TEAM
Laura Bigas
Amàlia Casals
Ester Serradell

COLLABORATORS
AIA Instal·lacions
   Arquitectòniques
COTCA
Eskubi Turró Arq.
Patrimoni 2.0
Joan Antoni Rodon

CONTRACTOR
Rehacsa

DEVELOPERS
AMB
Gavà Town Council
UE – FEDER

PHOTOGRAPHER
Adrià Goula

AWARDS
Shortlisted, FAD
Awards 2022

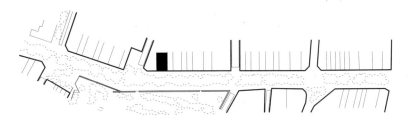

🕐 1/4000

Returning a building designed by Josep Lluís Sert and Josep Torres Clavé, members of the GATCPAC movement, to its original function and recovering a prime example of Catalan rationalist architecture: this is the two-fold aim of refurbishing the headquarters of the Unió de Cooperadors [Cooperators' Union], built in the 1930s.

The modifications to the building are channelled at restoring it to its original state and giving it the features of a contemporary public facility. Superfluous elements added to the building are removed and the compartmentalisation of spaces that had taken place over time is also removed; priority is given to the recovery of the main façade and the original colours; the open plan structure based on metal pillars, slabs with metal profiles and ceramic vaults is preserved, which allows for broad open spaces; and some of the remaining original finishes, such as the circular staircase, the railings and the door and window frames, are highlighted.

The adaptation to new uses requires an elevator that ensures access to all the floors from the street. They are also connected by the new staircase built in the rear bay, one of the spaces that has suffered the most transformations over time.

Ultimately, once adapted to current needs, the building is designated for multiple uses among the city's young entrepreneurs, in connection with its origins: the dream of a group of workers who left behind a legacy that is both a symbol of the cooperative movement and a testament to an architectural style.

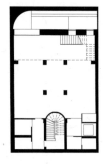 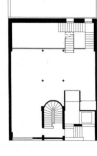 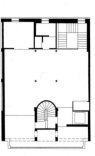

🕐 1/500   B-1   GF   F1

Sant Andreu Market

Barcelona

BLANCA NOGUERA
(AMB)

2018-2022
3,197 m²
2,670 m² (urban
development)
€8,228,156

**EXECUTIVE
MANAGEMENT**
Albert Dalmau (AMB)

AMB TEAM
David Aguilar
Francesc Germà
Vera Kolina
Albert Nogueras
Berta Romeo

COLLABORATORS
ICA Grupo
Manuel Arguijo
 y Asociados
Societat Orgànica

CONTRACTOR
UTE Rogasa - Alainsa

DEVELOPERS
AMB
IMMB
Barcelona
City Council

PHOTOGRAPHER
Simón García

The new Sant Andreu Market is intended as a replacement for the previous building, which dates from the early 20th century. Part of the original metal structure is reused, and the zinc is recovered as a material for the new roof. The so-called "retail area" – a single story building with stalls selling non-food items, which connects the porched Mercadal Square with Rubén Darío Street like a covered passage – is also being remodelled.

The main building maintains the distance from the porches around the square, while occupying a volume with reduced visual impact, achieved by adjusting the heights in relation to the surrounding buildings. The initial plane of the façade is a low-rise, transparent plinth and the taller volumes are set back from the perimeter.

The general configuration of the interior in three bays is reproduced. The bays are all the same height, with a sawtooth roof that takes advantage of the trusses from the old side bays and helps optimise natural light and ventilation. To adapt the market to current needs, a basement level is added to house all the building services and logistics necessary for its operations.

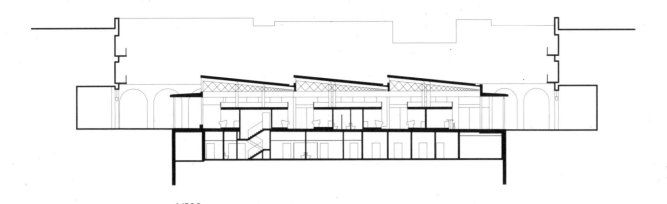

1/500

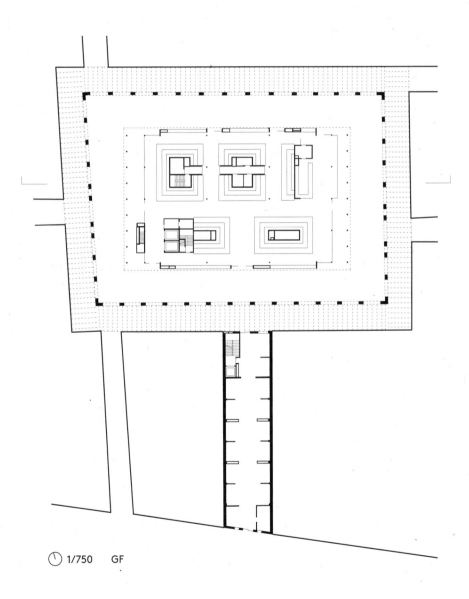

The transparency of the ground floor helps expand the commercial activity of the market into the square and the surrounding streets. The integration between the market and its vicinity is also emphasised in the redevelopment of the square: the pavement spreads across a single level that continues into the interior of the market.

The retail area is maintained on the ground floor, with a gabled roof outfitted with a central skylight and wooden trusses that reproduce the old ones. Next to the Mercadal Square, a building with two more floors has been planned to fill in the gap in the façade, where the market's administration services are housed.

In short, a new market is being built with all the comforts of the 21st century, while at the same time recovering one of its former characteristics: as an open market integrated into the urban fabric of the Sant Andreu neighbourhood.

1/750   GF

La Nau Youth and Arts Centre
Barberà del Vallès

MERITXELL INARAJA
(Meritxell Inaraja
Arquitecta)

2018-2020
888 m²
€1,147,656
€14,268 (facility)

AMB TEAM
Laura Gálvez
Marta Iglesias
Oriol Paluzie

M. INARAJA TEAM
Laura Bigas
Amàlia Casals
Josep Maria Cubí
Ester Serradell

COLLABORATORS
Ángel Gil Control y
Gestión de Obras
y Proyectos
Carles Montobbio
i associats
DSM Arquitectes
Teyle

CONTRACTOR
UTE Voltes Connecta
- Voltes

DEVELOPERS
AMB
Barberà del Vallès
Town Council

PHOTOGRAPHER
Adrià Goula

The transformation of an industrial building for use as a youth centre began a few years ago, dedicating part of it to a concert hall. Now, the other half is also being rehabilitated to accommodate spaces for workshops, classrooms and rehearsal rooms.

The entire structure is preserved except for the fibre cement roof, which is replaced to create harmony with the renovated section, and the virtues of the existing building are harnessed since it is a covered well-lit space, suited to any number of different activities.

A new *container* is built inside: a box made of wood and glass with the right dimensions for activities that need thermal and acoustic insulation, creating an interior wooden façade that looks out onto the rest of the space. Taking advantage of the difference in height between the street entrance and the ground floor of the hall, a large lobby is created that connects with this open interior space. Retractable stand seating is installed here, which can be used for performances and activities in different formats.

Cov-
ered
Space

With one foot in academia and the other in craftsmanship, Josep Ferrando (1972) from Barcelona is a defender of permeable cities and of buildings that draw on the *genius loci*, to which he adds local culture, techniques and materials. Director of the School of Architecture La Salle (ETSALS) in Barcelona, Ferrando defends open education, disciplines that mix together, and buildings with permeable edges to make the city a more human space. The interview was held in Barcelona, in an office full of architectural models, some of which have been built in Buenos Aires, where Ferrando has also taught.

What are the world's cities drawing today?

Rather than being drawn, cities are being erased, being blurred. Rather than zones being outlined, boundaries are being eliminated. It isn't "anything goes"; it's "everything is connected". It used to be that the boundaries between the public and private spheres were very clear. Now there are a growing number of thresholds. And the city, for the better, is increasingly disperse.

What is better about that?

The positive side of indefinition, flexibility, in-between places. Transition areas. I always say that I like those places: thresholds.

That's a nice sentiment, but a threshold is very narrow; you can't live in it. How do you prevent it from becoming just a place for passing through?

As I see it, an architectural threshold is an indefinite place or one that has more than one definition. A portico, for example. They're the setting for many little moments in your life. It might be a place where you take shelter as you're waiting for the light to turn green before you cross the street on a rainy day. It might be the place where you duck out of the wind to light a cigarette or where you pull the keys out of your bag before heading into your house. A place where you sit to wait for someone you've arranged to meet. Or a place where you sit down to eat a handful of sunflower seeds on the street. Those places that aren't destinations, but people use them to make the city friendlier. They make it more amenable.

Are those places, those architectural details, designed more with an eye to citizens' criteria than the form of the city?

Public space belongs to everyone. And there are a lot of us. That's why it often forces you to move on. It won't let you stay for too long. You can stay in a private space if you belong to it. But not if you aren't invited.

Is the city outlining a mix between those worlds of passing through and rest?

I think so. Partly because cities are slowing down. Their rhythms are changing.

Is that true or is it wishful thinking?

No doubt, it's still more a general desire than a reality. But it's happening in some places; more and more. And it makes so much sense that it will be unstoppable. Cities are places of change. The citizens change, the streets change, along with everyone and everything that inhabits them. Cars are going to change as much as cities will.

Cars or mobility?

Mobility. And cars. When we say, "In 30 years, cars should be…", what kind of cars are we talking about? Present-day cars or the ones that will exist 30 years from now?

"There's a word that's more important than sustainability: efficiency."

—Josep Ferrando

By Anatxu Zabalbeascoa

There has been a clear reduction of vehicles in the city by widening pavements or by doing away with car parks. If we managed to manufacture the non-polluting car of the future, would we go back to an individual mobility with cars at the centre?

If, on the way to that future, the car's transformation can avoid being at odds with other mobility resources and can strike a good balance, we'll see whether that return happens. If our debate about the future of mobility is just pitting one option against the other, we won't get anywhere. As usual. Anytime you choose to confront rather than cooperate, you get nowhere.

Are there universal recipes for better mobility?

There are common features, but Houston isn't the same as Barcelona. I haven't had a car for years because I live in Barcelona. I travel to Houston for work, and I can't live without a car there. In Chile, you need a car. In Argentina, you can live without one. Buenos Aires is a more European city; you can walk there.

Are there different speeds in how cars are disappearing from the city?

No doubt. But it's a trend. Although people talk about it in a way that is too generic, and that worries me. I always tell my students: what's important isn't learning recipes by heart, what's important is learning to cook. In urban planning and architecture we tend to focus on recipes and in reality, what we should be doing is teaching students how to think about what to do, rather than teaching them what to do. That's why recipes scare me: they aren't universal.

You defend permeability, the progressive dissolution of the limits between buildings or parts of the city. But architects like Moneo defend the perimeter when it comes to building the city.

Speaking of Houston, the Moneo Museum is that kind of building: hermetic. It occupies the entire plot. In contrast, if you look at earlier buildings like Louis Kahn's Kimbell Art Museum in Fort Worth, it's a project that stretches out across the territory instead of closing in on itself.

It's a landscape.

It's a landscape that opens out into the city while at the same time drawing it inward. Marvellous. There are architects who need clear definition and others who don't.

Is it more of a personal choice than an architectural one?

Perhaps. One example would be at the beach. A beach is an inhuman place in the sense that, when it's empty, it doesn't have a scale. But when you arrive and lay out your towel, that's an act of humanising the place: you're building an enclosure. As for that little piece of beach that everyone would step on if your towel weren't there, now one dares to step on it anymore. If you put up an umbrella, you're creating shelter and fortifying your presence. Most people understand and respect that code. The same thing happens in the city. There are architects who lay out a towel and pitch an umbrella, and there are others who, while acting in the city, are like someone at the beach without a towel, almost merging with the sand.

Do you think that we're coming to the end of the era of icons and that we are, at least on certain continents, working more on the construction of the context?

I think so. The era of icons and the star system in Europe is behind us. With the economic crisis, it became frowned upon. We've understood that, on the European continent and with its history, what's important is to continue drawing on top of an existing drawing, not drawing as though the canvas were blank.

Not ignoring history.

It's very important for architects to have constraints because these sharpen our ingenuity. If I were to say, "Let's go out and play", you would ask "Play what?" That "what" refers to understanding the rules of the game. Later you can ignore them, but first you have to know them. In Europe, history imposes positive constraints that hone inventiveness. There was a time when we were working almost as though we were a continent without history. Now we're adapting the context of what already exists, and we're working on palimpsests instead of blank pages.

Have buildings in Europe accepted a layered construction?

Yes, just like cities have. The buildings keep adding layers. That works in Europe. When China builds a new city for two million inhabitants, it's still working on a blank page. And in an iconic way.

There are more and more architects who build icons in layers.

Absolutely. It's a very European attitude. Preservation through transformation, entering into a dialogue with history. There are some major challenges in that coexistence. The CaixaForum in Barcelona has a historical portion that seems to float, almost like when something is left hanging in the air. The strategy adds space for the users while preserving history by updating it. Working in a non-iconic way doesn't necessarily mean that the buildings aren't attractive. Understanding the context means being contextual, not mimetic.

How do you interpret the context? Respecting the scale? The materials?

That's all part of it – but it means taking into account the present day when you're building. The type of brick people used 200 years ago isn't the same as what we would use today. The technological resources are different.

You're the dean of the La Salle School of Architecture. Do you impart those ideas there?

I always say that the best part isn't the position but the commission. I wouldn't have accepted the position if there hadn't been the commission of rethinking the school's educational model. We've changed everything, from schedules and calendars to how we approach the curriculum. We don't talk about courses, but axes of knowledge.

How does that change the education?

There are three axes: design, technique and culture. Design focuses on dreaming. Technique aims to turn those dreams into reality, and culture works to make those dreams shareable.

How?

Culture gives you objectivity.

Objectivity or subjectivity?

It gives you objectivity so you can be subjective. An oenologist may tell you, "I like that wine more than this one, but this one is a better wine." And they'll give you the criteria behind their judgment. That's what culture offers: the ability to value things objectively despite their being very diverse and removed from your own subjectivity.

The footprint of concrete in the city is now being called into question, whereas, due to its speed and low cost, it has been the quintessential material of modernity. Is there a better material for building cities?

It has to do with resources. When we built the university campus at the Torcuato Di Tella University in Buenos Aires, I asked if it would be possible to use wood as a material. And they answered: "Not if you want to win the competition, no." There aren't even any regulations for building in wood. We worked with concrete, and we couldn't use precast concrete because there isn't an industry there. In the end, the decision to use one material or another also has to be a social decision. Using existing resources implies activating society and involving it in the construction of the city.

Isn't ignoring issues of sustainability a shift away from society's needs?

You have to find a balance. In our case, the university has 600 identical recycled aluminium windows. With regard to concrete, our challenge was how to make the largest area of façade with as little concrete as possible. What wouldn't be sustainable would be importing wood from Austria to avoid using concrete in Buenos Aires. Sustainability is a balance. For me, there's a word that's more important than *sustainability: efficiency*. If you're using wood but you don't understand the industrial systems, that isn't sustainable. If the wood is coming to you in 2.20 panels, you have to adapt to those measurements for it to be sustainable; otherwise you're being inefficient and, therefore, less sustainable.

Do you learn from other people's mistakes when making cities?

Of course, and your own. When a certain trend appears in architecture, the temptation is to replicate it. But it would be better to study it, to understand the reasons behind it. If you follow along without a critical perspective, you can screw up. What Lacaton&Vassal do, for example, is extraordinary, but depending on where you're doing it and how you're doing it, it won't work.

What's one common mistake that has happened in the city?

High tech was accepted in an unconditional way. Norman Foster built several iconic buildings in the City of London. They looked like the future.

But it wasn't everyone's future.

Exactly, you can't fill the city with curtain wall buildings. It's inefficient and very expensive. In Barcelona, Mediterranean architecture offers a much more logical response: filters appear immediately – grape vines, porches, courtyards, water features – the idea of the threshold and the permeability that we talked about earlier.

Is a blurred limit condition more difficult to maintain from a climatic point of view?

Just the opposite. It's reinforced by using layers. And we learn from history, which is as good a teacher as innovation. Everything that arrives to us as tradition has withstood the test of time, otherwise it wouldn't have lasted.

How long should an urban building last?

As long as possible. But for that to be possible, it has to be structured spatially so that it doesn't have just one use. It should be easy to change its use.

Ricky Burdett, the director of the Cities Programme at the London School of Economics, says that London is built so that buildings last for 40 years.

You can tell. And that's a mistake. Buildings should stop having so many specific labels (early education for children from two to four, etc.) and be more versatile. What's good for anything can't be tantamount to what's good for nothing.

But modernity already tried that and failed because there was a lack of identity.

It failed because they were empty boxes. Like the Smithsons and Team Ten pointed out, you can't build something that has more value on the outside than on the inside. The habitation can't be worth more than the inhabitant. Not only does the box not work well climatically, it's totally finite. It can't be made smaller or expanded.

What would the alternative be?

The Smithsons worked on aggregative, which have a closer relationship to nature. And are therefore more human: finite and infinite at the same time.

Are buildings in Barcelona built to last?

I think so. The alternative is always a mistake.

Is today's Barcelona better or worse than that of 1992?

In 1992 there was a happiness and a level of citizen involvement that I'm seeing in Madrid today. The collective desire to make a place better is contagious.

And once it's better, what's left?

Maintenance and trying to understand what helped the city to improve.

What would make Barcelona better today?

Working on the density of the metropolitan area and blurring the limits between what is inside and outside the city.

Are some buildings more civic-minded than others?

Of course, the ones that invite you to come in. The library at Pompeu Fabra University, for example, invites you in because it's a unique but not uniform space. There's a question of versatility. You can hunker down to study or stroll among the books. Libraries in Barcelona have been the source of urban dynamism. The one that Pepe Llinás did in Lesseps Square is a square deployed in section. It is a civic space that teaches coexistence.

How many museums and how many hotels fit into a single city?

Phew. As for hotels, it depends on how spread out they are. 20th-century museums have been containers that signal that something is art because it's on display inside. There's no room for any more. However, when it comes to centres that help us learn, understand, there's room for any number of those. The city of Barcelona is already a museum. It can be a museum of peaceful coexistence or of human greed.

Can you promote social diversity through architecture?

Mixed uses in a city are absolutely necessary. That's as old as the hills. One problem is that the regulations are not very versatile. And the real estate market is governed by numbers. What gets built are the most profitable projects, not the best ones. In Japan, for example, restaurants are often stacked vertically. That creates a richness.

Cities are much denser there. Will we get to that density?

It's an option I find interesting. I think that the mixture between the horizontal and vertical city has yet to be explored in Barcelona. Why can't there be a restaurant on a third floor? We're used to seeing notaries or doctor's offices on higher floors, but not all kinds of commercial uses. Harnessing the vertical city is one way of activating it.

What activates a city?

The big difference is activity at night and lighting. Today, Barcelona is a much sleepier city than Madrid.

How can we increase porosity to create a closer relationship between urban planning and architecture?

By working on the ground floor, first, and the interiors of city blocks in cases like Barcelona. And also by working on the verticality we were talking about. The interiors of city blocks that aren't harnessed for the city are barriers. They should be green lungs. We should work on mobility on streets and greenery inside city blocks. Barcelona's greenery began with Cerdà. The streets are 20 metres wide. Ten of those metres are occupied by pavements shaded by trees. In summer there are green canopies, treetops that merge together. In winter, the leafless branches let the sun and the light through. We need urbanise rural areas and ruralise urban areas.

What aspects are important in ruralising urban areas?

Rather than planting greenery, roads and sidewalks need to be permeable. It isn't a question of vegetation but of water. The streets shouldn't be open sewers. And the interiors of city blocks should be green lungs.

And what about places where the city blocks don't have open interiors?

In that case, the greenery will have to be on the street.

Where would you put the trees?

In places were there aren't any cars. In Gràcia, for example.

In the paved squares?

Yes. But without turning our backs on tradition. We can't go to Lucca or Siena and admire their squares and then criticise our own. You don't even need to look at Italy. Would you put trees in our main squares?

Would you?

No. They're fantastic just the way they are. They can be improved with shade and made cooler with some vegetation, but they aren't places to plant a forest.

To what extent can a city be densified?

Again, each city has a its own code. Barcelona has a continuous cornice, only altered by the vertical additions that were built in the seventies. It looks like it was made from a mould. Cities like New York or Buenos Aires, on the other hand, don't work with a consolidation of limits but a play of heights, a negotiation.

Can that negotiation include fencing off streets?

It happens in Buenos Aires, but also in Majadahonda. Fenced streets are the end of the city. And gated communities are a fenced city. It's like going back to the medieval system. Those places are like *The Truman Show*. We associate that film with rowhouses and gardens full of flowers. But this idea of a series of mass-produced houses or flats, giving the appearance of a good life, is very harmful for the city because it eliminates commerce, mixed uses, the use of the streets as public space, the idea of the city as a meeting place. In the end, they're luxury prisons.

Can all that be changed?

Banks have changed. They shifted from being vaults to becoming living rooms. Everything can change; it's the only constant in life. What can change the most in cities is our trust in others.

How do we teach trust?

With transparency. With visibility, creating connections instead of limitations. At Harvard right now there's a common design space for knowledge exchange. Hermetic classrooms keep the knowledge locked in. Your ability to learn mathematics isn't limited to a window from ten to eleven a.m. You can learn math all day long by developing your perspective. It's a mistake to assume that only the student is learning in an educational context. The same thing is true in the city. Spaces that have just one use are closing the door to a lot of urban life.

How can that take place in the context of closed buildings?

By opening them up or, if they have to remain closed, by building filters using galleries, gardens, courtyards, etc., to connect them, opening and closing progressively.

Are 20th-century buildings a reflection of identity, the city or commerce?

If I were Venturi, I would say brands. I've heard there are so many Russians in London that they call it Londongrad. The sale of the city as an investment good – its *commodification* – empties out the city. And destroys it. The economic disparity between the different parts of the world is a factor that empties out cities.

What differentiates a cosmopolitan city

Vinçon helped to build a cosmopolitan Barcelona. The Massimo Dutti that replaced it does not. The global city doesn't serve the local sphere. And the cosmopolitan city is in the world to preserve its identity. The local sphere is receptive to the world, and it isn't mummified or closed off; it opens up to it.

0 500 1000   2000   5000 m

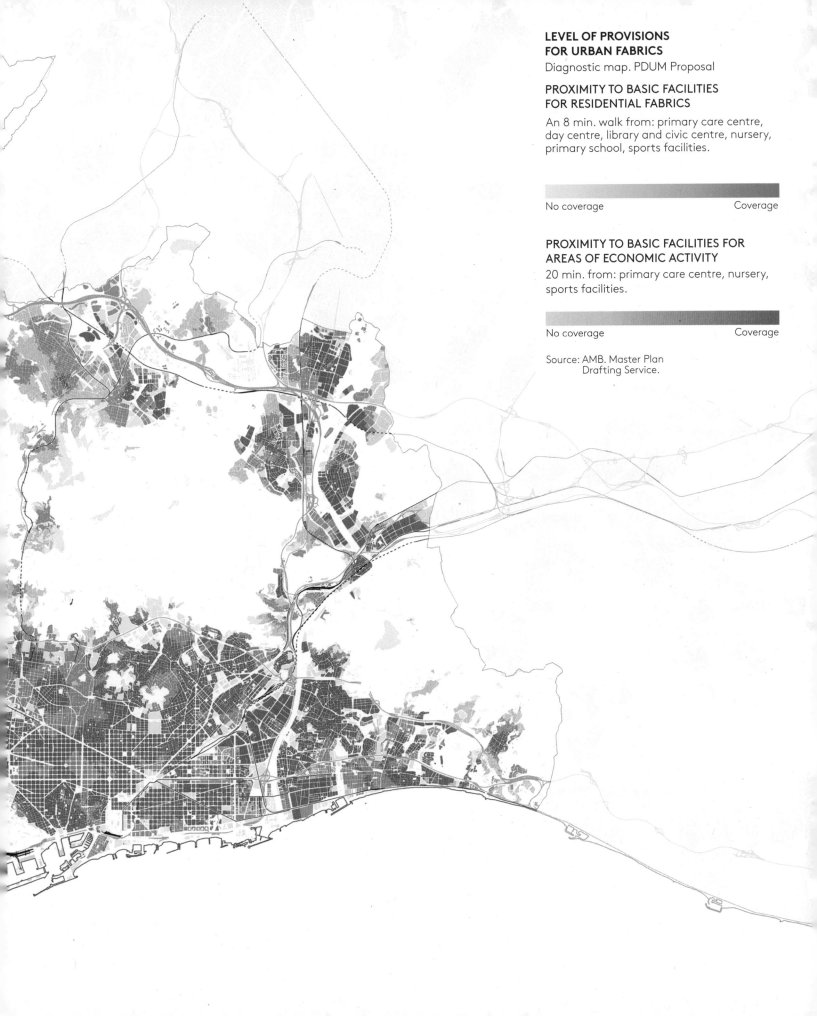

**LEVEL OF PROVISIONS
FOR URBAN FABRICS**

Diagnostic map. PDUM Proposal

**PROXIMITY TO BASIC FACILITIES
FOR RESIDENTIAL FABRICS**

An 8 min. walk from: primary care centre,
day centre, library and civic centre, nursery,
primary school, sports facilities.

No coverage   Coverage

**PROXIMITY TO BASIC FACILITIES FOR
AREAS OF ECONOMIC ACTIVITY**

20 min. from: primary care centre, nursery,
sports facilities.

No coverage   Coverage

Source: AMB. Master Plan
Drafting Service.

The architect Oriol Ribera (Barcelona, 1961) has been working in the Barcelona Metropolitan Area for 26 years. He has seen all kinds of changes in Barcelona, the surrounding municipalities and construction methods. He has been head of a design team since 2000. This interview was held at the AMB headquarters, not far from the sea.

Do cities focus more on the construction of the urban context than on monumental buildings?

We do not have a homogeneous idea of how to approach architecture at the AMB. Our way of working requires economic restraint – which is sometimes not as strict here as it is in other administrations. Given the budget limitations, monumentality has to be ruled out. That's why the architects who work for the AMB don't have monumental aspirations.

Because of their sense of reality?

Maybe. I don't know if architects have a sense of reality. I would say that it comes more from feeling comfortable in the exercise of their profession. One question we ask is: Would you be able to do something similar for half the price? Not in terms of the architects' fees but in the costs of implementation. The requirements are good design and construction, but with reasonable economic parameters that are different from the ones used in other areas of the city. The aim is to fulfil expectations, to be able to make the programmes a reality.

What kind of budget per square metre are we talking about?

It has gone through changes. Right now, times are hard. We still haven't been able to close out the latest projects we signed off on, which already seemed expensive for us. They're costing 20% more.

What were the ratios?

The cost of construction with VAT is €2,000 per square metre. From €1,800 to €2,000.

Isn't that a lot?

It is, but it isn't enough in many cases these days.

How do you learn to work with lower budgets? How do you set priorities when your resources are limited?

Our work has to respond to a programme. And the best design is the one that responds to the programme within the budget we have available, as long as the investment is reasonable – in other words, as long as it isn't less than what could be possible.

Is the best approach the boldest or the most reasonable?

Both. Architects need to know how to keep in line with normal prices without forcing it. The most common foundation type has a price; if you try something less common, you're incorporating an added cost. If the structure uses the habitual spans, the cost will be foreseeable; if they're out of the ordinary, the costs will increase.

Out of the ordinary means expensive.

Things that are uncommon in terms of form and materiality. Floors may be treated concrete, terrazzo, ceramic or natural stone. The difference has a direct effect on the price per square metre.

Is it the extraordinary or ordinary elements that are responsible for constructing the city?

I'm not great with quotes, but I think Oriol Bohigas said that instead of always talking about exceptionality, it would be great for someone to talk about ordinary things, which are what construct the city. If we could bring higher quality to the architecture

"The problem with copying Nordic models is that you can copy the form, but we aren't Nordics."

—Oriol Ribera

By Anatxu Zabalbeascoa

that we refer to as 'anonymous', the city would be better. The architecture that sells takes advantage of the mediocrity of the rest.

What do you mean?

Walking through the 22@ district makes me anxious because it's like a competition to see which is the most exceptional. It looks more like a showroom than a city. The architects have the excuse that the commission they've been given is exceptional for the area. And I think that's a simplistic approach.

Is that your opinion or that of the AMB?

There is no single structured thought at the AMB. The architects who work here don't have a brand or a pattern; our ambition is plural. The only directive is reasonable cost and money well spent. And if there are going to be novelties, they need to be proven. We can't build just anything.

What type of infrastructure is being built most often today, at a time when cities are already built up?

The AMB deals with the municipalities surrounding Barcelona, where that quality of being 'built up' isn't so obvious. We began with sports centres, and the facilities that we build the most often are sports facilities because there's an ongoing demand: football pitches, swimming pools – although at a slower pace – and then nurseries, libraries, civic centres...

What motivates the decision to build a nursery?

When the existing one doesn't offer decent conditions. They are built more often to replace existing buildings than as new construction.

How do we prevent large infrastructures from becoming white elephants, an element that is only used very occasionally but has a large and permanent footprint in the city?

The easiest way is to provide them with more than one use.

And are you doing that?

We do not have a decisive role in how the facilities are managed. We participate in developing programmes and, if we aren't sure about something or we think it's out of proportion, we'll say so. But multiple uses, unfortunately, are difficult to manage. A facility that has been put on hold in the Baix Llobregat area aimed to combine a research area and work spaces for the university with a shared lobby attached to a sports centre and a library connected to Barcelona's network of public libraries. In the end, every space has its needs, and the main problem for a library is to prevent the books from being stolen. Simple as that.

Not to promote reading.

If people steal your books, the library can't operate. Translated into architecture, that demands a closed space. The problem with copying Nordic models is that you can copy the form, but we aren't Nordics. And open architectural forms don't work without civic education. It's hard to have a successful 1,000-square-metre reading room if everyone's yelling. You have to be careful how and what you imitate.

So we're doomed to always be perpetuating the closed model and shouting at each other?

That isn't merely an architectural question. It begins with the educational model. That's what results in one type of society or another. Now there's talk about revising the educational model. But there's also a tendency to take things that have been around for a long time and brand them as new. And there are new expressions that we can't know what they may mean in 10 years, like 'designing from a gender perspective'.

What does that entail?

Being aware that the sports pitches in the schools are largely used by one sex.

That is already changing in society. The Barça women's team is doing better than the men's.

In schools, how sports courts are occupied is a fact.

Ball sports push people out because someone who isn't playing can get hit. It's harder to hurt someone else when you're skipping rope.

Right. But that would force out everyone who plays football.

Sure.

I went to an all boys' school and if you didn't play football, you couldn't use the schoolyard.

Isn't that more a question of management than architecture: maybe organising alternate days?

Sure, until you move into the realm of activism. I like to put flower pots on playgrounds. In other words, I break them up, to make sharing mandatory.

That's the microscale of what can happen in a city. When you can't arrive at a consensus, you have to set limits. But the buildings you defend are the ones that blur those limits, correct?

That was a very attractive and very civic option. But it hasn't taken off. It's hard for me to understand the fences that have appeared around schools in the Eixample. I went to school in the 1970s. There were already cars everywhere. It never occurred to anyone to install railings, the kind of guardrails that prevent children running out the door from ending up in the street. Now it seems like a guardrail is insufficient, and they build spaces like cages that are entirely at odds with the connection to the city meant to educate children in respect. By definition, schools are meant to educate and watch over children. In that sense, the space for parents to collect their children should be inside the building, not invading the street. An ideal school should be connected to the city.

How?

What better way than to open the sports pitch for everyone to use when the students aren't there. But that would require respect and civility. And, as I say, we aren't Nordics. And certain so-called progressive sectors defend fencing in schools, and even the streets surrounding them, instead of promoting educating through open spaces.

Are there any unfenced spaces that have been respected?

In the Almeda neighbourhood in Cornellà, the city council converted the old railway station into a civic centre. Next door is the library, and the proposal included an exterior semi-public space that could be used freely but could only be accessed from inside the library. It isn't fully open, but it's a first step.

As an architect, what might be an opportunity to open a building toward the city?

A library in a metropolitan park. You could pick up a book and be able to go outside and read. There are libraries with terraces, but then there has to be a protection so that no one can toss objects onto the street. The regulations are very strict because they anticipate all kinds of vandalism.

Is the idea to protect people or avoid conflict?

The main intent is to prevent theft. A library has more than just books: CDs, computers...

What determines the design of libraries is avoiding theft?

My colleagues would kill me if I said that. No, it isn't the top priority, but it is essential. And it limits more ambitious solutions.

The more civilized we are, the better our public spaces will be?

That's just the way things are.

The idea of the Metropolitan Area pursues the union between different municipalities, and it blurs the urban limits between them. Is this union also reflected in the contact between buildings and the city?

We aim for all the properties we build to have a good relationship with the space that surrounds them. In the case of sports centres, that can be easier to achieve through the bar area. In La Muntanyeta Park in Sant Boi, where Isozaki built the Agricultura Square, facilities were built within the area of the park. Although, in the end, the boundaries and gates make mixed uses very difficult.

Is the contact between buildings and the city – porosity – more of a theory than a feasible reality then?

In our culture, that may be true. It isn't easy. After years of being open – since 1996 – the Besòs Park will be fenced off.

What a failure!

After years of fighting to keep it open, it has become a space riddled with syringes. There has been no way to remedy it or to stave off the pressure from citizens, so it's going to be closed at night. That's a shame because it was a space that was perceived as natural. And now a perimeter fence will be put up to enclose the entire park.

It forces the park to close at night, and it closes the gates to homeless people who have nowhere to go.

When we started designing parks, there were no maximums stipulated for the length of park benches. Now there are. The benches are shorter so people can't sleep on them. Public space is full of 'sad things'.

Why is there a need to close off parks and buildings?

Because of vandalism. It's a very real problem. As I said, it's a cultural issue. We're working on the Sant Andreu market now, in Barcelona, which is inside a porticoed square. No one wanted an open square. The residents felt that it would generate more problems than comforts for the people who live nearby. It's hard to understand why someone would prefer not to have a public space near their home. But public space, in addition to being a gathering place, is also a place of conflict.

A square is a place of freedom, and freedom includes the expression of conflict when there is one.

Right. Translated into everyday life, it means that when you visit a city you also want to be able to sit in the street, have a drink on a terrace. But you don't want the terrace where you'd have that drink to be under your bedroom window. And you're willing to fight to have it shut down. What we enjoy somewhere else, we don't want in our backyard.

Do you tend to rehabilitate buildings rather than building new ones?

We're heading in that direction.

"Always reuse, never demolish" is the motto of Lacaton&Vassal. Do you share agree?

Mottoes are dangerous. I might agree, but I would never say 'never'. Or 'always'. Reusing is worthwhile but not everything is salvageable. In El Prat, construction materials were recovered from an existing building; the Palmira Domènech civic centre was initially an industrial building, and the entire structure was maintained. The question with reuse is whether it could end up being more expensive than starting from scratch.

That aspect isn't sustainable: it costs less to buy something new than to repair what we already have.

The same thing happens when it comes to recycling buildings. Saving isn't cheap. It's ecological. Old buildings have to be recalculated structurally to adapt them to new regulations. The costs of waste management and materials, etc. are reduced, though.

How is the memory of a building changed when its use is transformed?

It depends. In many cases in the Eixample in Barcelona it becomes superficial, because all that's left is the façade. And a building isn't just a façade. Plus, some old buildings are very poor in terms of materials. So if you don't take into account the cultural perspective, they aren't even worth saving.

What are the main difficulties facing the municipalities in the Barcelona Metropolitan Area?

Each municipality puts itself before the whole.

And the union is effective?

It's very effective in terms of transport, rubbish collection... less in terms of building construction. The towns continue to have their very clear borders. Investments around those borders are a harder sell because shared interventions are more complicated to implement. I've never taken part in the construction of a sports centre that belongs to two municipalities at the same time.

What's the difference between a cosmopolitan city and a global city?

Like Bertrand Russell in his writings, I need annotations: by 'global' I mean x... and by 'cosmopolitan' I mean y...

Global refers to a repetition of models. For example, Zara would be global. Cosmopolitan is local, related to a particular place that has its own voice and is therefore universally admired, because it speaks to you as something exceptional.

Global defined in those terms, as repetition, is disastrous. It's a monopoly. The advantage of traveling is to seek out difference and enjoy it. The alternative: travelling only to find the same things you have at home is empty. And sad. It loses all meaning. It's also true that when a brand is successful it's great that it can be accessible to the world. But in addition to expanding, it's beautiful when that same brand also adapts to the world. And it contributes to making the world a better place by respecting a variety of cities.

Is today's Barcelona better or worse than that of 1992?

Is it worse? I don't know. In 1992, the evolution of cities, the approaches being proposed, and the experts who intervened all happened to be aligned, and there was consensus. While today we might say that the ring road model isn't ideal, we can't say that it was a mistake in 1992. At the time, it was a salvation. On the other hand, I'd say that today we know more about what not to do.

What not to do?

I think it shouldn't be acceptable to generate spaces that aren't manageable. Because they can't be sustained with the resources of the places where they are going to be built.

Are you talking about empty museums?

No. I'm talking about something as simple as building a heated pool and then not being able to pay the gas bill. Before approving a project, its maintenance should be taken into account. The museums in the metropolitan area actually have close ties with their municipalities. In Gavà, for example, they're dedicated to prehistory... There aren't any 'art containers'.

Have you ever recommended against building a project?

Without naming names, the only time we recommended against a project, it was still built. But the recommendation was written down.

And did the mayor fail?

No. The infrastructure is still working.

So, you were wrong?

No. The fact that something works doesn't mean that it is well planned.

Where does the AMB have the most strength?

It's very strong in terms of the parks it manages, not so much in the buildings that are built. We provide a service, but we don't impose it. We've implemented a sustainability protocol that analyses the uses of the facilities we propose. But then the management is municipal. And a city council has to bring a lot of different political parties into agreement. The construction of cities needs to understand that making things sustainable should come before other criteria.

Sustainability should be a national interest and not a partisan one.

It is. And as such it should be made a priority. Our suggestion involves incorporating knowledge about what exists in the area. But the decision on whether or not to build an infrastructure comes from the municipality. The AMB works by offering information, talking about similar experiences in other municipalities to support more favourable decision-making.

How does the AMB decide which projects are designed internally and which are outsourced?

There are a series of criteria, but an essential one is our working capacity at any given moment. At present there are some 10 architecture teams. If we can't handle more work, we hold a competition. Architects and legislation are a bit at odds, but the Law of Architecture stipulates that we must convene a competition – restricted and in two rounds – beginning from a certain amount in fees.

How do you restrict who can compete?

Ideally, it would be by CV or, for someone without a track record, through a specific proposal. But contracting departments don't always see that as in keeping with the legislation. Everyone should be subject to the same criteria.

How can young people compete then?

Someone on the team needs to have a minimum of proven experience.

In Barcelona, the public libraries were a symbol of change in the city for everyone.

Yes, there's consensus on that front.

What other typology might do the same today?

Any public building should have that aim. All of them. Schools have long had that objective. We have historical schools where it seems like all you do is study, and more current ones that communicate a different idea of education: the buildings themselves aim to teach a way of living in the world. The Jesuits or La Salle have Harry Potter buildings. The schools that are being built today reflect a different vision of the world. The image they give to the city isn't one of authority; it's of a place for meeting and discovery. The atmosphere is more domestic.

Are some buildings more civic than others?

Absolutely. In the case of primary care centres, the visuals – the relationship between interior and exterior – are interrupted.

For privacy.

Right. It's only logical, but it creates secrecy and therefore distance. Privacy is a key value in healthcare buildings. But not everything needs that much distance. It's clear that someone lying on their back with their mouth open needs to be respected. But why are we able to see people working from the street but not nurses moving through corridors? Light can get in, but you can't see inside, and I think something is lost as a result. It means that primary care centres aren't as civic as they could be. The waiting rooms could still be open, but of course, that would force us to relinquish precious surface area.

How many hotels can one city sustain?

No idea. But hotels don't just serve tourists. They support business relations, visits.

There are more hotels than homes in some European cities.

There has to be some proportion. Until now, no one objected to universities being situated in urban centres. And they occupy a space that is unusable during the weekend. What characterizes hotels is that the city's residents are never users. That's a toll cities pay, and their implementation should be proportionate.

And limited?

Everything is limited in a city. If not by regulation, like in the case of pharmacies, by the amount of space.

Do a hotel and a coworking space contribute equally to building a city?

Not equally, but both build cities.

To what extent are passive systems for saving energy taken into account in the construction of new buildings?

That concern exists, and it's growing. Our sustainability protocol is five years old.

Only?

Yes. There were always certain minimums, inherent in the technical code and best practices. But the protocol was written to replace the certifications and labels that certain companies grant, and which are essentially a business. You have to be careful who teaches a methodology that people base their livelihoods around. Especially the labels that let you compensate unsustainable practices with sustainable practices. Our protocol begins with an analysis of the programme and the site. In other words, it looks at whether the construction is necessary or not. There may be municipal buildings with empty rooms that can absorb the proposed uses. In that instance, we offer a critical perspective, like better angels. We also try to salvage buildings for other uses. For example, repurposing an industrial building for use as a civic centre. The new buildings are also well insulated from cold and heat. In Sant Vicenç dels Horts, at the La Guardia Civic Centre, we tested out a type of structure that is unusual for our area: a wooden structure, which is considered more sustainable than concrete. They didn't let us install a green roof, however, because it would need to be maintained and they didn't have the resources to do so. Water recycling is much easier in parks than in buildings. Many of the sustainability measures can't be applied without a large budget for maintenance. I hope that sustainability advances towards cheap and easy solutions that can be applied in all buildings.

What is architecture changing?

At the AMB, we expect that more and more buildings will be refurbished and reused. Rather than building new ones. The goal is for buildings to become increasingly sustainable. We have programmes to improve insulation and to outfit public buildings with solar panels. That's a sustainable intervention that is also a restoration.

Has everything already been built?

Yes and no. There is something missing from every municipality, and there is some pretty poor construction. In other words, there's a lot that needs repairing. Also, sadly – or not, I'm not sure – a society is never finished. There are always new needs that appear.

Virgínia Amposta Cultural and Civic Centre

Sant Vicenç dels Horts

JOSEP MUXART (AMB)

2017-2021
2,361 m²
750 m² (urban development)
€4,288,505
€553,848 (facility)

EXECUTIVE MANAGEMENT
Albert Dalmau
Mireia Diaz (AMB)

AMB TEAM
Jordi Bardolet
Jordi Colom
Javier Duarte
Laia Ginés
Marta Juanola
Oriol Paluzie

DEVELOPERS
AMB
Sant Vicenç
dels Horts
Town Council

COLLABORATORS
Eskubi Turró
 Arquitectes
ICA Grupo
Ivana Rossell Acústica
PFP, disseny

CONTRACTOR
GrupMas

PHOTOGRAPHER
Marcela Grassi

AWARDS
Shortlisted,
CSCAE Architecture
Awards 2021

Located at one end of the Mamut Venux park, the building is intended to promote cultural revitalisation in the northern neighbourhoods of Sant Vicenç dels Horts. Its design has one strong determining factor: it must contain a multipurpose room that is equipped, among other things, for rehearsals of the human tower team.

The building itself bridges the difference in level between the main access, from the street, and the access from the park, which is situated on a lower level. The various spaces included in the programme – for young people, organisations, workshops or exhibitions – are distributed across the different floors around a large central, open triple-height space (14 metres tall) for use by the human tower team. A skylight that rises another full storey and captures light from above covers this interior courtyard. The ventilated double-skin façade is designed to reduce the energy demands, and it is outfitted with an external lattice made from ceramic pieces. The internal layer is either a curtain wall, ceramic or concrete walls, as the case may be.

The goal of the intervention is to achieve maximum integration of the building with the park and its surroundings, to bridge the existing height differences on the site and to guarantee connectivity. The result is a building that levitates above a perimeter plinth, which is set back with respect to the upper floors leaving the façades as large, latticed surfaces that do not rest on the ground.

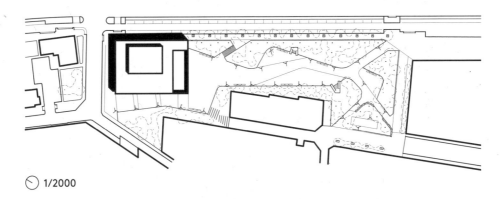

○ 1/2000

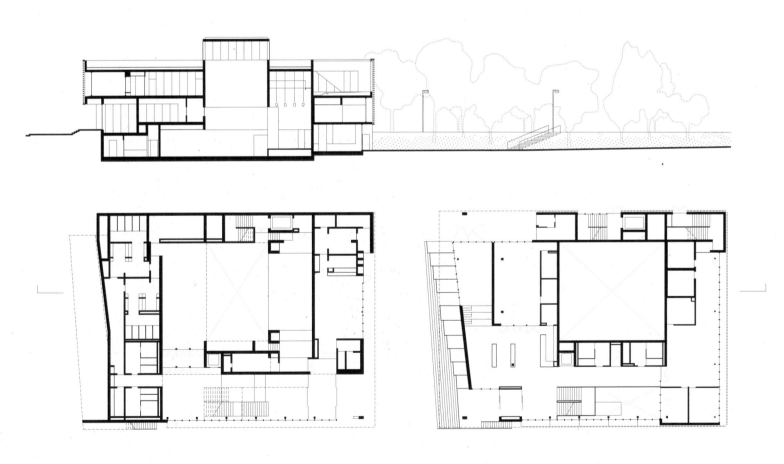

⊘ 1/500   PARK LEVEL

STREET LEVEL

La Guàrdia Civic Centre

Sant Vicenç dels Horts

BLANCA NOGUERA (AMB)

2018-2021
557 m²
2,492 m² (urban development)
€1,362,633
€58,280 (facility)

AMB TEAM
Vera Kolina
Cati Montserrat
Albert Nogueras
Oriol Paluzie
Berta Romeo
Mar Sierra

EXECUTIVE MANAGEMENT
Mònica Mauricio (AMB)

COLLABORATORS
BEST Costales-Jaén
Joan Gonzalez Gou
Lucía Feu

CONTRACTOR
CPM Construcciones, Pintura y Mantenimiento

DEVELOPERS
AMB
Sant Vicenç dels Horts Town Council

PHOTOGRAPHER
Simón García

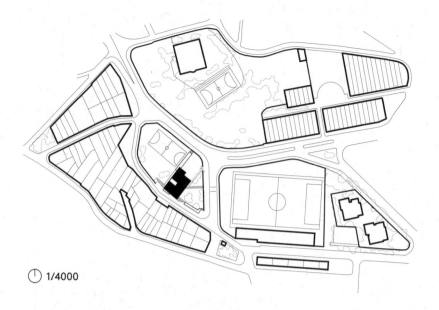

◔ 1/4000

The construction of a civic centre in La Pau Square in Sant Vicenç dels Horts is part of a wider transformation that will be taking place in the urban space of La Guàrdia neighbourhood.

The new building is located in the central part of the square, in front of the existing woodlands. It is designed in two volumes, with a central corridor with natural lighting that separates the classrooms – which seek a connection with the park – from a more closed-off back section that houses the multipurpose room and the facility's private uses.

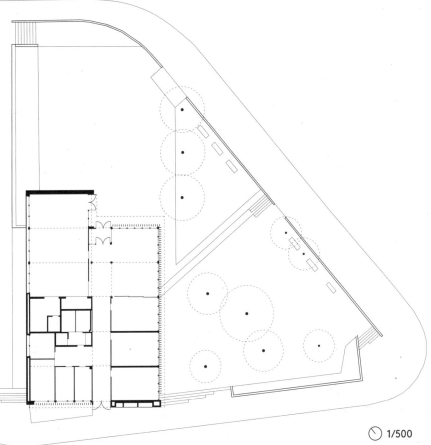

The design of the construction and materials is very much conditioned by the need to optimise costs, by the geological characteristics of the site, and by the desire to align the construction language with the surroundings. The structural solution is based on metal pillars, beams and ceiling structures in laminated wood, concrete façades with aluminium and glass doors and windows, sheet metal cladding and fixed wooden shutters on the south façade. Inside, the building elements are on display: the concrete block and wooden structure are combined with exposed building installations.

In the outdoor spaces, which incorporate new leisure and play areas, the urban development addresses the uneven ground and improves accessibility, while preserving a large number of the existing trees and adding new greenery.

1/500

Ricard Ginebreda Sports Area

Molins de Rei

ROGER MÉNDEZ
(AMB)

2013-2020
2,187 m²
2,391 m² (urban
development)
€3,435,397
€154,267 (facility)

**EXECUTIVE
MANAGEMENT**
Mònica Mauricio
Maria Sánchez (AMB)

AMB TEAM
Aïda Artiz
Susana Casino
Marta Juanola
Arnau Marimón
Cristina Pedreira
Gisela Traby

COLLABORATORS
Eletresjota
INTEC, Gestión
  Integral de Proyectos
Peris+Toral
  Arquitectes
Tectram Enginyers

CONTRACTORS
Sanjose Constructora
Certis
Gruas Constructora

DEVELOPERS
AMB
Molins de Rei
Town Council

PHOTOGRAPHER
Marcela Grassi

◯ 1/15000

The new sports complex in Molins de Rei focuses on the football pitch of a club with deep roots in the Canal neighbourhood. By expanding the facilities and adapting the surroundings, the aim is to accommodate other organisations and less common sports, such as weightlifting, judo, indoor climbing, and gymnastics, while connecting the complex to the city and the open spaces adjacent to the Llobregat River.

The construction of the new facility was carried out in different phases, conditioned by the availability of resources. The master plan for the complex defined the sequence of interventions over time and how the three different phases would fit together, as well as the materials that would be used throughout the process, which convey a certain industrial character that fits in well with the historical and urban context of the neighbourhood.

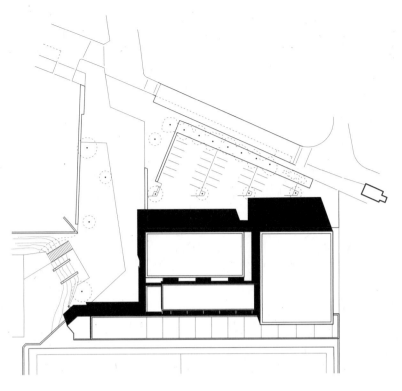

1/1250

The organisation of the new facility is based along a large canopy that runs the entire length of the football pitch: it groups together the volumes that correspond to the different rooms in the complex and serves as a roof over the publicly accessible spaces, such as the entrance, the café and the stands. A large open entrance to the neighbourhood is included in the design, accompanied by a new public space that fosters a relationship with the Llobregat park. The café provides service to both the inside and outside of the sports facility, which means it can be managed independently of the sports complex, making its use and opening hours more flexible. The stands are designed as a covered social space, steering clear of models that focus on a more professionalising aspect of sport.

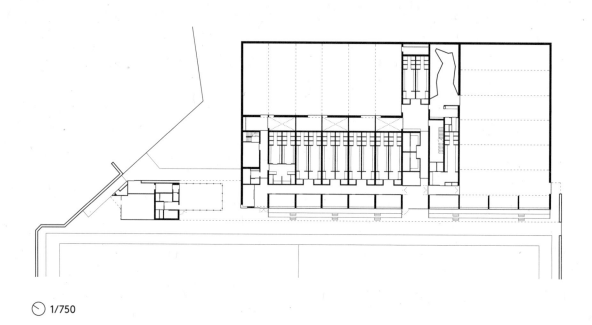

⊘ 1/750

The project's commitment to quality involved bringing in light and natural ventilation to all the rooms to ensure user comfort and promote energy savings in the facility. The size and topography of the site meant that the entire programme could be housed on the ground floor; and courtyards and differences in the height on the façades could be incorporated to allow light and natural ventilation into all spaces. The exterior façades are built in precast concrete at the bottom and, starting from a certain height, translucent polycarbonate modules protected by perforated sheet metal; windows are installed to ensure natural cross ventilation.

The challenge with the new facility is to optimise resources both in the management of the complex and by reducing the energy expenditure, as well as by trying to minimise the maintenance requirements. The concentration of different sporting activities into a single complex leads to an intensive use of the facilities, which, through the careful management of the changing rooms, helps maximise the facility's performance.

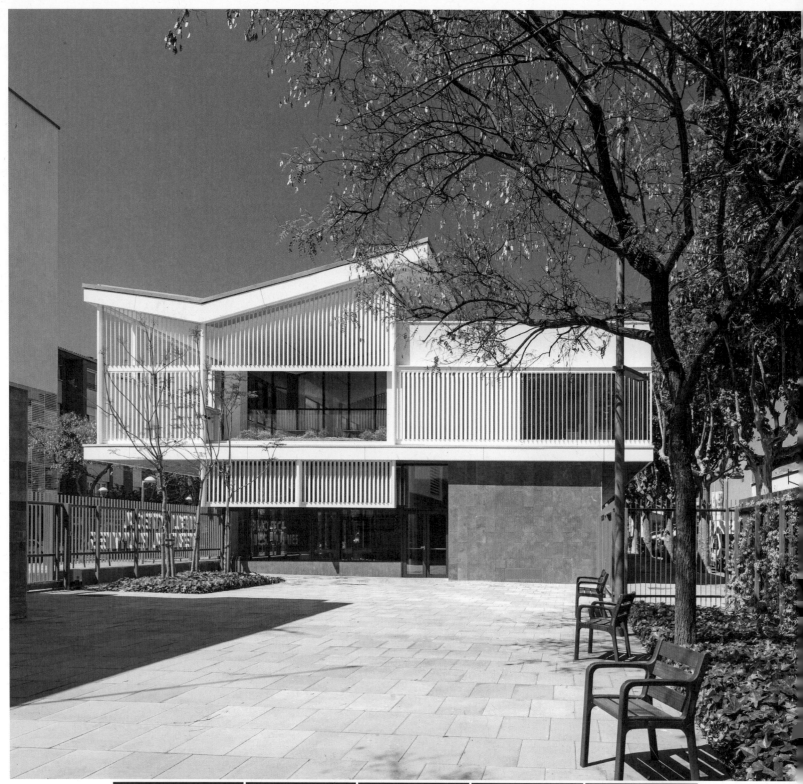

Teresa Pàmies Library

Cornellà de Llobregat

CARLOS LLINÁS
(AMB)

2017-2021
1,201 m²
2,004 m² (urban
development)
€2,741,927
€294,380 (facility)

EXECUTIVE MANAGEMENT
Maria Sánchez (AMB)

AMB TEAM
Jordi Bardolet
Tamie Delgadillo
Mireia Diaz
Marta Juanola
Ferran Roca

COLLABORATORS
Cómo Design Studio
Joan Gonzalez Gou
Martí Cabestany
 i Puértolas
Laura Coll

CONTRACTOR
Calaf Constructora

DEVELOPERS
AMB
Cornellà de
Llobregat
Town Council

PHOTOGRAPHER
Marcela Grassi

The new library for the Almeda neighbourhood in Cornellà de Llobregat is a small facility with the programme requirements of a local library. The site is meant to tie in with the existing day centre for the elderly, creating a courtyard garden shared by the two facilities where outdoor cultural activities like small-scale concerts, lectures, etc. can be held.

The entrance to the library on the ground floor has a double access: directly to the periodicals room and the children's reading area, or to the multipurpose room or study area, which has a separate entrance that allows the space to be used on a schedule that is independent of the rest of the facility.

The upper floor houses the general reading area, several classrooms for support and training, and the working area, as well as a terrace that offers views of the courtyard shared with the day centre.

The massing responds to the interior organisation, with a V-shaped roof over the general reading area and the terrace, and a flat roof over the other spaces. Between the two volumes, a horizontal north-facing window lets in natural light and offers a view of the tops of the nearest trees.

The building's permeability with the outside is achieved with a glazed façade facing the promenade on the ground floor, protected by a three-metre wide overhang that acts as an access porch. On the first floor, large windows, outfitted with a system of fixed or mobile slats that protect from the sunlight, are reminiscent of a shade house or a permeable filter.

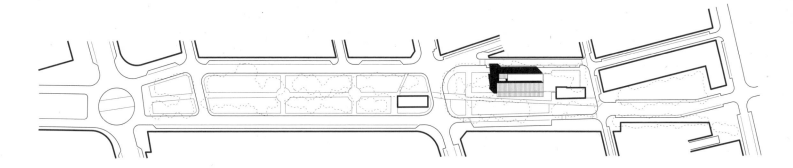

1/3000

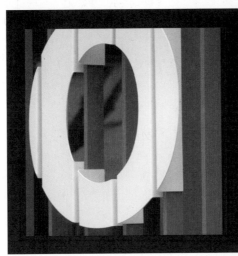

SIGNAGE

The graphic design for the signage at the Teresa Pàmies Library draws on one of the materials with the clearest presence in the project: plywood, which is also used for the construction of all the interior signage. In contrast, the letters in the sign marking the entrance are made from folded aluminium sheet and lacquered in white, and they are sized to stand out while perfectly fitting into the bars of the gate.

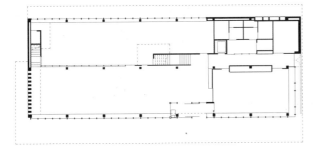

🕐 1/500   GF

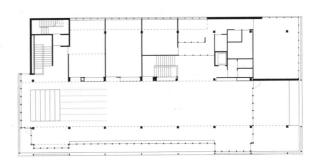

F1

Clara Campoamor Library

Cornellà de Llobregat

LUISA SOLSONA
NOEMÍ MARTÍNEZ
(AMB)

2017-2019
1,287 m²
1,379 m² (urban development)
€2,538,088
€304,683 (facility)

EXECUTIVE MANAGEMENT
Jordi Colom
Olga Méliz (AMB)

COLLABORATORS
Arau Acustica
Joan Gonzalez Gou
Manuel Arguijo y Asociados
Societat Orgànica
Gemma Domingo
Crisant Romans

AMB TEAM
Julen Arbelaitz
Jordi Bardolet
Virgínia Díaz del Río
Sara Fernandes
Ventura Godoy
Marta Iglesias
Cati Montserrat
Oriol Paluzie
Stela Salinas
Lídia Serrat

DEVELOPERS
AMB
Cornellà de Llobregat Town Council

CONTRACTOR
Calaf Constructora

PHOTOGRAPHER
José Hevia

The new reading room for the Fontsanta neighbourhood in Cornellà de Llobregat is a small facility with the programme requirements of a local library. It is located on a lot next to the Canal de la Infanta park, a green space that both separates and connects two neighbourhoods with very different realities.

The building, on a single floor, is elevated above the ground to account for an important condition: the plot is crossed by a collector which, under exceptional circumstances, can overflow and cause flooding. The main entrance, from the square and from public transport, leads into an atrium that opens onto the different interior spaces and the facility's central courtyard. From there, it descends in a series of steps to connect with the park, which sits on a lower level, passing under the building.

BIBLIOTECA
CLARA CAMPOAMOR

The energy consumption of the whole is close to zero, thanks to the natural cross ventilation that can be guaranteed in all spaces and with the use of other passive design strategies, in addition to harnessing energy from the ground. An expanded metal sheet wraps the entire building, blocking direct sunlight without interfering with the views. It provides a unified image, character and scale to the construction.

The facility has a particularity that makes it pioneering: there is a public area that is accessible 24 hours a day, 365 days a year, with no human supervision.

SIGNAGE

The graphic design for the signage in the different spaces of the Clara Campoamor library adapts to the particularities of the building's construction and highlights the original appearance of the "naked" materials. A new font is used, called La Santa, from the sans-serif family and with simple and geometric shapes, taking inspiration from the grid formed by the perforations in the wood.

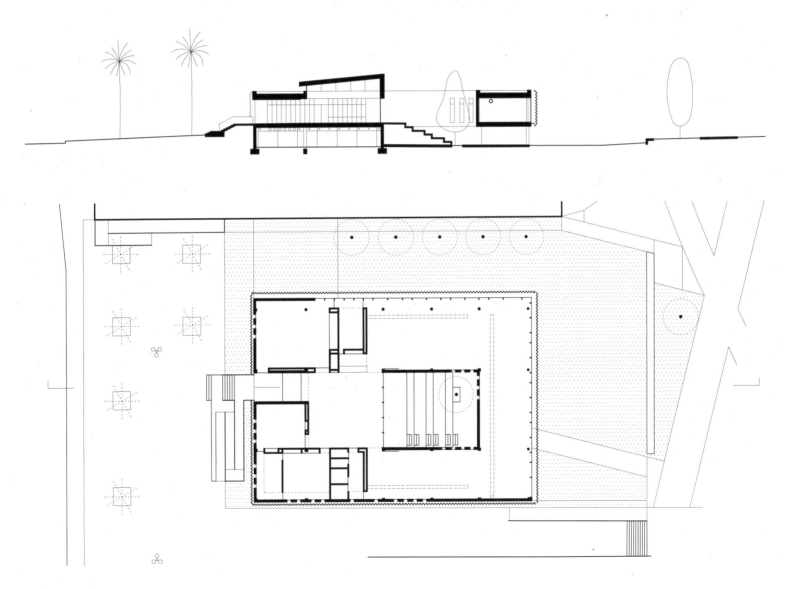

1/500

Can Xarau Sports Complex

Cerdanyola del Vallès

MOISÉS MARTÍNEZ-LAPEÑA
CARLES ESPAÑOL
(AMB)

MIQUEL ÀNGEL SALA
(Masala Consultors)

2018-2020
1,185 m²
€832,403

EXECUTIVE MANAGEMENT
Marta Juanola
(AMB)

AMB TEAM
Gisela Traby

MASALA TEAM
Jordi Cestero

COLLABORATORS
Proarquitectura

CONTRACTOR
Romero Polo

DEVELOPERS
AMB
Cerdanyola del Vallès
Town Council

PHOTOGRAPHER
Josep Casanova

One of the outdoor pitches at the Can Xarau sports complex needed to be covered so it could still be used in inclement weather. Bearing in mind that the roof structure could not be any larger than the current pitch, the designers proposed half-façades to offer protection from the sun and rain, along with a cantilevered porch over the users' path toward the entrance.

The portal structure contains eight steel frames on a micropile foundation, which support a structural sandwich panel made of wood. Skylights are installed in the roof to ensure natural lighting, and the two longer façades are made from translucent polycarbonate panels. The envelope on the short façades is made from opaque metal, which are clad on the inside with wood to provide more warmth to the space and improve the acoustics.

Sports
Courts
Pallejà

AMADO MARTÍN
(JPAM City Makers)

MIQUEL ÀNGEL SALA
(Masala Consultors)

2017-2020
4,846 m²
€1,106,875

EXECUTIVE MANAGEMENT
Marta Juanola
(AMB)

AMB TEAM
Gisela Traby

MASALA TEAM
Jordi Cestero

COLLABORATORS
AT3 Oller-Peña
MOSE Serveis
 d'Enginyeria

CONTRACTOR
Eurocatalana
Izer

DEVELOPERS
AMB
Pallejà Town Council

PHOTOGRAPHER
Jordi Surroca

AWARDS
Shortlisted, FAD
Awards 2021

Over the years, the Pallejà sports complex has expanded with several new pitches. As a result, it needed to be reorganised, and one of the pitches had to be covered so it could be used more intensively and continuously.

To preserve the openness and spatial continuity of the whole, the multi-sports pitch was covered but not closed off completely on any of the sides. The roof, slightly inclined and asymmetrical, is made from a metallic portal frame structure that rests on steel pillars at the back façade and atop a longitudinal truss on the side where it opens onto the football field and the views of the Llobregat valley.

The façades are suspended from the roof like skirting panels in different sizes and materials. The back and side façades, which are supported by a concrete base, removing the need for pillars at the corners, are made of corrugated perforated metal sheet; the main façade is made from translucent polycarbonate panels to provide maximum natural light for the pitch, in conjunction with the skylights in the roof.

A seemingly hermetic volume during the day, at night the roof's translucence is revealed and the light from the interior becomes a beacon and a landmark at the entrance to the town.

Marcel·lí Moragas Sports Pitch

Gavà

MARINA SALVADOR
(AMB)

2016-2018
3,137 m²
478 m² (changing rooms)
€2,129,119

EXECUTIVE
MANAGEMENT
Mireia Diaz (AMB)

AMB TEAM
Marc Alemany
Verónica Delgado
Marta Juanola
Gisela Traby

COLLABORATORS
BBG Estructures

DEVELOPERS
AMB
Gavà Town Council

CONTRACTOR
Calaf Constructora

PHOTOGRAPHER
Simón García

The renovation of the sports complex at the Marcel·lí Moragas school incorporates two important conditions: the preservation of a number of cedar trees near the street entrance; and the need to clearly separate and define the spaces – for teaching and sports activities – to differentiate between uses.

With the new layout, two sports pitches are installed with a single continuous set of stands; one of the pitches is covered with a three-dimensional metal structure and a sandwich panel roof with several skylights.

The changing rooms and lavatories adjacent to the pitch are grouped into three small rectangular modules with a light wooden frame structure: one with four changing rooms for athletes, which are differentiated by the use of colour; another for referees and administration; and a third with public toilets.

Urban
Space

An architect specialised in public space, Beth Galí (Barcelona, 1950) has designed quintessential spaces in Barcelona from the 1980s, including the Joan Miró Park (1989), the Túnel de la Rovira (1990), and the Sot del Migdia (1992), which she developed with Màrius Quintana. In this field, she has worked in Ireland on the redevelopment of Patrick Street and Grand Parade in Cork (1999) and in the historic centre of Dublin (2002); in the Netherlands, on the Piet Smit terrain in Rotterdam, where she designed a bike path (1996), and in the centre of' s-Hertogenbosch (1998). Our conversation took place a short distance from the studio where she works, at her home in Barcelona's Reial Square which she shared for decades with Oriol Bohigas.

How did your interest in public space begin?

It wasn't my interest. The interest was decided for me. I was pushed into it. There wasn't much talk about public space when I was a student at the School of Architecture. Manuel de Solà-Morales was the one who made the big shift. Urban planning used to be taught through zoning and as a very bureaucratic subject. Solà taught it through the form of the city, through design. Urban space can generate urban conditions that help cities to improve. At the time, no one called it "urban space". People talked about "stringing together outdoor spaces to construct the city". That was his great lesson and the great shift in urban planning.

Paying more attention to the city and its inhabitants than to the regulations.

Exactly. Designing the city not based on rules but based on what you want it to become – in other words, through design.

Is the city built through design today, or has there been another shift?

The most recent change has been widespread citizen participation in the construction of the city. I always ask which city they're talking about. The city made *for* citizens – where public responsibility prevails, the one made *by* citizens – which I'm not a big believer in, because I think action based on experience and knowledge is a better way to improve citizens' lives – or perhaps we'll find a middle ground that can be both *for* and *by*. But citizen intervention is a delicate issue.

Why is that?

Because decisions aren't made on a whim; they're outlining not only the immediate present of the cities but also their future. Offering an opinion on the design of the city requires having an informed opinion and being able to think collectively. That takes place in some countries, like the Netherlands, where people are accustomed to intervening and accepting that civic responsibility. Most people offer information, but they don't decide. The people who are meant to address the problems at hand are the professionals, after having listened to the citizens. For me, working for citizens, is what defines the best urban planning.

If there are complaints from citizens, doesn't that mean that something is failing in the city?

There is very little tradition of citizen participation in Spain, and there's a lot of protesting while offering limited effort and very few ideas. Citizens' demands are important. They have brought residents together to agree to build escalators or introduce neighbourhood parks. In the 1980s, in the early days of a democratic regime, a lot of neighbourhood associations were formed. That's when I started out.

"We're freer in public space than inside our homes."

—Beth Galí

By Anatxu Zabalbeascoa

And it was funny that, although citizen participation didn't exist, the residents of Barcelona were proud of their city. The question now is, if they're participating so much, why aren't they satisfied?

Why?

In Barcelona today, many citizens have lost their pride in the city, despite participating in decision-making.

Where does that detachment come from?

I think it comes from city management. In terms of design, not much has been designed in recent years.

Pedestrianisation...

Change is starting to happen now. But, up to now, we've been living off the legacy of the 1980s. The major improvements were made back then.

What were they, in your opinion?

Introducing the idea of a project for the whole city. The city can't be managed by zones. The project has to include all the details, designs for the benches and kerbs. Designing is very different from planning and codifying in an urban plan.

What do you think Barcelona needs for its residents to recover their attachment to the city?

I think what it needs is good management, which includes the maintenance of the spaces that are already built, the management of rubbish collection... Everything has declined so for that it's time to address that decline.

Has there been a change in who can use the city?

I don't know how many tourists we had in the 1980s and how many there are now. But no doubt the number is a lot higher. There are more tourists than inhabitants today. And management means addressing that.

How?

The problem is that tourists bring economic benefits that aren't shared by all citizens, and yet all citizens participate in maintaining the city. That's the problem.

And how can that be managed?

Cities need to establish an order of priorities. Decide what is most urgent. What is non-negotiable for people's quality of life.

What would your order of priorities be?

Right now, as things stand, the priority would be maintaining standards of cleanliness. Barcelona can't be as dirty as it is. It isn't an urban problem, it's a public health issue. In the end, we'll have to call in the sanitation department to fix it: to clean things up, get rid of the rats and sanitise. There's a waste management problem and there's a failure of civic responsibility.

Barcelona is one of the few cities in Spain with a civic ordinance.

It used to have one anyway. I don't know if it still exists. No one talks about it anymore. Any ordinance requires a certain control, a certain authority, and many current city councils are afraid of authority. If you can't send in the city police force, if they don't respond, there's a chain reaction and everything degenerates. Between the invasion of uncontrolled tourism, the experiments with rubbish collection that have been paralysed... The situation in Ciutat Vella (the old town district) is alarming.

The historic hearts of cities are always in-demand locations.

The neighbourhood belongs to everyone, and that makes it difficult. But there have been times when the city council has put in the resources, precisely because they know it's a complicated neighbourhood. Among other things, the mayor used to walk around here. He would walk around the streets.

Are you talking about Maragall?

Yes, although I would prefer not to. Because we always end up talking about him.

But you did.

Because he was the one who did those things. He understood the problems by being immersed in them. Then he'd arrive at the office and say: listen, the garbage collection isn't working. That's how you learn about cities, by experiencing them.

For you, as an architect, is that also the best way to understand cities?

Absolutely. Architects walk around with our eyes. We read the world around us.

In your walks, what's the best public space you've seen?	Something funny happened to me the first time I went to Holland for a competition. I couldn't understand why they wanted to make changes to the streets. They were fantastic! It was the first country to pedestrianise. Their streets were paved with bricks, an updated version of tradition. I think that's my favourite public space.
You talk about improving tradition. Do we need the same kind of public space today as we did in the eighties?	Maybe not. Today there are new issues that weren't even on the radar then, like sustainability. Although we misuse that word and it's losing value.
But it still needs to be accounted for.	Of course.
What does sustainability mean in a public space?	Easy and inexpensive maintenance, shade in summer and sunlight in winter, rainwater collection for irrigation or recharging groundwater. Also the durability of materials and not using them if coming from far away... We did a lot of that, just without calling it "sustainability": the granite pavements have held up impeccably.
And in buildings that are centuries old. You wouldn't put something fragile in public space!	Exactly. But we do. The Reial Square is made of sandstone that is continually breaking down. There was a lot of ignorance of materials. I've seen that young people today are very aware of their responsibility to the environment, to the future, and to taxpayers' money. Today we talk about *passive houses*, but we should also be talking about *passive streets* and *passive urban space*.
How can we ensure that the PassivHaus certificate doesn't become a stamp of approval that is a business in itself?	That's what's happening with certifications. When those certificates are a sales pitch, things get complicated.
Are there regulations on sustainability in public space?	I don't know if there are any legal mandates at this time. But I do know that there are a number of things that are mandatory in public spaces: facilitating maintenance, considering the durability of the materials and where they come from...
And greenery?	Greenery is also essential, of course.
So, do you think that hard paved squares were a mistake?	It depends. Hard paved squares was a political campaign. The mistake was the political campaign launched into angry criticisms of what the socialists were doing at that time. Paved squares construct the historic city. You go to Italy and all the squares are paved. Here only a few are entirely paved over. Nearly all have some greenery. They used the adjective "hard" because, not so long ago, our streets weren't paved. They were dirt. And paving them made them harder. But think about it. Dirt translates into mud: you'd come home with muddy shoes. Nobody wanted that in a city. But that what Barcelona was like. Most of it. We'd see it when we walked around neighbourhoods on the periphery: there were more dirt roads than paved ones. And that means dirt at home. In the 1980s, the decision was made to asphalt and pave.
Now asphalt is the enemy.	Because it causes a lot of heat accumulation. But there are alternatives. Even making sure pavements can drain or collect water.
When the pavements are torn up, many citizens think: they're doing construction again to take a cut off the top.	That happens when they don't perceive the results. Citizens should always be critical, and the City Council needs to demonstrate whether its decisions are appropriate or not. Today, it doesn't make sense to install pavements that are impermeable and that don't absorb heat. Dealing with those issues should be a sine qua non.
Can private space be intended for public use?	It depends. I am very much in favour of private buildings being open to public passage. In New York, it is very common for pedestrians to get from one street to another through a building lobby. There are some here, like as the Design Hub, which not only connects two streets but also overcomes a significant difference in height. It's something new here, but it makes the city more porous, more civic and more walkable. I think that everyone wins: the city, citizens, and the buildings that may

have cafeterias or small shops inside. Some buildings are set up for that to happen, like the MNAC, and passing through would save people a lot of time. It would avoid having to go all the way around large city blocks. There are architects who focus on connection, who think about the city at large rather than focusing on their own work.

Jordi Garcés connecting adjacent buildings to expand the Picasso Museum.

That's outstanding. What he did was connect all the palaces along another parallel street. Only someone who walks around the city would be able do that.

And someone who understands the city's residents.

Definitely. There's another way to connect the city: through the interior courtyards of the blocks in the Eixample district. Lots of them are already parks, squares, public spaces. But it would be great if they were permeable, if you could cross through them.

Is that possible?

It's easy from a management standpoint: a ground floor has to be expropriated and opened to make the connection.

Was Cerdà's plan designed to be able to cross through city blocks?

The Cerdà Plan has many variables. The first proposal was parallel blocks with an open centre. Later, he suggested changes. For example, the arrangement into macro-blocks formed by nine city blocks. In other words, the idea of *superblocks* comes from there. Cerdà already foresaw that, in the future, traffic wouldn't affect every part of the city. He always included proposals centred on permeability. The current density... he couldn't even have dreamt of it. Although... I quite like the density.

What do you mean?

Well, when it comes to Cerdà's initial plan... I find it, I don't know, not very "city-like". It was simply the façade of a huge main street connected to the side streets. I see that big street crossing through the interior as constructing a somewhat disjointed city. It has been shown that density, in addition to being more urban, is more sustainable.

Sustainability has three main workhorses: density, the return of greenery in the city, and water management.

That's essential for lowering temperatures. And producing oxygen. Green canopies make cities liveable.

Have you learned to work with greenery?

I didn't start out working with greenery mainly because I didn't know how. I didn't know about trees.

And you didn't know how to collaborate?

Perhaps not. In a profession you learn almost everything by doing, and by taking an interest in what other people are doing. No one is born wise; we don't know much of anything in fact, early on. When you're young and insecure it can be hard for you to admit, but when you get older... you gain perspective. I've been learning, but I still have a lot to learn. That's why I always work with agronomists. I know what I need and want – for example, shade – and they translate shade, city and a Mediterranean climate into a type of tree. Architecture is teamwork.

The image of a genius designing all alone has done a lot of damage.

There are no geniuses who design all on their own. Anyone who claims that is a lying genius. And even more so today. The profession has become so complicated that it's impossible to practice alone.

Is everything related in the city today?

And the regulations are stricter in terms of building services, structures, etc.

What have you learned from designing public space?

One thing that I love, the goal and the knowledge that what I do will be used and experienced by thousands of people. There's nothing sadder than making a public space that no one uses. Success is represented by people occupying those places. A public space can't force citizens out. You feel very free designing public space, and that leads to experimentation and not always repeating the same thing. It's gratifying to be able to advance.

Is it easier to advance in public space than in architecture?

I think so. Architecture is a slower process, and it's rife with conflict.

Is generating more empty space always an objective when designing public space?

Sometimes you have to fill it up. It depends. But it's always a blank canvas, and it allows a lot of freedom.

Thinking about the regulation that has been in force in the United States for years, dedicating 1% of the budget for new buildings to urban art: Would you dedicate that to vegetation?

No. I'd continue dedicating it to art. Greenery is cheaper; it will come, eventually. But art, quality art, is harder to come by. Trees, plants, seating and lampposts will always be in any project. What's never included a public space design is culture. That's why, when I talk about art, I don't just mean sculptures and murals. Art is theatre, a raised platform, stands in public space. That's demystifying culture and making it easier for citizens to access. Bringing culture into public squares responds to and represents change.

It's curious how you defend organisation, planning and design and, at the same time, change – that is, chaos.

That's my fundamental truth. Things have to admit change if they're going to be alive. Extreme order isn't life, it's an imposition.

How does the city communicate that it belongs to everyone?

Through the fact that you can do basically whatever you want in public space as long as it does not threaten the freedoms of another person. For that to be possible, there have to be norms of coexistence that come either from education or from a certain municipal authority that acts when the education isn't effective. But the principle of public space is "I feel free here" – freer than in private space, even.

When is a city fully built?

That's the great drama of the city: the finished city. Barcelona was a finished city. It was a city that couldn't grow because of the boundaries of the mountains and the sea. It couldn't get much denser either. All you can do is refurbish, refurbish, refurbish.

And what refurbishment mean in urban planning terms?

The opportunity to think about different grouping systems. I am interested in the *metapolitan* area – not a collection of municipalities but areas that are joined together and have many things in common: for example, geography if they''re on the coast, or the type of vegetation, or corridors of animal species, and which tend to blur the boundaries between them. That union interests me. Much more than the segregation of municipalities that breaks down what was once united by nature.

You defend territorial spaces over and above municipal ones.

That's right. It's like the beads of the necklace exist but, somehow, the thread is missing. I'm in favour of building that thread.

Are cars the great enemy of the city?

I don't think so, but everyone says so today.

Why don't you think so?

Like everything, if cars are well managed, they aren't an enemy; they can be an aid. Almost nothing is just good or just bad. Management makes it better or worse. Electric cars have their own problems, many of them, that will need to be solved. But what needs to be impeccable is public transport. It has improved. I always travel by subway or bus, and I've noticed it. But it needs to be improved to the point that you prefer it because taking a car is difficult, or expensive, or too much of a hassle. That's the natural way for people to leave behind their cars. They'll do it when it's more comfortable for them.

Should public space compensate for domestic deficiencies?

Absolutely. Public space is like our second home. I've said it before, we're freer in public space than inside our homes.

Isn't that a bourgeois notion? Doesn't it assume that we can't be free inside our homes?

Inside our homes we tend live in close proximity to people we want to avoid offending, and everyone is different and has their different interests. We can put up with noise in the street, but noise inside our homes becomes unbearable. There's a different kind of freedom in public space. The other day there were some tourists wading in the fountain until the city police showed up and spoiled their fun.

It's funny, you talk about the need for police authority, but you also paint them as killjoys.

Both are true. Like almost everything in life!

Cb

Cr_L2

Cr_L1

SAB_CCAT

SAB_L1

PCv_L1

Pp_L1

Cv_L1

Pr_L1

MR_L1

Be_L1

SVH_CCLV

To_L1

SCC_L1

SF_L1 SF_L2

SCl_L1

SJn_CEJG

SCC_L2

SJl_L1

SB_L3

SJn_L1

SJn_TVHB

SB_SJD

SJn_L2

Es_L1

SB_L1

Es_L2

Ga_L1

SB_L2

Vi_L1

Co_L1

Co_L2

Es_Hp_L1

Cf_L1

SB_CCAL

Co_PLG

Co_CICM

Cf_CUC

Ga_CCBS

Vi_CC

Vi_CCV

Hp_L2

Hp_L4

Pr_L1

Hp_BIO

Hp_PEF

Pr_L2

Pr_AER

0   500 1000   2000   5000 m

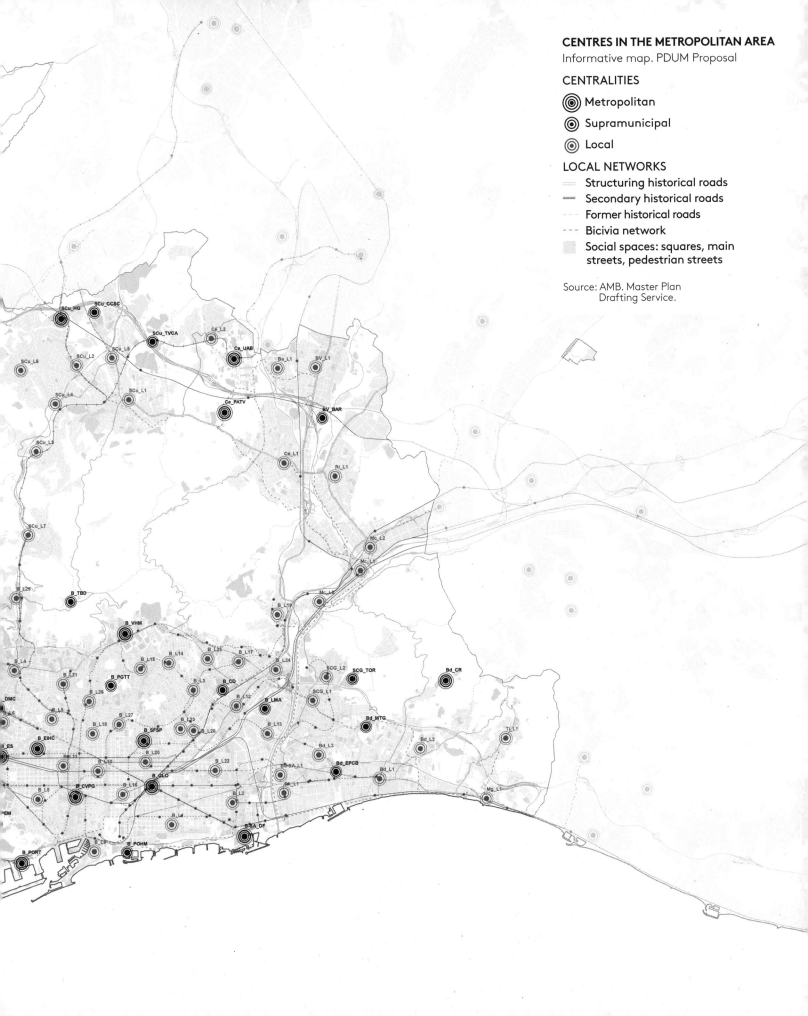

CENTRES IN THE METROPOLITAN AREA
Informative map. PDUM Proposal

CENTRALITIES

◎ Metropolitan

◎ Supramunicipal

◎ Local

LOCAL NETWORKS

Structuring historical roads

Secondary historical roads

Former historical roads

Bicivia network

Social spaces: squares, main
streets, pedestrian streets

Source: AMB. Master Plan
Drafting Service.

Claudi Aguiló Riu (Barcelona, 1951) became an architect while working at the mid-1980s equivalent of today's AMB: the Barcelona Metropolitan Corporation. "I had left school but the director of the Public Space Service, Jaume Vendrell, demanded that the entire team be qualified." Among his career milestones, he cites a proposal by Jon Montero to transform the AMB from a controlling institution into a propositional one. "He got the AMB to design, to organise competitions in which young people could participate. Until then, public spaces were the territory of engineers," he recalls.

Architect Eva Pagés (Vic, 1979) began working as an intern on the team of an already established Claudi. After completing her training at the ETSAB, working at the Barcelona City Council, participating in the Erasmus programme, and earning a degree in landscape architecture from the UPC, she returned to the AMB where they have been collaborating for years.

In consolidated cities, do small changes improve our lives?

Claudi Aguiló Riu: Small changes exist within a larger context. On the regional level, there have been major interventions in Collserola, the Besòs and the Llobregat, which are gigantic. But what's interesting today is the sum of green spaces. The city isn't a village or a forest, but connecting these green spaces makes it healthier and friendlier. In the 90s, Germany was already working to infiltrate water to prevent major flooding. Here, we've channelled rainwater instead of infiltrating it, which is why we see such dramatic scenarios with heavy rains. In the days of Pasqual Maragall, large lamination tanks were built. But when a city grows considerably, you have to be careful because everything is connected.

You're talking about problems of excess water, while other departments are talking about issues with too little water.

C.A.: There are contradictions. We say we want green, but we have to know what kind of green to put in. Under Mayor Porcioles the city was paved over. Then the green came in the form of grass, which is the worst possible thing for our climate: it needs care and water. Today we're constantly talking about sustainability, but we continue to put in grass in a climate where it isn't sustainable.

What would be sustainable?

Eva Pagés: We did a park, Can Rigal, at the end of Diagonal Avenue, between Barcelona and L'Hospitalet, where one of our biggest challenges was deciding how to irrigate the vegetation. We didn't want to use metered drinking water, even though it's cheaper in the short term than building an entire system.

C.A.: The Besòs River, for example, is an open channel that was an open sewer until 1992. Today, it's a pleasant place to take a stroll. The city and the geography undergo transformations. The Llobregat isn't a strict channel because we've naturalised the landscape. But it's a fake river. The problem is all the urban development, the large transport infrastructure that has been built. Today, a city wouldn't be designed that way.

"We work from a bird's-eye view so that the landscape isn't interrupted."
—Claudi Aguiló and Eva Pagés

By Anatxu Zabalbeascoa

When did we start getting things right?

C.A.: When we took control. For example, there's a project to connect Gavà and Viladecans with a green corridor.

Those connections used to be created through construction, and now we're using vegetation?

C.A.: Exactly. The AMB was created to coordinate the plans of the various municipalities and to ensure the territory was respected. We work from a bird's-eye view so that the landscape isn't interrupted, and the streets remain continuous.

E.P.: When Claudi was first starting out, the AMB began trying to repair what had been destroyed, by connecting the landscape. What was just an intuition then is now the foundation for a more sustainable way of building and caring for the land.

You defend the bird's-eye view that connects everything, but a lot of architecture has been designed from a distance instead of on the ground.

C.A.: At the end of the 80s, there were changes to the criteria for mobility and roads in the city, and public space began to be projected. It was decided then that cars shouldn't be given such a fundamental role.

But the ring roads were built in 1992…

C.A.: Sure. But that was to keep cars out. And, furthermore, it broke with the trend in previous plans of building five lanes in both directions. The ring roads have been criticised because they're small, because their relationship with the metro or tram was not taken into account.

Why not?

C.A.: Money is usually a valid response to almost everything.

E.P.: It was purely economic.

C.A.: The Catalan government gave strong support to the tram because the investment in the metro would have been much higher. Even though the metro is better for the city.

When we think about urban space, we rarely consider underground space, do we?

C.A.: We do. In 1992, Barcelona opened toward the sea, but we continued to dump rainwater into the sea through the sewage system.

E.P.: In designing parks, we've always considered what to do with rainwater. It's not just the fact of wasting the water by diverting it into the sewer system, it's also that the sewer overflows. It's a consequence of our Mediterranean climate. We get almost the same amount of rainfall as in England, but over the course of just a few days. Cities were made impermeable. Mistake. Because we're close to the sea, the salinity of the groundwater gets very high if it isn't mixed with rainwater. I have learned a lot from Claudi because he has watched the city grow very quickly, and he understands the mistakes that he has spent his life trying to correct.

How do institutions react when everything is called into question?

C.A.: They thought we were crazy when we were designing Els Pinetons Park, in Ripollet. The mayor wanted a rose garden like the one in the Cervantes Park in Barcelona and a lake. And the land had been industrial, abandoned lots. We did a little research on its history. She's the one [referring to Eva] who researches almost as far back as prehistory. And from there, we proposed something very different.

E.P.: Politicians sometimes come to us with ideas that may or may not be viable. In our profession, you have to think not only about how to build things but how to maintain them, because they're maintained by public funds.

What did you propose to the mayor who wanted the rose garden?

C.A.: To build a Mediterranean landscape. Since the city was still being developed, there wasn't any water or a sewer connection. So, we had to find groundwater for irrigation and infiltrate rainwater into the soil. It was my first experience dealing with geologists. At the time, the Ripoll River was polluted by chemical industries, not by sewage.

What can show us that the city belongs to everyone?

C.A.: I'm a cynic. People are selfish. Air conditioners are still being hung out people's windows. And it's prohibited.

Where are they supposed to go?

E.P.: On rooftops. Or we need spaces on the façades where they can be installed. It's a design problem. But since that would be more expensive than adding it later, it doesn't get done. Many good and useful things are studied at university and later not applied.

C.A.: The thing about air conditioners on the façade is as bad as misunderstanding sustainability. Can solar panels be installed anywhere? What about bicycles hanging from balconies; they're everywhere. Why don't buildings bicycle parking areas if they're supposed to replace cars? The regulations don't account for that. We've made flats so small that my wife always says: if you buy something, you have to get rid of something.

If cars are kept out of the city, what will happen to carparks?

E.P.: We have great capacity for reinventing spaces. During the pandemic, more than one resident would go down for a run.

What can and can't be done on the street?

C.A.: We should be able to park bikes, hang clothes, and store junk in our homes. But, again, there's the question of money... Since flats are always getting smaller... When you build a park, there are people who come to complain to you about dog poop. Listen, take it up with the dog-owners!

E.P.: The Administration has to come in and offer a solution for everything. People occupy public space because we all pay for it. But it's a double-edged sword: precisely because it is yours, you should take care of it and, since it belongs to everyone, you have to share it.

C.A.: It's like beating your rug off the balcony. Where do you think the dust is going? There's a devastating lack of civility.

Is public space compensating for the deficiencies in residential spaces?

C.A.: It should. During the lockdown, there were some buildings that organised so residents could walk on the roof. In other buildings, complaints were lodged. There are two ways of living: working together or against one another.

E.P.: When we all do our civic duty, everybody wins. At certain crosswalks, cyclists are supposed to get off their bikes and walk. But who actually does that?

I always think, if we were able to ban smoking in certain places (planes, classrooms, etc.), then anything can be changed.

C.A.: That's true. There is less and less dog poop in the street. It's a cultural issue. When I was little, there were signs in bars and on public transport that said: "No swearing or spitting." Today spitting is back.

Spitting or urinating?

C.A.: That too. I've seen it mostly at night.

I've seen it mostly from men.

E.P.: Earlier you asked how the city shows that it belongs to everyone. Well, through respect when you cross the boundary between the public and private sphere. There should be intergenerational and intercultural spaces for coming together rather than for clashing.

How do you go from clashing to coming together?

E.P.: With respect. You give and receive. How? By making the city more welcoming. I'm thinking both about water management and about benches outside schools so parents can sit down while they wait for their children and talk to each other. Semi-public/private spaces have always existed. They are shared places that teach us about civility. Bet Capdeferro and Ramon Bosch widened the sidewalks on a street in Turó de la Rovira (Barcelona) to transform them into small squares. And people pulled out their chairs to get some fresh air. That's a good, collective, respectful gesture of occupying the city.

Benches are often replaced with individual chairs in public spaces. Why is that?

C.A.: One reason is to prevent drinking on the street. Instead of motivating young people to stop, we try to make it difficult for them.

Is the fear of change more visible in public spaces?

E.P.: Definitely. Resistance to change is almost the baseline state.

Does public space change too often in Barcelona?

C.A.: No. When we design kerbs, we shouldn't be thinking about the average citizen but about seniors who use walkers to get around. That's social change.

E.P.: People question whether public space should be luxurious. For us, the value is durability; what we do should be useful and lasting. That's quality – which is very different from luxury.

Are you in favour of the *superilles* [superblocks]?

C.A.: When properly executed, yes. Barcelona isn't a village. It's a cosmopolitan city. When Le Corbusier proposed the superblocks based on Cerdà's Eixample, even breaking with the layout, he was thinking of mobility and circulation criteria. He also imagined a garden city for Castelldefels.

E.P.: Actually, Cerdà already foresaw some of the values defended by the superblocks. The problem is how little is left of that original plan with so much private, carfocused space. Chamfered corners are uncomfortable for citizens. They were designed for cars. Bike paths are great, but they need to be managed. It would be interesting to connect different municipalities by bicycle, like in the Bicivia project, whereas at present they can only be connected by car.

C.A.: Painting lines on the ground isn't enough. You have to study the context. The most important thing today is to make public transport more comfortable and cheaper than private transport. That would change everything.

Is it only possible to build large parks before the city has been built?

E.P: No. There are moments of transformation when it's also possible. The investment is always the problem. Who's going to pay for those big parks? The last ones in Barcelona were compensations. Towers that were given permission to be taller in exchange for building open public parks instead of private gardens, like in the case of Diagonal Mar neighbourhood. Mixing public and private investment is often the way to progress.

How can parks be improved?

E.P.: Partly through citizen surveys, which are done annually. Sometimes through accessibility. Other times, it's a question of maintenance. And almost everything can be remedied. The idea of a park is not to kick anyone out. The objective is to co-exist.

When is a city finished being built?

E.P.: Never. A city is always constantly evolving.

C.A.: An important chapter of the Barcelona of the future will be rehabilitation. We have to understand that there are areas of the city that were poorly built. We built cheaply, with materials that have an expiration date. The word sustainability refers to hygiene and health. Today it's a requirement, whereas in the past it was avoided. Improving what was done poorly is synonymous with progress and justice.

Does design mean reconciling contradictions?

C.A.: Definitely. Cati Montserrat wants to put trees everywhere. As for us, we don't want trees that don't have enough space. That's why we have a love-hate relationship, and we've all learned that building a city is a team effort.

E.P.: And repairing it, even more so.

Salzereda Avenue

Santa Coloma
de Gramenet

CLAUDI AGUILÓ RIU
EVA PAGÉS
(AMB)

2017-2021
30,376 m²
€8,150,258

SITE MANAGEMENT
Jordi Larruy (AMB)

AMB TEAM
Carles Español
Francesc Germà
Ainhoa Martínez
Mireia Monràs
Cati Montserrat
Daniel Vázquez

COLLABORATORS
Proiectum
VVV Proyectos y
 Servicios con Ingenio

Pepe Gil
Jordi Pruna

DEVELOPERS
AMB
Santa Coloma
de Gramenet
City Council
UE – FEDER

CONTRACTOR
Copisa

PHOTOGRAPHER
Jeroen Van Mieghem

As part of the Pinta Verda plan, the redevelopment of Salzereda Avenue supports Santa Coloma de Gramenet's strategy to promote more sustainable mobility and the physical and visual connection between the city centre and the Besòs River. Moving away from its former condition as a road and a barrier between the city and the river, the BV-5001 becomes a green promenade along the city's river front.

In the section where it crosses Llorenç Serra Boulevard and the bridge over the river, the underpass for road traffic is eliminated and the section is turned into a *ha-ha*, a landscaping strategy that allows views of the river above the protective wall required for large avenues.

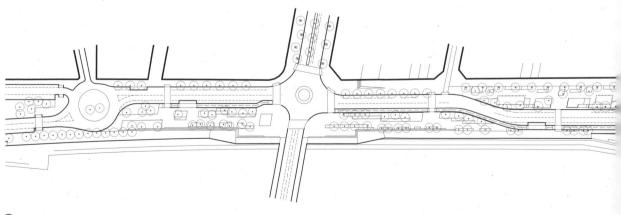

1/2500

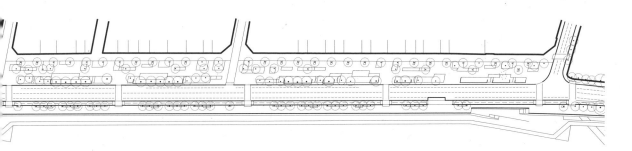

In a second section, the relationship between the city and the river is improved by making the promenade more accessible and enhancing the views: the promenade is maintained along the built façade, the differences in height and the barrier formed by existing walls are removed, and the landscaping is reorganised. The line of false pepper trees between the road and the promenade is preserved, and trees along the pavement closest to the river are replaced, substituting the linear arrangement that created a visual barrier with intermittent groupings that improve the connection between the two spaces.

Biodiversity and ecological connectivity are enhanced through the combination of different species of trees and shrubs: the false pepper trees recall the willows that give the promenade its name [salzereda means "willow grove"] and the poplars and plane trees consolidate the site's character as a riverbank. Techniques to improve the urban greenery are implemented, and the landscaped surfaces serve as drainage and infiltration points to avoid overloading the storm sewers.

PINTA VERDA PLAN

Organising the city based on its open spaces while linking neighbourhoods together and connecting the Besòs River with the Marina mountains. This are the main goals of the Pinta Verda plan for Santa Coloma de Gramenet. Since 2017, the plan has guided the approach to urbanising streets that, due to their location, serve as the main connectors for the network of open spaces and facilities.

With less space for vehicle traffic, circulation is treated as a necessary element of the city, and parking, loading and unloading, public transport and rubbish bins are all redistributed. On a level halfway between the road and the pavement closest to the river space, a two-way bike lane is added as part of the metropolitan cycling network that connects Santa Coloma with Montcada and Sant Adrià.

Ultimately, Salzereda Avenue is a prime example of a design that works on two scales at once: it is both a local renovation and a metropolitan strategy project.

Streets of the Historic Centre
Castellbisbal

CRISTINA SÁEZ
(AMB)

2015-2018
2,432 m²
€1,015,892

SITE MANAGEMENT
Joan Roca (AMB)

AMB TEAM
Cinta Alegre
Sara Arguedas
Susana Casino

DEVELOPERS
AMB
Castellbisbal
Town Council

CONTRACTOR
UTE Siccsa - Archs
Constructora

PHOTOGRAPHER
Jordi Surroca
i Gael del Río

The urban transformation of the old town of Castellbisbal, which is being implemented in phases, is founded on the morphology of its streets: a comb-shaped structure with a main axis, Major Street. Being less than four metres wide and with a single central traffic lane, streets are gradually transitioned towards a model that gives priority to pedestrians. Intersections and points where the streets widen are adapted to create small squares, one of the few outdoor leisure spaces in the historic centre.

The intervention has a common theme that ties it together: a systematisation of the streets' section and the materials that are used. On the one hand, streets are made kerb less, with a single neutral paving material. On the other hand, the same prefabricated concrete element is used throughout, which is arranged in different layouts depending on the street, and which offering a solution to the differences in height and creating small landscaped areas.

The action focuses on four points in the historic centre: the stretch of Major Street between Gaudí Avenue and Sol Street; Orient Street, where a small square is created at a widening point; Sant Marc Street, which ends with an overlook taking advantage of the site's location, and Miquel Blanch Street, which ends at Joc Square, a space that is used for civic activities like concerts or traditional dances.

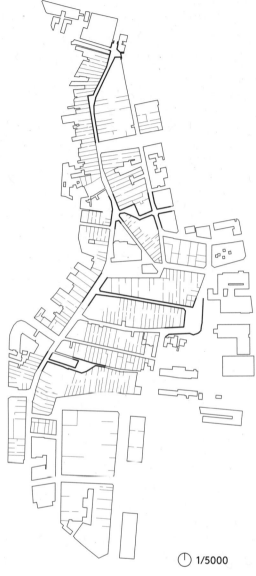

1/5000

Església Square

El Papiol

MARTA PERIS
JOSÉ MANUEL TORAL
(Peris+Toral
Arquitectes)

2017-2018
1,851 m²
€616,747

PERIS+TORAL TEAM
Miguel Bernat
Ana Espinosa
Miguel Ángel
Gorrochategui
Albert Rubio

SITE MANAGEMENT
Núria Herrero (AMB)

COLLABORATORS
AB Paisatgistes
Bernuz-Fernández
Arquitectes
Eletresjota

CONTRACTOR
Coynsa

DEVELOPERS
AMB
El Papiol Town
Council

PHOTOGRAPHER
José Hevia

The aim is to recover the memory of the site in El Papiol by connecting the church and the square in a single urban space, despite the differences in height between them. Where there was once a steep descent, the stairs are renovated using prefabricated concrete pieces to create a leisure area with stand seating and a planter, adjacent to a fountain that also serves as a reference to the past.

The new square, on a single level, integrates Major Street and is paved with the same materials as the rest of the old town. Two new trees are planted to make the space more appealing, and a large garden area with shrubs and climbing plants is planned for the opposite end, bordered by a precast concrete bench that allows users to contemplate both the church building and the views over the landscape.

Thus, a disorderly space once occupied by cars is turned into a pleasant gathering place where pedestrians are the main focus.

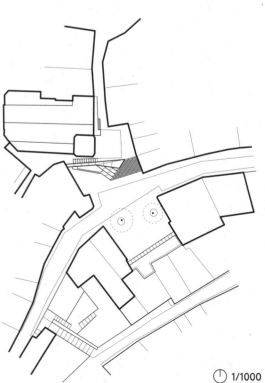

1/1000

Matas Street

Tiana

ROBERTO APARICIO
ROGER JORNET
SÍLVIA OLLÉ
(AR47)

2016-2018
3,407 m²
€588,058

SITE MANAGEMENT
Albert Dalmau
Marta Juanola
(AMB)

COLLABORATORS
Ingenieros Asociados

DEVELOPERS
AMB
Tiana Town Council

CONTRACTOR
Amsa

PHOTOGRAPHER
Josep Casanova

AWARDS
Shortlisted,
El Maresme
Architecture
Exhibition 2021
Shortlisted,
FAD Awards 2019

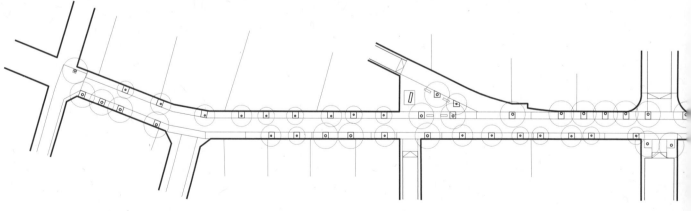

1/1000

Once used as the road to access Tiana from the south, the uniqueness of Matas Street comes from the two rows of century-old plane trees that, especially in summer, provide a canopy of green leaves overhead and a pleasant space for strolling.

The redevelopment stipulates a kerbless street with a central lane of traffic, where cars, bicycles and pedestrians coexist, along with two permeable strips on the sides that accommodate the existing trees as well as new seating areas equipped with benches and chairs. The same prefabricated concrete element is used as a paving material throughout, laid with separations between the pieces in some sections along the edges to permit rainwater infiltration.

The lighting installation uses a hanging system, based on a zigzagging catenary that disappears among the leaves of the trees and situates the fixtures above the middle of the street.

Thus, the street's character as a greenway and a space for socialisation is enhanced by improving the conditions for the growth of the plane trees, reducing vehicle traffic, eliminating parking, and expanding the leisure spaces for residents.

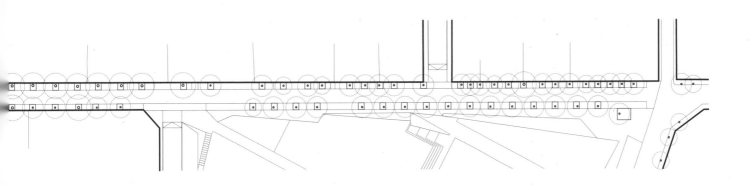

Environs of Torre Balldovina Museum

Santa Coloma de Gramenet

CLAUDI AGUILÓ RIU
EVA PAGÉS
(AMB)

2018-2020
3,720 m²
€1,264,644

AMB TEAM
Carles Español
Francesc Germà
Ainhoa Martínez
Mireia Monràs
Cati Montserrat
Daniel Vázquez

SITE MANAGEMENT
Maria Sánchez (AMB)

COLLABORATORS
BIS structures

CONTRACTOR
Copisa

PHOTOGRAPHER
Jeroen Van Mieghem

DEVELOPERS
AMB
Santa Coloma
de Gramenet
City Council

AWARDS
Shortlisted,
Catalonia Construction
Awards 2021

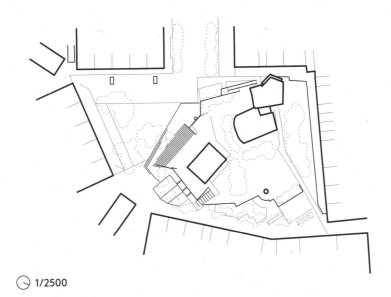

⊘ 1/2500

Just outside the main building of Torre Balldovina, and on a lower level, sit the archaeological remains of Molí d'en Ribé, which are part of the museum and will eventually be connected to it on the basement level.

The building being built above the ruins of the old flour mill forms a new square on the level of Torre Balldovina gardens. It integrates the concrete slab and the wooden roof that were built a few years ago to protect the ruins. To ensure the ruins remain visible from the outside, a skylight is set above one of the wells used to provide falling water for the mill, and a wall is built to form a semi-basement level to provide views of the other sections of the ruins. Natural lighting for the lower level is ensured through a side skylight and the installation of six prefabricated tubes that bring daylight into the main room.

A series of prefabricated elements are used to articulate this covered square and bridge the differences in height with the surrounding area, especially with Pau Casals Square: a set of stands that face the square and the main entrance, and concrete steps and ramps that lead into the gardens or towards the independent access to the future classrooms on the east façade.

The entrances to the museum are redesigned with an accessible ramp and stairs, and the visual impact of the walls required to compensate for the difference in height is softened by a landscaped slope. This creates a more open space that helps to broaden the square, providing more visibility for the museum building and a direct path leading to the hypogeum, the shelter that once extended from Torre Balldovina to the lower part of the square.

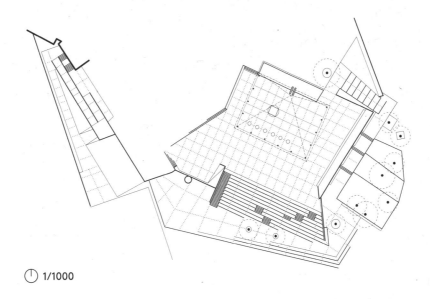

🕐 1/1000

Cerdanyola Avenue
Sant Cugat del Vallès

ANTONIO MONTES
(AMB)

LOLA SIMÓN
MARIA BLANCO
(SBS Simón i Blanco)

2018-2020
3,450 m²
€1,275,433

SITE MANAGEMENT
BT arquitectes

AMB TEAM
Natalia Castaños

DEVELOPERS
AMB
Sant Cugat
del Vallès
Town Council

CONTRACTOR
Voracys

PHOTOGRAPHER
Jon Arruti

The transformation of Cerdanyola Avenue is limited to the sections included in the expansion area near the Sant Cugat Monastery, where there is a great deal of commercial activity that needs to be preserved. The proposal involves a complete modification of the section of the street, making it kerb less and giving priority to pedestrians, and re-arranging the trees and street furniture.

The uses of the space are differentiated by changes in the paving materials, which tie in with the ones used in the renovation of the historic centre: neutral with respect to the surrounding buildings and of high quality. A strip for pedestrian circulation runs adjacent to the buildings, and it remains continuous through the road crossings, which helps to reduce the speed of passing vehicles. There is a circulation lane for authorised vehicles only and a strip with seating areas and flowerbeds for trees and shrubs on the side with more sun exposure.

Following guidelines similar to the ones used for the redevelopment of this initial section, the entire street is being remodelled in phases to turn it into a new civic axis.

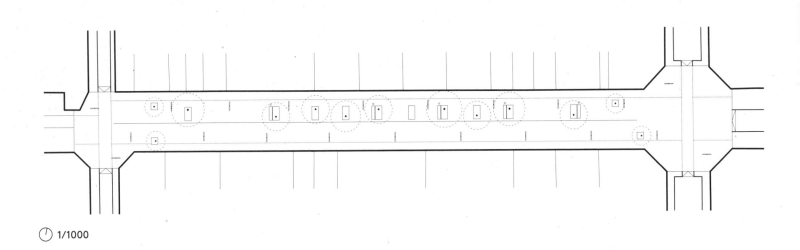

1/1000

Green Space on Claverol Street

Sant Vicenç dels Horts

ROGER MÉNDEZ (AMB)

2018-2020
3,030 m²
€549,577

SITE MANAGEMENT
Núria Herrero (AMB)

AMB TEAM
Jonatan Álvarez
Aïda Artiz
Arnau Canyes
Susana Casino
Arnau Marimón
Cristina Pedreira

COLLABORATORS
Societat Orgànica

CONTRACTOR
Roig

DEVELOPERS
AMB
Sant Vicenç
dels Horts
Town Council

PHOTOGRAPHER
María José Reyes

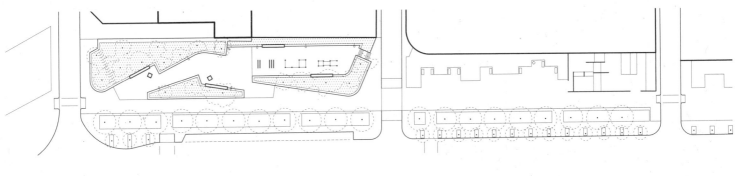

⊘ 1/1000

A redevelopment is taking place on a section of Claverol Street between two different prior interventions, an unpaved space that was being used as an unregulated car park. The aim is to improve the street's integration with the urban fabric and to turn it into a comfortable leisure area with abundant vegetation and an outdoor fitness circuit.

The design includes a line of grevilleas and dogwoods adjacent to the road to shade the path. Accessibility is improved, and increased protection against heavy traffic is provided with a long and landscaped tree pit. Within the green space, all strategies are aimed at the sustainable management of rainwater: vegetation is encircled by gabions that capture water and let it infiltrate slowly, pavements are permeable, and excess rainwater is channelled into two infiltration wells.

Access to the Railway Station

Barberà
del Vallès

MAIRA GONZÁLEZ
(Maira Arquitectes)

2016-2019
6,410 m²
€1,018,052

COLLABORATORS
AVANT
Eletresjota
MVA despatx
  d'arquitectura i
  estructura
SBS Simón i Blanco
VVV Proyectos y
  Servicios con Ingenio

DEVELOPERS
AMB
Barberà del Vallès
Town Council

CONTRACTOR
Eurocatalana

PHOTOGRAPHER
Gabriele Bortoluzzi

As part of the process to improve accessibility to the Barberà railway station, which sits at a lower level than the streets around it, a series of ramps are designed that adapt to the current topography while respecting the existing pine and cypress trees. The edges of this wooded area are arranged to accommodate parking for disabled people and bicycle parking, and the street along the tracks is extended for pedestrians, bicycles and service vehicles.

Vehicle traffic in the new Josep Badia Square is reorganised and the asphalt surface is reduced to form a square that combines paved and landscaped areas. The site is transformed from an intersection into a space that combines leisure areas with areas for the circulation of vehicles and pedestrians and that aims to generate continuity with the adjoining city.

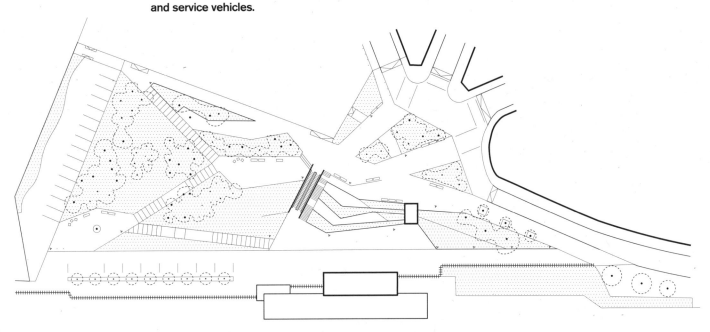

1/1000

Joan Salvat-Papasseit Gardens

El Prat de Llobregat

CARLOS LLINÁS (AMB)

2018-2019
5,932 m²
€1,091,300

SITE MANAGEMENT
Jordi Larruy (AMB)

AMB TEAM
Jonatan Álvarez
Arnau Canyes
Susana Casino
Tamie Delgadillo
Oriol Paluzie
Ferran Roca

DEVELOPERS
AMB
El Prat de Llobregat
Town Council

CONTRACTOR
Benjumea

PHOTOGRAPHER
Jon Arruti

The new square shaped by the Joan Salvat-Papasseit gardens offers more leisure space for citizens in a dense residential neighbourhood with several nearby schools. The barriers that once hindered access are removed, including parked cars and the hedge around perimeter, and two of the streets bordering it are made kerb less to form a single shared platform, thus improving permeability with the urban surroundings.

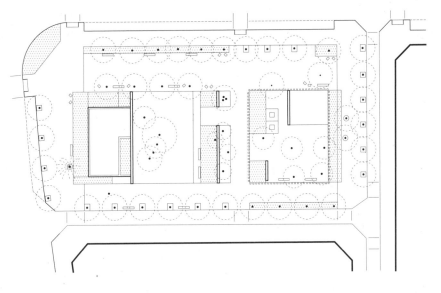

1/1000

The spaces are organised into a large central strip, where most of the existing trees are retained and several areas paved in decomposed granite are outlined, as well as the inclusive children's play area and the pond. Groups of shrub species of different sizes are interspersed between these elements, which help create the atmosphere of a *garden*. Adjoining Pompeu Fabra Avenue there is a large paved open space for multipurpose uses (socialising, play, small performances, etc.), with a row of trees and bushes that protect the pedestrian circulation area from street traffic.

Andalusia Street

Castelldefels

CRISANT ROMANS

2016-2018
2,540 m²
€523,263

COLLABORATORS
ICA Grupo
MOR arquitectura
 tècnica

DEVELOPERS
AMB
Castelldefels
Town Council

CONTRACTOR
Gicsa

PHOTOGRAPHER
Adrià Goula

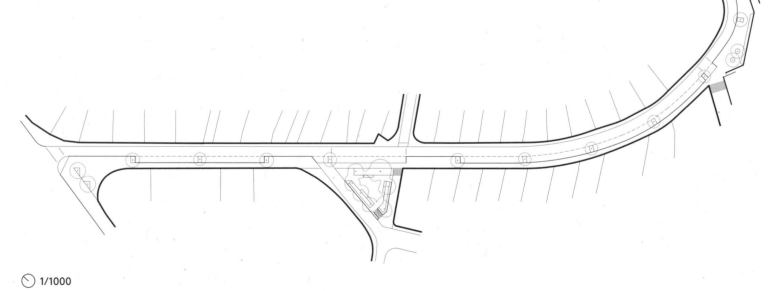

◔ 1/1000

A MODEL FOR OPEN SPACES

To improve the urban structure of Castelldefels, there is a need to define a city model that can serve as a framework for implementing urban, social and environmental policies. Drawing on the form and organisation of the territory, the proposal recognises and enhances six structuring axes that will reconnect the city in the mountains-to-sea direction, crossed transversely by the current C-245 turned into a metropolitan avenue.

The renovation of this street is part of the urban transformation of the Vistalegre neighbourhood in Castelldefels. To give pedestrians more space and comfort and to organise parking, the new section of the street is asymmetrical. There is a narrow pavement flush with the road on one side and a wider, raised pavement on the other, which, in some places, devotes all the space to seating areas with benches or incorporates lamp posts and planting pits for new trees.

Halfway down the street there is a small triangular square, bounded by uneven slopes. To avoid damaging the existing trees, the square is preserved at the current level, and the perimeter walls are adapted to improve transitions with the surrounding area. The wall along Andalusia Street is turned into a landscaped slope, and the other two walls are made invisible from the interior of the square by reducing their height.

To reinforce the continuity of the public space, the same concrete element is used as cladding for the walls and as a paving material for the street and the square.

Azorín Street and Square

Badalona

JAVIER ZALDÍVAR
(JZ Paisatge i
Arquitectura)

2018-2021
2,510 m²
€566,509

AMB TEAM
Jonatan Álvarez
Jordi Bardolet
Núria Saura

JZ TEAM
Quim Bosch

COLLABORATORS
Lourdes Romeo
Elisabeth Torregrosa
Carmela Torró

DEVELOPERS
AMB
Badalona
City Council

CONTRACTOR
Roig

PHOTOGRAPHER
Quim Bosch

Expanding and improving the public space in the neighbourhood, while making it more accessible and sustainable. This is the aim in remodelling Azorín Square in Badalona. Given the difference in level between the streets surrounding the square and the fragmentation of the current space, an intermediate level is generated for the new square to give it the maximum possible flat surface.

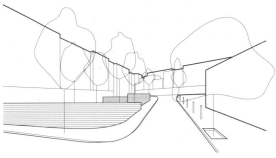

PREVIOUS STATE

CURRENT STATE

The edges of the main esplanade are defined by landscaped slopes, which help to bridge the differences in level with the surrounding streets while guaranteeing physical and visual continuity between the different parts of the square. These green spaces, which incorporate ramps or stairs, contribute to the biodiversity and sustainability of the site.

The transformation removes the section of Pérez Galdós Street that once divided the space in two, and it includes Azorín Street, which is transformed into a kerbless street with just one traffic lane.

Francesc Macià Square

Sant Feliu de Llobregat

FRANC FERNÁNDEZ
(Franc Fernández
Arquitectura)

2017-2020
2,173 m²
€632,058

**FRANC FERNÁNDEZ
TEAM**
Andrea Caparrós
Maite Moya
Jordi Sancho

COLLABORATORS
Atis Obres i Projectes
Factors de Paisatge
JSS Efficient
 Engineering
Masala Consultors

DEVELOPERS
AMB
Sant Feliu
de Llobregat
Town Council

CONTRACTOR
Artífex

PHOTOGRAPHER
Andrés Flajszer

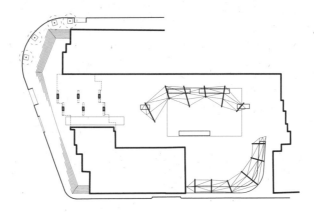

⏱ 1/1000

The redevelopment of this small interior square, which is accessed via a passage under one of the buildings and by a street that runs at a lower level, responds to a demand for public accessibility as expressed by residents in a participatory process.

The central part of the square is remodelled on a single level, so that the public space can be more easily shared: it can be used by both adults and children, with a space reserved for very small ones, fostering the intergenerational interaction

that offers so many benefits to neighbourhood life.

Greenery plays a major role throughout the intervention, whether along the access ramp, where the flowerbeds adapt to the sloping topography and minimise the visual impact of the change in level, or in the square, where metal pergolas are installed to support climbing species that help dampen the noise generated by the activities while, at the same time, adding colour and life.

Mobil-
ity
Space

An urban planner for the Paris metropolitan region, Paul Lecroart (1962) is an expert in large-scale sustainability. Among other work, he developed the Green Plan for the Paris metropolitan region and the Paris Olympic project, promoting the renovation of highways and the pedestrianisation of the banks of the Seine. A professor of Strategic Planning in Paris (Sciences Po - École Urbaine and École d'Urbanisme de Paris), he has consulted on mobility in cities such as Bodø (Norway), Cali and Medellín (Colombia), Tehran (Iran), Tripoli (Libya), Vitória (Brazil), Changzhou (China), Moscow (Russia), Rabat (Morocco), Johannesburg (South Africa) and Montreal (Canada).

You've transformed the mobility in cities like Seoul with the recovery of the space occupied by highways. Is it true that traffic decreased by 82%?

What happened in Seoul was that the mayor, Lee Myung-Bak, wanted to spearhead the recovery of the Cheonggyecheon River and he did everything necessary to achieve that. It included reducing vehicle traffic. He did it in several different ways. To begin with, he increased the frequency and speed of the bus system, generating traffic lanes for exclusive use. He created express bus lines. And then he worked to discourage drivers of private vehicles through an incentive system. In Seoul, if you don't drive for one day out of 10, you get discounts on petrol and free tickets for public transport. That was key to reducing traffic. Another strategy was limiting parking spaces. In short, he made it difficult to use private transport. The combination of all those measures led to a spectacular reduction in urban traffic.

Through penalisations?

There were also psychological motivations. Many drivers imagined the result would be chaos, and it deterred them. It changed their habits. The 82% that people refer to is the reduction in vehicles entering the city.

The reduction of traffic in other cities, like Paris or New York, using similar measures, only reached 25 and 27 percent. If Seoul is the model example, what worked best there?

The mayor had control over all the factors involved in mobility. He is ultimately responsible for traffic, public transport, urban development and parking, and he made sure that there would be other ways to access the city centre. He managed to change the big picture by making small changes. But there's something else. Much of the traffic could be chalked up to street vending, so the mayor eliminated the practice by relocating it to the outskirts of the city. The idea was to transform the city centre into a space for offices and residences.

Does altering mobility have a social cost?

In Seoul it came at a cost, without a doubt. The street vendors who were displaced were specifically selling electronic components. The mayor determined that, in this case, proximity was not as important and he relocated them. What I don't know is how things are going in the area that was designated for that business.

Is displacing certain business activities to improve circulation a form of gentrification?

In this case it wasn't. Many of those businesses occupied buildings that were in poor condition. Some could be regularised and stayed. The rest relocated to low-rent locations.

"Changing how we work has altered how we move around the city."

—Paul Lecroart

By Anatxu Zabalbeascoa

Is reorganising mobility and urban traffic easier to do in Asian countries, where there is a more developed idea of collectivity than in most Western countries?

In truth what fuels the biggest change is when life becomes unsustainable somewhere. Carved up by elevated highways criss-crossing the urban centre, the heart of Seoul had reached its limit, and people were abandoning it. That often happens when, instead of repairing the existing centre, another centre is developed. People and businesses move out, and that's the time to act. In order to revitalise the historic centre, it was essential to remove the highway that crossed through it. And divided it.

You defend drastic ideas to alter the mobility in cities.

Altering the mobility of a city takes time. Even minor changes take months to show results. But they are always worth it.

Always? How can that benefit be assessed?

I don't know of any mayors, in any city in the world, who have altered access roads and reduced the presence of cars and who wouldn't say that it was worth it. And that they would do it all over again. Not one. Altering mobility is a complex process. It takes time, listening and planning. But it always pays off because restricting car traffic, curiously enough, makes the city more accessible. The mayor of San Francisco is convinced that limiting the presence of cars, by diverting the highway, was the best thing he did in his entire term. And the mayor of Seoul, Lee Myung-Bak, who brought life back to the Cheonggyecheon River, which had been buried under the old highway, ended up becoming president of the country. He was a controversial mayor, of course. He was quite authoritative.

If limiting vehicle access to the city centre is effective all over the world, why is it so difficult to implement?

Taking cars out of the city centre lets us recover the urban core for pedestrians. People keep arriving, but in a different way. The big highways through cities were built when cities were industrial centres, and they needed roads for the traffic that came in to pick up or deliver goods. Today we work in different ways. People work in offices, in cafés, and now, increasingly, at home. Changing how we work has altered how we move around the city. We don't need big highways running through cities anymore.

The process of reducing the impact of major roads is always similar: it begins with closing them on Sundays – for pedestrian use, then traffic is limited, many end up disappearing, and the efforts are always a success.

Exactly. But the success is slow. And it requires all those phases. The first phase is the most essential. And it's impossible to achieve without conviction on the part of mayors. That's because it tends to stir up a lot of opposition, a lot of doubt, and politicians are terrified of eliciting doubt and disapproval. Today we applaud the pedestrianisation of the banks of the Seine in Paris. But when the previous mayor, the socialist Bertrand Delanoë, made the decision, there was a lot of controversy. And opposition.

Why is that?

The greater region and some city councils around the periphery wanted to be able to cross Paris by car. There were also some loose ends in the proposal. Loose ends are dangerous because the opponents of a proposal tend to latch onto them. The measure asserted that removing cars from the riverbanks would reduce pollution. And they presented an opposing study, which showed that pollution would not be reduced because the presence of cars on the streets bordering the river would increase. They clung to that data until Mayor Hidalgo and her team studied the issue again and offered another compelling argument: the recognition of the Seine as it passes through Paris as a UNESCO World Heritage Site. Cars weren't compatible with that designation.

Do cultural or economic criteria have more weight than public health when it comes to making changes to mobility?

So far, yes. That has been the case. The legislation would need to be altered.

You have worked all over the world: China, North Africa, North America, etc. When private vehicle traffic in cities is reduced, are poorer people the ones who are left out?

The poor generally don't use cars to get to the city centre. They use public transport. If they do have a car, they'll use it to go to work on the outskirts of cities – where the jobs are. In that sense, the rich tend to see more changes in their lives with the alteration of urban mobility.

Do you think mobility today has more to do with the boundaries that limit movement or with vehicles themselves?

Mobility is fundamentally related to how you perceive your movements. If you have the idea that using public transport will be difficult, or very slow, or very uncomfortable, you will look for alternatives. Anything that makes travel difficult – a lack of information on bus lines, timetables or the city map – complicates mobility. In truth, a lot of people get lost driving their own cars, but driving is initially perceived as more comfortable. Cities developed along railway lines or rivers precisely because they could be used for the transport of people and goods. Streets were added to the confusion and then, often elevated above the streets, came roads and highways. All this made walking through cities difficult, if not impossible. There are places in metropolitan areas that pedestrians can't access.

Have cities become disconnected from the inhabitants to connect with their vehicles?

Something like that, although there are people travelling in the vehicles. In the 1960s, we thought that cars would be the way to get around the city. And we built up that idea. We did our best to facilitate movement by car. Eventually this planning turned against city inhabitants: many don't have cars, and the people who do use them create congestion that impacts everyone. We've complicated our lives trying to make them easier, and now it's very hard to go back: highways run across cities; and they're one more layer of construction along with roads and utilities. Reorganising all of that is difficult.

How do we plan future cities now without relying only on short-term solutions?

Initially, cars were going to save us. So we built highways. Now we believe that being able to walk and ride bicycles will make our lives better.

How can we think for the long term?

It's difficult because of political and industry pressures. The idea was to shift from cars powered by gasoline or diesel to electric cars. But now we know that isn't going to be the solution. Pollution would be reduced, but not traffic or the disproportionate amount of space occupied by cars in cities. I don't think that the widespread use of electric cars is the future.

What will it be then?

Beyond public transport, we need individual mobility, but it can take many different forms: smaller cars, motorcycles, bicycles, scooters, etc. Now we need to work on plural systems, where several individual means of transport can coexist. Cars need to be in the minority. The dominant form of mobility in urban centres should be on foot, walking. We need to reverse our priorities.

How do you move around Paris, your home city?

On a bicycle.

Since when?

For the past 30 years.

You're a pioneer!

There weren't as many bike riders before.

Have you ever had an accident?

No. Fortunately.

Does your wife also ride a bicycle?

She walks. And she uses the subway. It's question of habit. Ten years ago I lived in Santa Monica, in Los Angeles. I had to ride 11 kilometres to get to my office at UCLA. The first day I thought it might be crazy. But I started talking to other teachers and students who were doing it too, and I got used to it. The fact that there are other riders is a good thing and, little by little, it helps drivers adjust.

Are you in shape?

It's a beginning, but it isn't enough.

Do you dress different since you started riding?

I do. I don't wear a jacket. I was in Iran in 2005, and I realised that wearing a tie was a symbol of colonialism. I took it off and I haven't worn one since. Why would I? We repeat actions without asking ourselves why.

How do you know that transport by bicycle or scooter isn't just a fad and that it won't disappear if a space is created to promote it?

Well, we've been pedestrians for three million years.

You don't think we nearly left that behind?	That's true for many people, yes. And that has translated into the obesity epidemic affecting the West. Many people can no longer walk without getting tired because they've lost the habit.
Pollution doesn't help either. Or the lack of shade.	True. That all has to do with how easy it has been to use cars. It has been the norm up until now. As for what we'll be seeing in the future, we can only venture hypotheses. We have talked a lot about carsharing, and even shared motorcycles. But we don't live in a society that knows how to share. We live in a society that is accustomed to commerce. And those are very different goals. We have to think and plan realistically.
And based on a realistic perspective, what do you predict?	We can drive from Paris to Barcelona today because the streets are connected to the highways. And the highways are conditioned so that cars can drive on them. That means that streets function on different scales. The architect Christian de Portzamparc says that the streets always work because they're easy to understand. The edges orient the circulation in one direction or another. There's no other option. If there aren't any streets, there are more options. But people get lost. It's hard for us to move around without boundaries. We need to design flexible streets so that they can accommodate various forms of mobility.
What is more difficult to change, cities or the mentalities and habits of citizens?	I think both things go together. I have analysed cities that have managed to change their mobility. Barcelona is one of them. It has been transformed in the last 30 years.
Do you think that Barcelona is improving as a city?	You don't?
It's still a wonderful city, but it is losing population and gaining tourists.	That's a very common problem. Barcelona has been much smarter than other cities in Spain because it hasn't developed its periphery as an extension of the city but as separate neighbourhoods. That's an achievement. In France, cities have grown along the extension of the tramway lines and density has been neglected, except in Strasbourg or Nantes. Do you think the Barcelona model is obsolete?
What do you think?	Barcelona has a very human scale. Large metropolises tend to be associated with more authoritarian administrations.
As an urban planner, do you question the model of an endless city?	We try to show that the large metropolises that prospered between 1990 and 2010 have added the global economic crisis to their usual problems of segregation, pollution and poverty. There are jobs in cities; that's why people want to live in them. But it can be hard to live in cities today. Few people can afford it. I think the price of housing is the reason for the progressive abandonment of some cities. More than problems with quality of life. There are a lot of metropolises on the planet that have seen improvements, in that sense, in recent years.
What has changed?	In the 1980s, most businesses left urban centres. Think of New York. Back then, 85% of jobs were created outside the city, in the metropolitan area. Since the year 2000, 85% of jobs have been created in New York.
What caused that shift?	The economy is more based on knowledge and financial products than on industrial production. Offices have replaced factories in many cities. It's very difficult to predict urban changes. Degrowth – in terms of traffic, population, business – isn't something politicians tend to have in mind.
Isn't the 15-minute city a way to reduce travel, and traffic as a result?	I don't know what the 15-minute city is.
You're kidding. It's a French invention.	I know. But I don't like it. In Bilbao, they asked me to talk with Carlos Moreno about it. And I refused. There are so many things to talk about; I refused to discuss that topic with him because it has become a political slogan.

What do you mean?

Paris is a 15-minute city. Traditional neighbourhoods are too, and always have been. So where's the novelty? In the name? My son has always gone to school, from nursery to secondary school, three minutes from home. That isn't a novelty. That's why I don't like talking about it, but I do like talking about how much time pedestrians waste at intersections. We can design with that in mind: improving pedestrian waiting times. There are large avenues in Paris that can take 10 minutes to cross. You can't have a 15-minute city if it takes you 10 minutes to cross a single street!

You published the book *Cities Change the World*. What changes cities?

The economy changes cities. Paris today is founded on exchange. It always has been, but we had forgotten about it. We built laboratories and research centres 30 or 40 kilometres outside cities, and we moved knowledge out of them. When they had to come back, in response to changes in mobility, those industries and research centres settled in the east of the city. Why? Because that's where the new life is, the stimuli, the coexistence, the city that has yet to be built. Today, I believe ours is an economy of stimuli. We need to interact, relate, continuously.

The liveliest neighbourhoods in cities are usually the poorest, with small shops and people on the street.

That's true.

Among other things, because the richest parts have been sold to the highest bidder, not to be inhabited but as investments.

That's a reality. Housing can be protected. If we don't protect it, international investors will end up buying the whole planet creating a distortion in the market, putting the real estate market out of reach for city dwellers. The fiscal system should combat that. An investment in housing should be for living in it. Otherwise it will be the end of cities. I don't know if it's the main problem in cities, because there are a lot of them, but it's certainly one of them. In Vienna, 80% of the population lives in public housing. Many of them are renters. What will happen if they're sold or rented to the highest bidder?

As we've said, you've worked all over the world. In your opinion, what city has the best mobility?

I think Italy has changed a lot with the low emission zones. Of course, Tokyo, Singapore and Hong Kong have always rejected cars. But they don't have good public spaces. In terms of public space, I think Barcelona wins. And in terms of mobility, the Scandinavian countries are very interesting. Their trump card? The population is very educated. Civics is taught in schools, which are public, and as such they are also founded on coexistence. Education is simple if there's an interest in forming free and engaged citizens.

We always praise Scandinavian civility, but they're dealing with smaller populations. There are a lot more of us in the Mediterranean, and we're much noisier. Could their formula work for us?

Education always helps. Barcelona and Bilbao have made big improvements to their public space and the awareness of mobility. The Scandinavians have a small and relatively homogeneous population. It's easier for them to reach an agreement, but they're still a benchmark. When you buy a flat in Malmö, someone from the town hall visits to inform you about the neighbourhood and mobility options. That could be implemented everywhere, right? Big changes can start with small actions.

0 500 1000   2000   5000 m

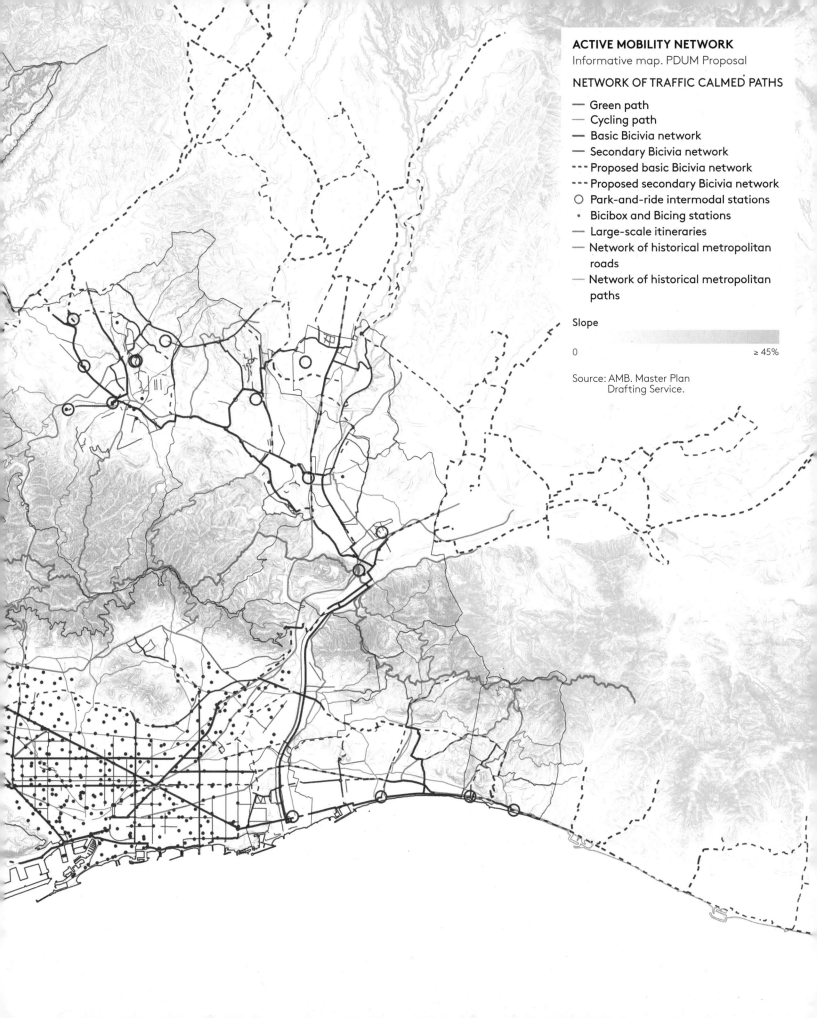

ACTIVE MOBILITY NETWORK
Informative map. PDUM Proposal

NETWORK OF TRAFFIC CALMED PATHS

— Green path
— Cycling path
— Basic Bicivia network
— Secondary Bicivia network
--- Proposed basic Bicivia network
--- Proposed secondary Bicivia network
○ Park-and-ride intermodal stations
· Bicibox and Bicing stations
— Large-scale itineraries
— Network of historical metropolitan roads
— Network of historical metropolitan paths

Slope

0   ≥ 45%

Source: AMB. Master Plan Drafting Service.

Civil engineer Javier Ortigosa (Badalona, 1982) has always been interested in the city. He obtained a PhD from ETH Zurich with a thesis on urban traffic and is an expert in urban mobility. With a cross-disciplinary education and interests, he defends recovering the human scale of cities rather than fine-tuning algorithms to maximise the traffic light systems. In other words, he wonders what we lose and what we gain when the priority is moving through the city quickly.

You've spent half your life facilitating mobility for motor vehicles. Now you're questioning it?

Absolutely, but the science of mobility was based on optimising the circulation of cars, and that's difficult to change.

Were pedestrians not included under the scope of mobility?

They were protected by separating them and circulation was facilitated for cars. There's no economic logic to pedestrian mobility. It's more difficult to control. A car travels in a lane. A pedestrian has more freedom of movement. When it comes to pedestrian mobility, you have to account for many factors: ease of movement, safety, and the air they're breathing.

Your discipline started by trying to increase the flow of cars, and now it's doing the opposite?

I don't know if it's the opposite, but mobility today is trying to adapt to a new world. It started in the US, making it easier for cars to move around. I read that during World War II, the Americans understood that the highway network in Hitler's Germany had helped him gain ground. There was a consensus that the modern way of getting around was going to be by car rather than rail, which was rigid. Cars were free and personal. But cars were just a hobby for some. The first one to arrive in Barcelona was called "the Pedralbes fireball". It's a resilient invention when you think about it: it works the same in the Sahara as it does in Norway, it runs for at least 10 years, etc.

But it causes problems that we didn't foresee.

Of course. It has been the victim of its own success. Cars were viewed as a way to achieve modernity. The construction of expressways across cities was applauded and upheld as the advent of progress. Having powerful traffic networks makes economic development possible. There is still a link between GDP and traffic.

What happened?

In the 60s, a fear of cars began to emerge because regions were unprepared for them. In 1963, Colin D. Buchanan declared that cars would cause cities to collapse. And to prevent that from happening, cities were occupied with infrastructure.

Cerdà's urban plan wasn't suited to cars?

The major arteries – Gran Via, Diagonal Avenue, and Meridiana Avenue – that formed the structure of the grid were meant to exit Barcelona and continue on throughout the region. But there came a time in the 60s when those infrastructures were considered insufficient. More and more roads began popping up to increase the flow of traffic.

There were warnings of the risks while the expansions were going on at the same time?

With the idea that the problems could be solved with more infrastructure. The issue we were seeing was gridlock traffic, not pollution or streets being occupied by parked cars. But of course, the problem is that if you build more infrastructure, you

"The future is thinking about mobility on a metropolitan scale."
—Javier Ortigosa

By Anatxu Zabalbeascoa

create more demand. You make it easier to fit more cars on the roads. And when you promote one type of mobility, you marginalise another. The ring roads in Barcelona were meant to alleviate traffic, but by facilitating access to the city they shifted the population toward the Maresme area, among other places, and generated a demand for urban parking. Traffic doubled.

When did people start to realise that so many cars were unsustainable?

In the 80s we started thinking about how to limit the number of cars in the city.

They didn't disappear en masse...

Speed limits in the city have been progressively reduced to increase safety and reduce pollution. But it's true that today there are *superblocks* in Barcelona in some places and traffic junctions in others. The space for cars doesn't just disappear, it gets relocated.

How many types of mobility coexist in the metropolitan area?

We generally talk about three: active mobility – walking and cycling; public transport; and private vehicles. Today there is a general awareness of air quality. People think, if I live in the Eixample I'll be breathing polluted air and if I live in Sant Vicenç dels Horts, I won't. But how are you going to get there, and how are you going to move around there? That will affect the air quality!

Active mobility used to be called passive.

Right. Or slow mobility. And we turned it around. It's urban mobility. In a city, you can easily get in 10,000 steps a day. In a village, people rely more on their cars.

Where do electric scooters fit in?

They're a type of personal mobility that some consider active and others don't. I don't think they're a passing fad because they make sense. They're a hybrid between the traditional scooter and the motorcycle. In Barcelona, there are no shared electric scooter rentals. But there are for motorcycles. Electricity is gaining ground.

Isn't that just substitution in terms of fuel? New vehicles may not pollute, but their presence can still be overwhelming.

Electric cars require less labour. The industry loses workers. You gain in air quality. And you occupy the same space. That's the drama of cities: the fact that only 1.2 people move around using a device that takes up so much space. One of the interesting things about new forms of mobility is that they will occupy less space. The key will be in how they are regulated.

If scooters are successful, will they pose the same problem as cars?

Probably. But cars are very autonomous and fast, which is why they can respond to a regional demand that scooters cannot. In the future, I think we'll have a single lane for cars. They will be the exception. And, if they're limited to a single lane, the speed limit will be reduced. Induced demand entails increasing traffic with better conditions. Reduced demand means decreasing it. Some people call it 'traffic evaporation'.

How can that be achieved?

There isn't a single solution. The idea is that restricting the space available for cars makes people reconsider using them. But it doesn't always work like that. Mobility is an intermediate good. We have the right not to movement but to reaching our destination: accessibility. When it comes to mobility, people choose what suits them best. There will always be people willing to deal with traffic and pay for parking. Public transport will always win out in terms of cost. And ecological awareness. But when it comes to time...

Is it a matter of what your time is worth?

Yes. And whether or not the difference is acceptable to you. Improving public transport and making car parking more expensive are effective measures to keep cars out of the city. Reducing the space for them sometimes just redistributes the same traffic.

Are you in favour of urban tolls?

That's one measure. They did it in Stockholm. They charged 10 kronor, the equivalent of one euro, to enter the city. After two days traffic had dropped by 20%. And it hasn't gone back up.

So the rich can enter, and the poor cannot?

Having fewer cars on the road benefits all citizens. The biggest investment in health is the reduction of pollution. That protects public health. Along with public transport, which moves more quickly with 20% less traffic.

And is more crowded.

Probably. Or not, because there could be a higher frequency.

What does friendly mobility mean?

It's also known as healthy or sustainable mobility. It's a type of mobility that generates zero cost for the city: for example, walking. The idea is that it doesn't have a negative effect on others. And active mobility, walking, accounts for 50% of daily mobility in the metropolitan area of Barcelona.

Has that changed in recent years?

It has always been the case, but it tends to increase during financial crises or during the pandemic, for example.

If half the population moves on foot, why are pedestrians given so little consideration?

There is work-related mobility (30%). The rest is within neighbourhoods. And it's sustainable. It involves walking. That includes walking to school and to the shops. It has to do with proximity. There are still parents who drive their children to school, but with neighbourhood schools all that changes.

How have cars taken over the city then?

That's the big question. They've done it by constructing metropolitan barriers through their infrastructures.

Is it your job to break down those barriers?

Partly. We work in urban planning. I bring mobility and urban planning together. We strive for the mobility that we generate – access to schools, recreation, and hospitals – to be as sustainable as possible.

Driving to the grocery store was once a modern thing to do; today it's backward.

In Mediterranean cities, that was never fully the case because of the urban fabric. In the US they've recently started building neighbourhoods. Washington, for example, is being expanded following criteria from 19th-century Europe: the human scale, Paris, the Eixample. In the United States, people wanted more space for less money, and that model of the city based on semi-detached and single-family houses leads to mobility by car that the city cannot absorb today. The 15-minute city is essentially an old-fashioned neighbourhood.

How is it possible to promote neighbourhoods without segregating uses – working in one place and living in another – in the city?

By thinking ahead 30 years from now. Since it is so slow, urbanism operates with a lot of inertia. Cars were questioned in the 80s and were only seeing their departure today. The future of mobility is efficiency of economic cost, time cost, and environmental cost. Anything inefficient will either be very expensive or prohibited.

How do you think ahead 30 years from now?

In the 19th century, they were worried about cleaning up horse droppings. Today, its cars. In 30 years' time maybe everyone will be running through parks playing sport and that will be the source of our problems. We'll see.

Are those parks already being designed?

We're designing more balanced neighbourhoods, where work and facilities coexist with daily life. That should reduce movement. You can't implement urban development without thinking about public transport. And we want to recover networks on a human scale with urban density, diversity, a social mix and mixed land uses (schools, hospitals).

Why is a social mix important?

Because everyone has a job. And if all the residents of a neighbourhood did the same thing, there would be more forced mobility.

But neighbourhoods have personalities: university-based, commercial, etc.

Sure, there's a certain specialisation. The city is sectorised for economic reasons. But if a baker can't afford to live in the neighbourhood where he bakes bread, his life will be worse and so will that of the neighbourhood. If everyone on a given street is a lawyer, who will make the coffee? The more diversity you have, the more demands intermingle, and the more mobility improves. A typological mix is a social mix. My partner walked to the hospital when she was in labour because we live nearby. We moved there because she works at the hospital.

You made a decision based on mobility.

More and more people are doing that. We used to choose schools based on education, and now we do so based on proximity to our homes. That is prioritising mobility. The dream is for everyone to have everything they need in their own neighbourhood.

It that something new?

It has always been an issue: a human scale and local commerce. Manuel de Solà-Morales said that Barcelona is still reaping the benefits of the Eixample. That structure mixes so many uses, the human scale, and public space that it is exemplary. Now, experts in public space, construction and mobility are working together. And it shows. We're learning to coexist.

And we're becoming more sophisticated.

There used to just be cars and pedestrians. Now there are various types of mobility that operate at different speeds.

What's an example of good mobility today?

The priority given to pedestrians in Barcelona is a success story. Wide squares and sidewalks were already planned in the 80s. The trend of creating space for pedestrians dates back to Bohigas and Busquets. It's a question of small details, like aligning crosswalks with the edges of streets to facilitate pedestrian circulation, for example.

Is it possible to slow down mobility without slowing down life?

You can have a fast-paced life with active and sustainable mobility. It's a question of accessibility. What can't be acceptable is moving through the city like you're on a highway.

How do you get to work?

I use Bicing. Or I take the bus. In 2016, when I started working here, that wasn't possible. Today there's a bike lane and Bicing. I have mobility options.

And between municipalities?

That's the challenge. On a metropolitan scale, active mobility – walking or cycling – is still a challenge. We're working on improving the connections between nearby municipalities. Zona Universitària is just one kilometre from Esplugues. There shouldn't be a barrier for pedestrians. Esplugues is closer than Francesc Macià Square, which is three kilometres away, and yet I can get there on foot. But, until very recently, I couldn't get to Esplugues. That's the challenge. Most trips within the metropolitan area are less than 10 kilometres. What we need to create is a metropolitan city. Sabadell and Nou Barris are 15 kilometres away from one another, a standard distance for an electric bicycle. We need to build channels to connect the metropolis.

You design from a bird's-eye view.

Gran Via is the C-31. It's the same street turned into a highway, a major avenue that could have a tram and sidewalks to connect with the larger region. The scale of the large axes is connection; the small scale supports neighbourhood coexistence. Both are crucial. I believe that's the future, continuity: thinking about mobility on a metropolitan scale. That creates the city.

Pere IV Street
Barcelona

JOSEP MUXART (AMB)

2015-2017
15,549 m²
€7,012,138

EXECUTIVE MANAGEMENT
David Aguilar (AMB)

AMB TEAM
Javier Duarte
Francesc Germà
Laia Ginés
Cati Montserrat

COLLABORATORS
CTP 1999

DEVELOPERS
AMB
BIMSA

CONTRACTOR
UTE Acciona
Infraestructuras -
Copcisa

PHOTOGRAPHER
Adrià Goula

Historically connected with the routes leaving Barcelona toward the north, the character of Pere IV Street is currently more associated with neighbourhood life in Poblenou; hence the need to transform its structure to integrate it better as a pedestrian axis with a larger number of activities, where trees help to generate pleasant leisure areas.

The renovation that is underway in this stretch of street, which is meant to serve as a model for subsequent phases, expands the spaces reserved for pedestrians and active mobility and reduces the space occupied by vehicles: five lanes for traffic and parking are reduced to two.

The new street design is symmetrical with pavements more than five metres wide and a central roadway with a single lane for circulation, a service lane (parking,

rubbish bins, etc.) and a two-way cycling lane. This symmetry is reinforced by the lines of trees along the pavements and the streetlights installed at two different heights: one to light the roadway and the other for the pedestrian areas.

The cross section of the street distinguishes between the character of the two sides. The pavement on the mountain side, closest to the bike lane, is flush with the road and has more seating areas: in certain sections, the borders around the tree pits are raised and finished with wood to serve as benches. The pavement also widens at the intersections with La Llacuna and Castella streets, where there are more trees and additional chairs and benches to sit on.

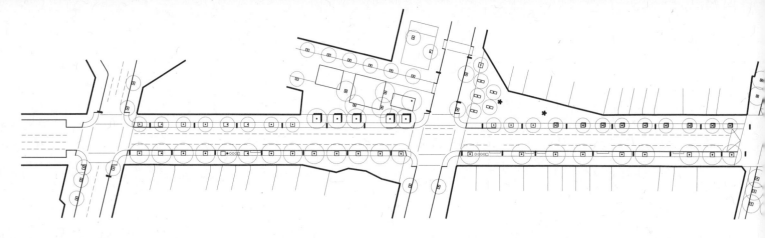

⊘ 1/1500

The pavement on the sea side, which is closer to vehicle traffic, is outfitted with raised kerbs to better delimit the space for cars and to promote proper drainage of rainwater. The trees there are also planted in a single row, but always in tree pits at the same level as the pavement.

At the intersection of Pere IV with the Rambla del Poblenou, priority is given to pedestrians across the entire width of the street: the roadway and the pavements run at the same level as the Rambla, turning the space into a square that acts as a point of articulation between the two streets.

In short, with the redevelopment of Pere IV Street, the aim is to enhance public use of a street that has always played a significant role in the development of the Poblenou neighbourhood.

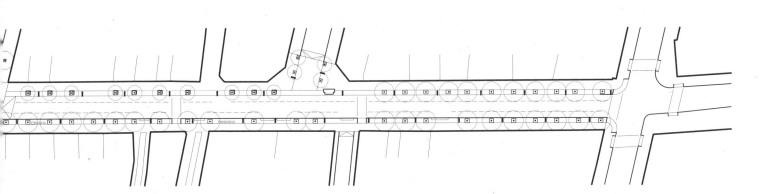

Cycling Connection

Various municipalities

ENRIC BATLLE
JOAN ROIG
IVÁN SÁNCHEZ
(Batlleiroig)

2015–2018
15,230 m²
€1,552,949

AMB TEAM
David Aguilar

BATLLEIROIG TEAM
Yago Cavaller
Dolors Feu
Antoni Monté
Francesc Montero

COLLABORATORS
SBS Simón i Blanco

DEVELOPERS
AMB
Barcelona City C.
Esplugues de
Llobregat Town C.
UE – FEDER

CONTRACTORS
Rogasa
Agrotècnica del
Segrià

PHOTOGRAPHER
Jordi Surroca
i Gael del Río

AWARDS
Shortlisted:
Bicycle Architecture
Biennale 2020
BCN Architecture
Exhibition 2019
Construmat 2019
FAD Awards 2019

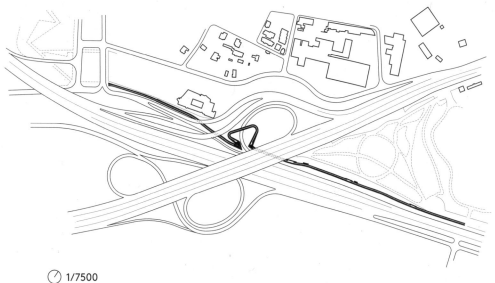

⊘ 1/7500

The construction of a connection for pedestrians and cyclists linking Diagonal Avenue in Barcelona and Països Catalans Avenue in Esplugues de Llobregat involves passing through a junction that is one of the most complicated sites in the metropolitan road network: the intersection of the B-20, the B-23, and the interchange formed by the different connections and access roads to the two cities. Sometimes an overpass and sometimes a tunnel, the new path redefines the edges of the highway, enhancing the urban greenery to soften the harsh qualities of an environment dominated by transport infrastructure.

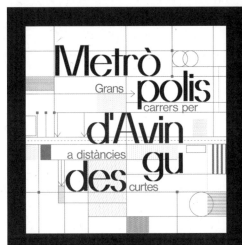

Under the motto "Long Streets for Short Distances", the exhibition *Metropolis of Avenues* portrays an imaginary city where streets, highways and roads have been transformed into accessible, sustainable and integrated public spaces. It displays the resulting ideas from the Junctions and Crossroads competition, a reflection of multidisciplinary teams on the idea of "metropolitan avenues", outlined by the Metropolitan Urban Master Plan.

The route is designed with gentle slopes that adapt to the different ground levels, ensuring comfort for both cyclists and pedestrians. The urban development stipulates a total width of 4.5 metres and differentiates the cycling path from the pedestrian spaces using two adjacent strips of pavement differentiated by colour and texture.

Thus, the cycling path can be continuous and homogeneous along the entire route, while pedestrians can walk through a renaturalised environment planted with greenery and make use of a number of rest spaces in widened areas that adapt to the geometry of the landscaped slope and the existing trees.

Llorenç Serra Boulevard

Santa Coloma de Gramenet

CLAUDI AGUILÓ RIU
EVA PAGÉS
(AMB)

2017-2019
12,600 m²
€2,037,030

SITE MANAGEMENT
Jordi Larruy (AMB)

AMB TEAM
Carles Español
Francesc Germà
Pepe Gil
Ainhoa Martínez
Mireia Monràs
Cati Montserrat
Daniel Vázquez

DEVELOPERS
AMB
Santa Coloma
de Gramenet
City Council
UE – FEDER

CONTRACTOR
Copisa

PHOTOGRAPHER
Jeroen Van Mieghem

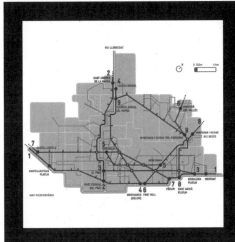

A new section of this old road that belonged to the network of local routes is being redeveloped in keeping with the same criteria, materials, and elements used until now to remodel the first section of the boulevard and other streets in the urban centre of Santa Coloma de Gramenet.

The street is designed to be asymmetrical, where the pavement on the north side, the sunniest side, is wider; a two-way cycling lane is set up in the centre of the boulevard, close to the median planted with trees and grasses, and the roadway is reduced to one lane of traffic and one service lane (parking and rubbish) in each direction. Deciduous trees are planted in three staggered rows, one on each side of the road and one down the centre, and different species of vegetation are combined on the surfaces that are also drainage points and zones for rainwater infiltration. The project fosters ecological connectivity between the city centre and the Besòs River, and it formalises the introduction of green infrastructure into the urban fabric.

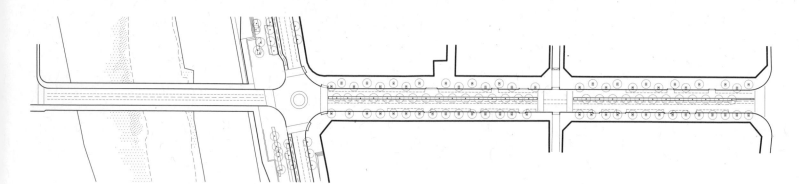

⏱ 1/2500

When it reaches the river, the promenade incorporates the roundabout that connects with Salzereda Avenue, and the cycling path continues, crossing the Besòs River to reach Barcelona, as part of the Bicivia – the metropolitan cycling network. The pavements and lighting on the bridge over the Besòs are renewed. A row of lamp posts is installed on the pavement of one side, tying in with the same elements used on Llorenç Serra Boulevard. As a counterpoint, an illuminated handrail is placed along the railing on the side that offers views of Collserola.

In short, the remodel of the Llorenç Serra Boulevard and the old Santa Coloma bridge makes a commitment to more sustainable mobility and to enhancing green infrastructure in the city.

Access to Bètica Street
Badia del Vallès

CARLES ENRICH
(Carles Enrich Studio)

2017-2019
1,000 m²
€354,990

COLLABORATORS
Brufau Cusó
MA+SA arquitectura
TRAM

CARLES ENRICH
TEAM
Anna de Castro
Joan Martí

DEVELOPERS
AMB
Badia del Vallès
Town Council

CONTRACTOR
Voracys

PHOTOGRAPHER
Adrià Goula

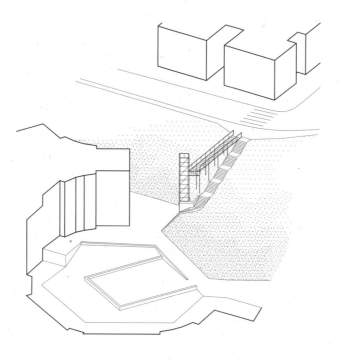

The topography of Badia del Vallès has significant differences in height at some points, which obstructs connections between streets and makes it difficult for residents to access all the city's facilities. To address this problem between Mediterrània Avenue, where there are several residential blocks, and Bètica Street, which concentrates services such as the municipal market and schools, a lift and stairs are proposed with a design that respects the existing slope and trees.

The lift has a light tubular structure, and the envelope is built from micro-perforated steel sheet and glass, giving a feeling of transparency and integrating easily with the surroundings, similar to the walkway that connects with Bètica Street.

METROPOLITAN PASSAGES

Passages are fundamental connecting elements for moving around the city; they can lend form and urban content to metropolitan spaces by working on a small scale, through immediate interventions, and over short periods of time. The Metropolitan Passages ideas competition focuses on six areas characterised by barriers and discontinuities that also have the potential to foster soft mobility and slow speed connections.

On the lower level, the space between the buildings is reorganised, as it tended to flood in rainy weather due to the steep slope and lack of drainage. Permeability of the soil is encouraged by slightly inclined planes to help control rainwater, by pavements in decomposed granite, and by planted meadow areas. In the centre, the new children's play area has a soft pavement and a perimeter of gabions that serve a double purpose: to help with rainwater infiltration and to act as benches to encourage gathering.

The intervention improves mobility in the neighbourhood and gives local residents access to an area for leisure and play that was previously often flooded by rain.

Connectivity in Mas Rampinyo Neighbourhood

Montcada i Reixac

ARIADNA PERICH

2017-2019
453 m²
€496,898

AMB TEAM
Natalia Castaños

COLLABORATORS
Eletresjota
March-Rius
 Arquitectes Tècnics

DEVELOPERS
AMB
Montcada i Reixac
Town Council

CONTRACTOR
Constructora del
Cardoner

PHOTOGRAPHER
José Hevia

Divided by the railway, the neighbourhood of Mas Rampinyo in Montcada i Reixac needs new elements that generate connectivity between the residential fabrics on both sides. The current underground passage near the station is being remodelled to incorporate a lift at each end, thus ensuring accessibility for the entire population.

The outdoor structures of the lifts have a double façade: an opaque layer for the cabins themselves and a much lighter outer layer, made of metal mesh, which gives them a more sculptural look. The sloping roofs either follow or contrast with the current canopies that protect the escalators at the exits.

On the lower level, the waiting areas for the lifts are arranged at a tangent to the path of the underground passage, widening the corridor to create small enclaves that provide comfort and a sense of security.

Ultimately, the intervention reinforces the universal accessibility of a path that overcomes the barrier of the railway tracks and contributes to the cohesion of a disperse and poorly defined urban space.

As a result of its geographical situation, Montcada i Reixac has become fragmented over time, to the point that the city's internal connections have been compromised. The proposed urban planning model takes this fragmentary nature and turns the situation upside down, promoting a clear structure to reconnect the municipality, reinforcing its morphological richness and enhancing dynamism and connectivity with the surroundings.

Access to Ciutat Cooperativa

Sant Boi de Llobregat

ROBERTO APARICIO
ROGER JORNET
SÍLVIA OLLÉ
(AR47)

2016-2019
2,106 m²
€917,060

SITE MANAGEMENT
Núria Herrero (AMB)

COLLABORATORS
B-lap
Eskubi Turró
 Arquitectes

DEVELOPERS
AMB
Sant Boi
de Llobregat
Town Council

CONTRACTOR
Rogasa

PHOTOGRAPHER
Josep Casanova

As part of the comprehensive remodel of the public spaces in the neighbourhood of Ciutat Cooperativa in Sant Boi de Llobregat, the entire urban frontage along the highway and the river is being transformed based on three elements: a staircase, a ramp and a lift, which must overcome a difference in height of more than six metres.

To create a slope that offers a more comfortable path, the ramp runs the entire length of the frontage. It is supported by gabion walls and connects the different landings of the stairway. The spaces that remain are infilled and planted with recovered fan palms and new shrubs and climbing vines. Two cross walls, in concrete covered with Corten steel plate, outline the new main slope between the lift, located next to the footbridge that leads to the railway station, and the staircase that unfolds from an old section remaining on the other side. On the upper level, a public square of decomposed granite is generated, with views towards the river and paved on three sides to provide access to the blocks of flats, the neighbourhood, and the lift and footbridge connecting with the railway station.

In short, the new access to the neighbourhood forms a large green façade based on a series of landscaped slopes that incorporate mobility elements that ensure accessibility for all.

Access to Central Park

Sant Andreu
de la Barca

**SERGI CARRULLA
OSCAR BLASCO**
(SCOB Arquitectura
i Paisatge)

2017-2019
1,151 m²
€493,683

SITE MANAGEMENT
Jordi Larruy (AMB)
Gerard Yubero

SCOB TEAM
Olga Saro

DEVELOPERS
AMB
Sant Andreu
de la Barca
Town Council

CONTRACTOR
Archs Constructora

PHOTOGRAPHER
Quim Bosch

The connection of the Central Park with the historic centre of Sant Andreu de la Barca needs to reach the level of the covered railway tracks, a difference in height of more than six metres from Anoia Street. This barrier to pedestrian mobility is overcome through a combination of ramps and stairs that follow the outline of the current western boundary of the park. The positioning of the ramp, necessary to ensure slopes in keeping with accessibility criteria, runs parallel to the railway track.

The row of existing trees along the railway will be preserved and new grass and shrub species will be planted to soften the visual impact of the walls needed for the construction of the ramps and stairs.

Ultimately, the new entrance to the Central Park provides a more direct access from the streets of the historic centre for pedestrians and active mobility vehicles.

La Clota Street under the Highway

Cerdanyola del Vallès

MIREIA MONRÀS
(AMB)

2018-2020
9,387 m²
€325,955

AMB TEAM
Montserrat Arbiol

COLLABORATORS
Pi Enginyeria Civil
i Urbanisme
STATIC Ingeniería
Josep Cónsola

DEVELOPERS
AMB
Cerdanyola del Vallès
Town Council
UE – FEDER

CONTRACTOR
UTE Drim - Talio

PHOTOGRAPHER
Joan Guillamat

To improve the connection on foot or by bicycle between the municipalities of Cerdanyola del Vallès and Badia del Vallès, a segregated path is built following La Clota Street and passing under the AP-7 highway to connect with the bridge that crosses the Sec River.

The path, three metres wide, is paved with concrete and follows a winding course as it adapts to the topography and the existing elements. There is a landscaped margin on one side, planted with shrubs, that separates the path from road traffic and ensures the drainage of rainwater coming from the street; on the side closest to the river, the difference in height on the slope is used to plant riverside vegetation in the lowest parts, where the different species are arranged in layers depending on the moisture level. Benches are placed sporadically along the route to form rest areas.

Thus, a new greenway is developed along the Sec River, contributing to promoting active mobility in spaces where the infrastructure makes it difficult.

Car Park in the Cemetery Area

Santa Coloma
de Cervelló

**ISIDRE SANTACREU
SANDRA MOLINER**
(Santacreu-Moliner)

2018-2019
3,896 m²
€298,154

SITE MANAGEMENT
Joan Castellví
Laura Gálvez
(AMB)

AMB TEAM
Jordi Bardolet

**SANTACREU-
MOLINER TEAM**
Víctor Navarro
Albert Rabaza

COLLABORATORS
Eva Blanco

CONTRACTOR
Civilstone

DEVELOPERS
AMB
Santa Coloma
de Cervelló
Town Council

PHOTOGRAPHER
Joan Guillamat

A section of the plot adjacent to the cemetery in Santa Coloma de Cervelló, which was paved in decomposed granite and steeply sloped, is made suitable for its continued use as a parking area. Due to the provisional nature of the intervention, the arrangement of the rows of cars between the trees is respected, but the slope is adapted to prevent rainwater from continuing to cause damage.

A series of stepped terraces is added, formed by draining planters, which promote the infiltration of rainwater while helping to moderate the slope of the terrain. The site is paved with different materials depending on the use: the vehicle circulation areas are asphalted; the parking areas are paved with open jointed cobblestones; and between these two pavement types there is a strip of white concrete that signals pedestrian crossings.

This area characterised by parallel strips – trees, planters and the different paving materials – has two sides that are clearly limited by streets. The junction with the rest of the surrounding green areas is much more indefinite and is resolved through a slope that separates it from the circulation road around the perimeter of the car park.

OVERVIEW OF THE PERIOD 2018-2022

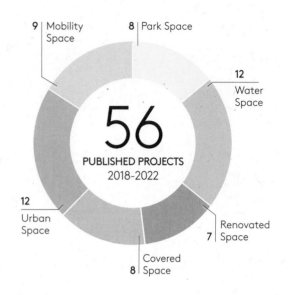

9 Mobility Space
8 Park Space
12 Water Space
7 Renovated Space
8 Covered Space
12 Urban Space

56 PUBLISHED PROJECTS 2018-2022

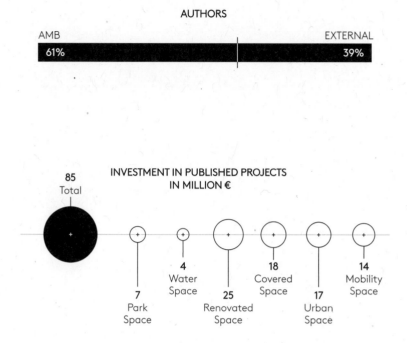

AUTHORS

AMB **61%**
EXTERNAL **39%**

INVESTMENT IN PUBLISHED PROJECTS IN MILLION €

85 Total
7 Park Space
4 Water Space
25 Renovated Space
18 Covered Space
17 Urban Space
14 Mobility Space

PROJECT TYPOLOGY
Published | Built

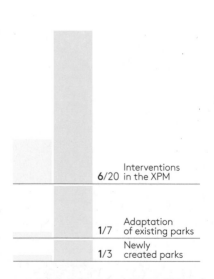

6/20 Interventions in the XPM
1/7 Adaptation of existing parks
1/3 Newly created parks

PARK SPACE

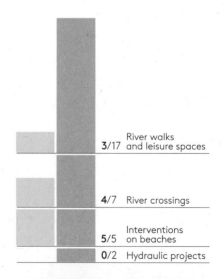

3/17 River walks and leisure spaces
4/7 River crossings
5/5 Interventions on beaches
0/2 Hydraulic projects

WATER SPACE

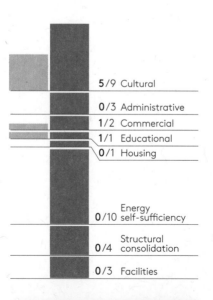

5/9 Cultural
0/3 Administrative
1/2 Commercial
1/1 Educational
0/1 Housing
0/10 Energy self-sufficiency
0/4 Structural consolidation
0/3 Facilities

RENOVATED SPACE

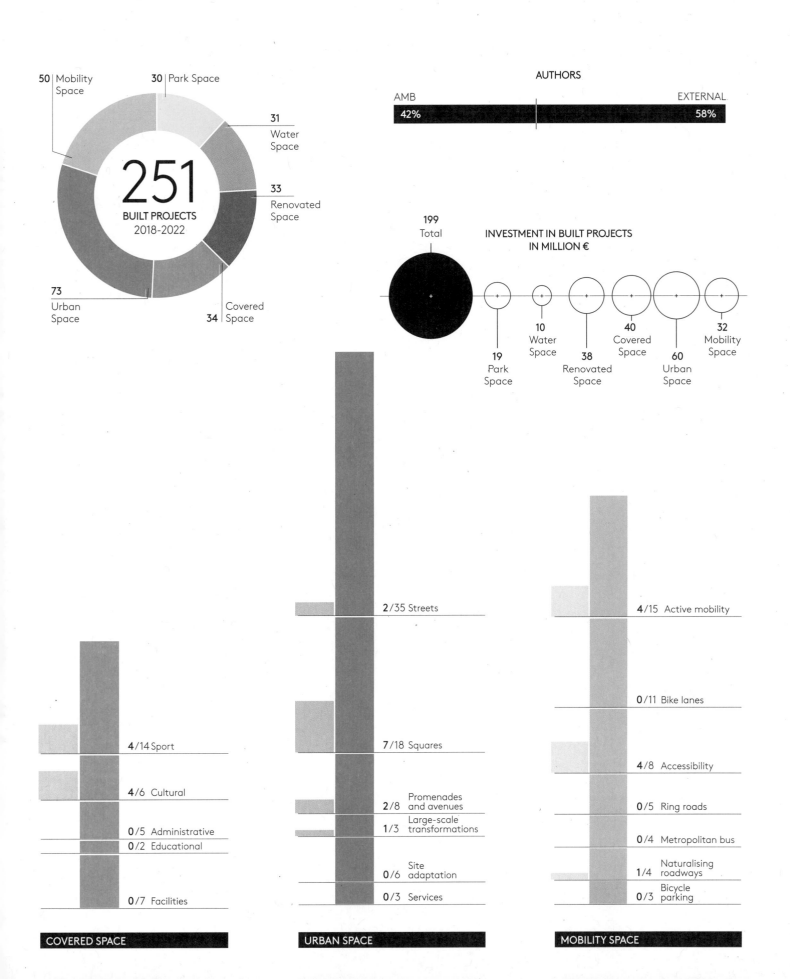

50 | Mobility Space

30 | Park Space

31 Water Space

33 Renovated Space

34 | Covered Space

73 Urban Space

251
BUILT PROJECTS
2018-2022

AUTHORS

AMB
42%

EXTERNAL
58%

199 Total

INVESTMENT IN BUILT PROJECTS IN MILLION €

19 Park Space

10 Water Space

38 Renovated Space

40 Covered Space

60 Urban Space

32 Mobility Space

4/14 Sport

4/6 Cultural

0/5 Administrative

0/2 Educational

0/7 Facilities

COVERED SPACE

2/35 Streets

7/18 Squares

2/8 Promenades and avenues

1/3 Large-scale transformations

0/6 Site adaptation

0/3 Services

URBAN SPACE

4/15 Active mobility

0/11 Bike lanes

4/8 Accessibility

0/5 Ring roads

0/4 Metropolitan bus

1/4 Naturalising roadways

0/3 Bicycle parking

MOBILITY SPACE

A sort of shared vision, a somewhat latent collective spirit, surrounds us and gives our projects at the Barcelona Metropolitan Area (AMB) a natural, spontaneous coherence. For years, this relaxed architecture, not at all jarring, is what has been transforming metropolitan public space – to highlight it, to give it its own particular character, and to advance towards a new city model.

That is why we have been saying, for a long time now, that public space is, first and foremost, for people,[1] that it should support pedestrian mobility, that it should be easy to understand, safe, accessible and inclusive. We advocate free, open and fluid public space that is compatible with multiple uses, flexible and adaptable to changes so that it can transform, evolve and engage with new needs. And this, using just the essential elements and taking special care in the choice of materials, to make it as functional, durable, efficient and sustainable as possible. And finally, and now more than ever, it should tend towards self-sufficiency, minimal energy consumption and efficient management of water and other resources. These criteria – the direct result of the work and the reflections of all the experts who participate in AMB's projects and construction – form the spirit I was talking about and lend the projects their character.[2]

Writing a book about built work always entails talking about the past. Time flies, and things are always changing. In some respects, we're further along than we were when those projects were conceived and executed. Because, in the time that has passed, various initiatives have led to a transformation in the ways we think and work. Initiatives that we've shared with other professionals because we understand that they help us address new challenges. Some have to do with processes and procedures, aspects that don't tend to appear in books like this, but which help us to do our work better. Among them, the definitive incorporation of digitisation has brought about the most radical change. It is truly a shame that, for commercial reasons, it has taken us so many years to embrace the benefits of a technology that has been available for decades. At the AMB we began our journey with BIM in 2015. Today, seven years later, we can say that it is a methodology that plays a role in our daily work. It doesn't change how we approach architecture, of course, but it does give us more accurate control of what we design, both in terms of the geometry and the data we obtain from the three-dimensional models. And everything that helps you work better helps you make better designs.

This book is appearing at a complex time, and in an environment that is increasingly fragile and difficult to understand, given the inevitable and terrible reality of climate change. A reality that has been appealing directly to our responsibility for some time now. That responsibility ranges from the personal sphere to the global community and, unfortunately, it seems difficult for many to accept. But addressing this challenge does directly affect how we design our projects. Because the construction and use of buildings accounts for 38% of greenhouse gas emissions, and cities are responsible for 75% of CO_2 emissions worldwide. The global warming caused by these emissions has direct and obvious effects on the water cycle, on biodiversity, and on people's health.

[1] When I talk about public space, I mean both open spaces (parks, rivers and coastal areas, streets and squares) and covered spaces (both rehabilitated and newly built), like in this book.

[2] I would have liked for all the projects in this book to be accounted for in this text, in one way or another; they are all examples of what I'm trying to express. The problem is that there are 56 of them. And so, similarly to the book, which highlights just a selection of the more than 250 works that we carried out during this period, the projects that appear in the text are ones that exemplify some very specific aspects that I wanted to highlight.

Challenges

Albert Gassull

Director of Public Space Services, AMB

We can say, with certainty, that the urban model we've built does not live up to what citizens demand from their environment. The pandemic has made this very clear, and it has brought out a sensitivity that I don't think will disappear. But in addition, we know that the lack of urban green spaces and air pollution lead to thousands of premature deaths every year in our immediate surroundings; that biodiversity is tied to health, beyond being indispensable for ecological balance, and that the heat island effect, in addition to having a direct impact on the consumption of resources and on the urban ecosystem, affects the most at risk populations.

For all these reasons, we have been taking environmental sustainability very seriously for a few years now. So much so, that we have drawn up our own protocol to cover those areas that are still unregulated, for the purpose of addressing, among other things, global goals for the year 2050 that may seem impossible to achieve. That is how the Sustainability Protocol was created, out of professional and institutional responsibility in the face of the climate crisis, with the aim of giving our internal experts, and anyone developing projects for the AMB, the resources to respond to the sustainable development goals promoted by the United Nations in the international context of the 2030 Agenda. The Protocol is a cross-cutting tool with a comprehensive vision that lets us assess the environmental impact of the decisions that are taken in the drafting of the designs and the execution of the works. It is a guide that, with specific values for three time spans, helps us to improve resource management, to advance in reducing the demand for water and energy, and to promote biodiversity, sustainable mobility, renewable energies and urban regeneration; all of this to mitigate climate change and adapt to it.[3]

[3] You can find the Protocol on the AMB website (www.amb.cat).

However, the Protocol by itself is insufficient: it is an instrument that can help us, but together we all need to reflect, decide and act to create the city model we desire, a model that responds to all our needs. Several factors come together here. The first is to remember that mobility is not only fundamental but indispensable and that, given the current circumstances, it is a genuine problem. Although at the AMB we are working to create an infrastructure for sustainable mobility, and we have carried out notable actions that are stitching together the territory,[4] I have colleagues who are committed to environmental sustainability who come to work by car. That's because taking public transport means tripling the travel time for them or because, from certain towns, getting to Barcelona's Zona Franca (where we have our offices) by bicycle is unthinkable. That fact, which can certainly be extrapolated to almost any city in the world, highlights that mobility is the aspect we must focus on if we're hoping to progress in other fields.

[4] For example, the connection for pedestrians and bicycles between Barcelona and Esplugues de Llobregat, or the incorporation of a bike lane onto Llorenç Serra Boulevard and its connection with the other side of the Besòs River via the old bridge in Santa Coloma de Gramenet.

The second factor is to clarify what we mean by renaturalising the city. I say this because, going back to the previous point, a street is a street. It isn't a park or a forest. You see what I mean. So, I think we need to provide urban space and buildings with as much green infrastructure as possible without diminishing other fundamental aspects of the city. The metropolitan urban fabric is compact and dense, in some cases with streets that aren't wide enough to plant trees on. But that's difficult to change; it's the reality we have to work with. In contrast, 52% of the metropolitan area corresponds to open spaces. Two rivers, the Baix Llobregat Agricultural Park, the Garraf Massif, Collserola, the Marina mountains and the beaches surround and divide the urban fabric, while generating a 900-kilometre contour, and creating spaces of opportunity to bring vegetation into the urban fabric.[5] Initiatives like Cornellà Natura, which includes the Alps Avenue project, or the Pinta Verda in Santa Coloma de Gramenet, with Salzereda Avenue as its central element, are examples of how, by harnessing open spaces, we can bring green infrastructure into cities. These kinds of actions, which combine the generation of urban green connectors with the provision of spaces for sustainable mobility, are how we should transform the metropolitan urban territory.

[5] The regeneration of beach dunes or projects focused on riverbanks should also be highlighted as belonging to the realm of open spaces.

The third factor is water management and its role in urban regeneration. There is a water shortage, and we're hoping to fill the city with greenery. So, we need to understand what the most suitable greenery is and how we should manage water to make the most out of it. The idea would be to close the water cycle without the need to connect to either the sewer network or the network of drinking water. In this sense, the Can Bada Park or the Tortuguer Stream are examples of using groundwater for irrigation, where systems have also been built to manage and control rainwater and runoff to increase infiltration into the soil and prevent it from ending up in the sewer network and being lost.

The fourth factor is maintenance, which is essential to meet all the criteria we are talking about so that the spaces can offer maximum benefits. Let's forget about zero maintenance. At the AMB, we're responsible for metropolitan beaches and parks, and we try to reduce the environmental impact of our management by employing sustainability criteria that respect the environment. We avoid artificiality, and we tend towards naturalisation following ecosystemic, biological criteria that enhance biodiversity. We use more resilient native plants to avoid the need for phytosanitary treatments, we employ biological means of pest control, and we simulate natural systems to reduce the frequency of mowing and weeding, while also returning any green waste into the soil.

The fifth factor has to do with construction. What, how, how much, where and why should we be building? Ideally, building nothing is more sustainable than building something, and building less is always the way to go. This is particularly relevant in construction projects, because the most significant ecological footprint of an architectural intervention is determined by decisions related to the site and the functional programme – two issues that directly affect mobility and the built environment. It's also important to find synergies with the surroundings to share or optimise the use and management of water and energy resources. As a result, determining factors include the choice of location, whether or not existing buildings are repurposed, or the optimisation and multiple uses of the spaces that are occupied by facilities.[6] Finally, if we have to build, let's use materials with a minimum carbon footprint, that promote carbon absorption and that combat the heat island effect.

With these ideas in mind and the Protocol as a tool, we are moving towards the metropolitan model that we believe will respond more and more to the real needs of citizens. Earlier on, I said this book was about the past. I've talked about the present and the issues that concern me. But where are we heading? Now I'll try to take a step into the future, towards an immediate future.

The Environmental Sustainability Plan (PSA, for its initials in Catalan)[7] has given us the opportunity to tackle projects that put us on the path toward a more sustainable future. Aside from urban regeneration, the promotion of renewable energies or sustainable mobility, there are two initiatives that exemplify where I think we should be heading.

The first involves climate shelters, an example that offers a direct, immediate response to a growing need, with adaptation to climate change as the goal. The PSA is being used to create a secondary network of local climate shelters.[8] We're talking about accessible spaces that, during episodes of extreme heat, can provide comfort, rest and safety to the population through quality shade, preferably generated by layers of vegetation, permeable soil, air circulation and, if possible, the presence of water. These spaces, which have social, ecological and environmental value, also have a direct link with the renaturalisation of the city. The aim is to identify the places in the urban fabric where they can be implemented.

[6] The Molí building, in Molins de Rei, is one example. The original idea was to build the library on a lot near the former factory. Ultimately, in addition to the library, the building will contain study rooms, exhibition spaces, and other uses open to the public.

[7] The PSA is a €100-million investment plan for municipalities, launched by the AMB in the wake of COVID-19, and which aims to promote projects that improve our surroundings from an environmental perspective.

8 We call it "secondary"
because there is already a
metropolitan network of
climate shelters (XMRC),
which combines municipal
facilities and public spaces
that can provide comfortable
thermal conditions during
episodes of extreme
temperatures.

The second has to do with the questions I mentioned before: what, how, how much, where and why we should build. Under the umbrella of the PSA, we'll implement measures that respond to those questions, and many more, through a project that is transformative from both an environmental and social point of view. The remodel of Can Bertrand, an old industrial colony in Sant Feliu de Llobregat where we will intervene in a 3,800 m² building, is a clear example of the direction our work should be taking. Under the premise of energy efficiency and a minimum carbon footprint, an innovative functional programme will transform the building to house two main uses: a hospitality and tourism school; and a municipal programme to promote agroecology. There will be shared spaces and joint activities, training restaurants run and managed by students, and spaces for outreach. In addition, the participation of agricultural cooperatives from Collserola and the Agricultural Park will allow schools in the municipality to be supplied with local fruits and vegetables, with a shop and convenience store open to residents, and a library and multipurpose spaces. All of this will be spread throughout the public space surrounding the building, thus fostering activity through markets, talks and workshops. In short, it is an ambitious heritage recovery project that follows sustainability criteria with the aim of shaping, disseminating and acting as a catalyst for local agricultural economies. Fantastic!

In the end, it seems like the population at large is becoming increasingly aware of the dramatic situation we are up against. Certainly, there is a growing level of awareness of the climate crisis. But how many of us have changed our habits? We can build sustainable surroundings, with efficient buildings that optimise resources, but if we want to take maximum advantage of them, we need to start living in keeping with those ideas. And that affects everything from waste to sustainable mobility, including how we use and manage spaces. Let's all keep that in mind. There's no point in changing our surroundings if we aren't capable of living in accordance with them.

EVOLUTION OF THE METROPOLITAN SPACES COLLECTION 1989-2022

Metropolitan Public Space
1989-1999

83 projects

Metropolitan Spaces
2000-2004

51 projects

NUMBER OF PROJECTS

1   3   5   7

AWARDS

1 – 1998 Solidaritat Park
FAD Awards. Fostering Arts and Design

2 – 1999 Canyadó Stream Park
Rosa Barba International Landscape Prize

3 – 2004 Torrent d'en Farré Park
Catalan Architecture Exhibition

4 – 2004 AMB wastepaper bin
Delta Awards. ADI-FAD, Industrial Design Association
and Fostering Arts and Design

5 – 2006 Mil·lenari Park
Torsanlorenzo International Prize

6 – 2008 Turó del Sastre Park
Catalan Architecture Exhibition

7 – 2011 Word Search Puzzle, Ramon Fernàndez Jurado Library
ADG Laus Awards. ADG-FAD, Graphic Design
and Visual Communication and Fostering Arts and Design

8 – 2012 Llobregat River Park Signage
ADG Laus Awards. ADG-FAD, Graphic Design
and Visual Communication and Fostering Arts and Design

9 – 2015 RIM-AMB bicycle parking racks
Delta Awards. ADI-FAD, Industrial Design Association
and Fostering Arts and Design

10 – 2015 Els Encants school
FAD Awards. Fostering Arts and Design

11 – 2016 Micro-interventions in the network of metropolitan parks (XPM)
AJAC Awards. Young Architects' Association of Catalonia

12 – 2016 L'Escorxador municipal swimming pool
Catalan Architecture Exhibition

13 – 2016 Joan Oliver Park
FAD Awards. Fostering Arts and Design

14 – 2022 Metropolitan Dunes
New European Bauhaus Prizes

1973 1975 1977 1979 1981 1983 1985 1987 1989 1991 1993 1995 1997 1999 2001 2003 2005

1 **2**   **3** **4**

CMB (Barcelona
Metropolitan
Corporation)

28 municipalities

PGM (Metropolitan
Land Use Plan)

28 municipalities

The CMB
is dissolved
and replaced
by:

→ EMA
(Environmental
Agency) is created
33 municipalities

→ EMT
(Metropolitan
Transport Agency)
18 municipalities

→ MMAMB (Union of
Municipalities of the
Metropolitan Area of Barcelona)
31 municipalities

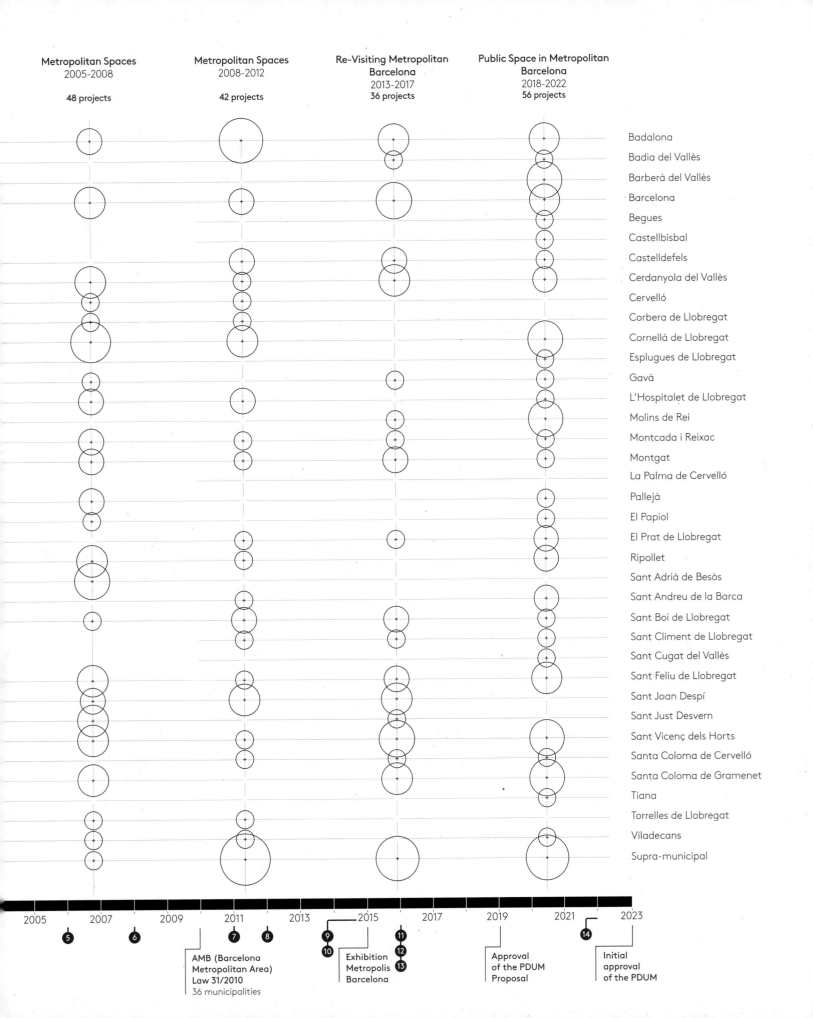

Metropolitan Spaces
2005-2008

48 projects

Metropolitan Spaces
2008-2012

42 projects

Re-Visiting Metropolitan
Barcelona
2013-2017
36 projects

Public Space in Metropolitan
Barcelona
2018-2022
56 projects

Badalona
Badia del Vallès
Barberà del Vallès
Barcelona
Begues
Castellbisbal
Castelldefels
Cerdanyola del Vallès
Cervelló
Corbera de Llobregat
Cornellà de Llobregat
Esplugues de Llobregat
Gavà
L'Hospitalet de Llobregat
Molins de Rei
Montcada i Reixac
Montgat
La Palma de Cervelló
Pallejà
El Papiol
El Prat de Llobregat
Ripollet
Sant Adrià de Besòs
Sant Andreu de la Barca
Sant Boi de Llobregat
Sant Climent de Llobregat
Sant Cugat del Vallès
Sant Feliu de Llobregat
Sant Joan Despí
Sant Just Desvern
Sant Vicenç dels Horts
Santa Coloma de Cervelló
Santa Coloma de Gramenet
Tiana
Torrelles de Llobregat
Viladecans
Supra-municipal

2005   2007   2009   2011   2013   2015   2017   2019   2021   2023

5   6   7   8   9   11   14

10   Exhibition   12
Metropolis   13
Barcelona

AMB (Barcelona
Metropolitan Area)
Law 31/2010
36 municipalities

Approval
of the PDUM
Proposal

Initial
approval
of the PDUM

ORGANISATION CHART

PUBLIC SPACE SERVICES DIRECTORATE

Xavier Segura, director
through August 2019

Albert Gassull, director
from August 2019

Administrative Office
Núria Samsó

Eva Acosta
Raquel García
Marta González
Elena López
Maria Navajas
Flor Racero
Laura Villero

Technical Office of Public Space Management
Javier Duarte

Mònica Arch
Andrea Caparrós
Jose Sánchez

COORDINATION OF MANAGEMENT SERVICES FOR PARKS AND BEACHES
Jordi Bordanove

Mónica Burgos
Aida Girona
Nuria Machuca
Marta Sánchez
Esther Sebastián

Parks Service
Dina Alsawi

— **Office of Installations**
Sara Arguedas

José Antonio Alcaide
Jordi Martínez

— **Office of Gardening**
Jaume Fornés

Cristina García
Ángel Segura

— **Office of Construction and Claims**
Paco Sánchez

— **Office of Civil Works and Furniture**
Eulàlia Codina

Javier López
César Martín
Eduard Redondo

COORDINATION OF THE ARCHITECTURE, ENGINEERING AND LANDSCAPE SERVICES

Architecture, Engineering and Landscape Service I
Francesc Pla Ferrer

— **Architecture Teams**

Helena Arnaste
Aïda Artiz
Rosa Bertran
Laura Castany
Alexandra Ciscar
Laura Coma
Tamie Delgadillo
Verónica Delgado
Carles Español
Laia Ginés
Vera Kolina
Carlos Llinás
Cristina Magallón
Arnau Marimón
Ainhoa Martínez
Moisés Martínez-Lapeña
Roger Méndez
Josep Muxart
Anna Nadeu
Blanca Noguera
Eva Pagés
Cristina Pedreira
Irene Puig
Jordi Rodríguez
Cristina Sáez
Olga Salve
Mar Sierra

— **Engineering Projects and Works Section**
Joaquim Ventura

Jordi Giralt
Martí Magrinyà

Architecture, Engineering and Landscape Service II
Víctor Ortiz

Marc Alemany
Joan Castellví
Oriol Garcia
Albert Nogueras
Oriol Ribera

Former Directorate workers
Mariano de Gracia, service coordinator
José A. Megías, service coordinator

Claudi Aguiló Riu
Eustasio Capilla
Jordi Colom
Jonathan Ibeh Ojei
Esteban Manjón
Mireia Monràs

Antonio Montes
Jordi Navarro
Montserrat Periel
José Antonio Reina
Berta Romeo
Álvaro Sainz

Marina Salvador
Manel Santoyo
Isabel Sebastián
Antonio Vallès
Carles Villasur

Design, Documentation and Communication Section
Noemí Martínez

Virgínia Díaz del Río
Lídia Serrat

— **Office of Design**
Luisa Solsona

Sara Fernandes
Stela Salinas

Beaches Service
Daniel Palacios

Alba Barrera
Marta Cabello
Salvador Clarasó
Estela Guàrdia

Office of Projects for Parks and Beaches
Jona García

Julen Arbelaitz
Montse Garcia
Francesc Pla de Casacuberta
Miquel À. Soriano-Montagut

Quality and Environment Section
Isabel Martín

Rosa María Alcalá
Jordi Arqué
Jaume Campos
Helena Casals
Ana Gracia
Rocío Mesa
Aida Novau
Eric Peramos

Innovation, Technology and Sustainability Service
Eva Bernadí

— **Building Engineering Team**

Albert Dalmau
Mireia Diaz
Margarita Espinós
Laura Gálvez
Marta Iglesias
Marta Juanola
Mònica Mauricio
Maria Sánchez
Núria Saura
Cèlia Viladot

— **BIM Office**
Olga Méliz

Andrea Contreras
Maria Duran

— **Civil Engineering and Topography Section**
Jordi Larruy

David Aguilar
Maria José Alberich
Natalia Castaños
Luisa García
Núria Herrero
Francisco Javier Pérez
Joan Roca
Carlos Utrillo

— **Building Engineering Section**
Gisela Traby

Jonatan Álvarez
Arnau Canyes
Francesc Germà
Oriol Paluzie
Rosa Pla

— **Green Engineering and Biodiversity Section**
Cati Montserrat

Montse Arbiol
Jordi Bardolet
Susana Casino

Sustainable Mobility Interventions Service
Xavier Nogués

Alvar Diego
Nèlida López
Mina Sanatgar
Daniel Vázquez

Interventions for the Environmental Sustainability Plan (PSA)
Francesc Puig

Marta Belando
Virginia Campos
Ricard Coma
Sara Ferrer
Rosa Romero

STUDENTS

Francesc Albert
Albert Alcàzar
Johanna Andrade
Ivan Ballesteros
Maria Barniol
Alba Baroja
Raúl Benítez
Antoni Bisanyes
Bernat Bonet
Faiza Boutabouzi
Genesis Valeria Bravo
Sonia Carazo
Esther Casamayor
Francisco Cespedes
Hind Cheikh Saad Bouh
Joan Cortiella
Jose Costa
Guillem Davila
Laura Deulofeu
Anna Escoda
Ruben Farró
Julio César González
Joana Graells
Martina Griful
Arantxa Guerrero
David Hernández
Katia Hidalgo
Elisabet Huguet
Ana Jiménez
Ruslan Kalachov
Oriol Lafarga
Òscar Latorre
Bruna Lima
Marc Llin
Andrea López
Jenaro López
Dídac Mar

Ester Martí
Ana Alicia Martín
Manel Martínez
Marta Martínez
Joan Miquel
Oriol Montero
Jonathan Monterrey
Laia Montserrat
Mercè Mullerat
Agustín Nahra Abi Samra
Katherine Lizeth Narváez
Arturo Nguema Onufriev
Inmaculada Oliva
Eloi Pallarès
Maria Fernanda Pierre
David Piquer
Mariona Pizarro
Anna Pons
Oriol de Quintana
Lorena Ramírez
Félix Rebollo
Xavier Romera
Alba Rubio
Magdalena Ruiz
Pol Sánchez
Santiago Sauqué
Jorge Scarano
Marianna Sedrakyan
Berta Sellarès
Arnau Soto
Eulàlia Suárez-Fuster
Oriol Vallbona
Andrea Vilar
María Viteri
Jaume Xicola
Arpi Zohrabyan

TECHNICAL TEAM

AMB TEAM

David Aguilar	40, 143 urb, 266 (CS); 260 (CM)
Claudi Aguiló Riu	44, 212, 228, 272 (DCM)
Cinta Alegre	218 (DCA)
Marc Alemany	132, 198 (DCA)
José Alonso	77, 104, 100 (DCM); 91 (DA)
Jonatan Álvarez	234, 238, 244 (INS)
Julen Arbelaitz	186 (DCA)
Montserrat Arbiol	77, 94, 96, 98, 100, 104, 286 (GI)
Sara Arguedas	50, 52, 57, 60, 94, 98, 218 (INS)
Eloi Artau	77, 94, 98, 100, 104 (DA)
Aïda Artiz	173, 234 (DCA)
Jordi Bardolet	52, 132, 164, 180, 186, 244, 288 (GI)
Alba Barrera	81 (DM)
Paula Beltrán	124 (DA)
Rosa Bertran	124 (DCA)
Jordi Bordanove	81 (DM)
Arnau Canyes	234, 238 (INS)
Susana Casino	118, 173, 218, 234, 238 (GI)
Natalia Castaños	52 (CM); 232, 279 (CS)
Joan Castellví	52 (DM); 288 (CM)
Eulàlia Codina	50, 57 (CM)
Jordi Colom	164 (BDT); 186 (PM)
Albert Dalmau	132, 143, 164 (PM); 225 (CM)
Tamie Delgadillo	118, 180, 238 (DCA)
Verónica Delgado	132, 198 (DCA)
Mireia Diaz	124, 135 lib, 164, 198 (PM); 180 (CA)
Virgínia Díaz del Río	186 (DA)
Javier Duarte	164, 260 (DCA)
Julieta Duran	60 (DA)
Carles Español	84, 86, 192 (DCM); 212, 228, 272 (DA)
Sara Fernandes	186 (SIG)
Sara Ferrer	52 (DCM)
Jaume Fornés	50, 57, 60 (GI)
Laura Gálvez	148 (CS); 288 (CM)
Montse Garcia	50, 57 (DCM)
Jona García	50, 57, 60 (DCM); 88 (DA)
Francesc Germà	44, 143, 212, 228, 260, 272 (INS)
Pepe Gil	272 (CA)
Laia Ginés	164, 260 (DCA)
Aida Girona	81 (PP)
Ventura Godoy	186 (CA)
Estela Guàrdia	81 (DM); 88 (CM)
Núria Herrero	222, 234, 282 (CM)
Marta Iglesias	148, 186 (CS)
Marta Juanola	48, 124, 164, 173, 180, 198 (QC); 192, 194 roof (PM); 225 (CM)
Vera Kolina	143 (DCA); 169 (DA)
Jordi Larruy	212, 238, 272, 284 (CM)
Carlos Llinás	118, 180, 238 (DCM)
Nuria Machuca	81 (PP)
Cristina Magallón	52 (DCA)
Arnau Marimón	173 (DCA); 234 (CA)
Ainhoa Martínez	44, 212, 228, 272 (DCA)
Jordi Martínez	50, 57, 60 (INS)
Noemí Martínez	186 (DCM)
Roberto Martínez	77, 104 (INS)
M. Martínez-Lapeña	84, 86, 192 (DCM)
Mònica Mauricio	118, 140, 169, 173 (PM)
Olga Méliz	186 (PM)
Roger Méndez	173, 234 (DCM)
Mireia Monràs	44, 212, 228, 272 (DA); 96, 100, 286 (DCM); 102 (CM)
Antonio Montes	124 (DCM); 232 (DM)
Cati Montserrat	44, 169, 186, 212, 228, 260, 272 (GI)
Aida Munsó	94, 98 (DCM)
Josep Muxart	164, 260 (DCM)
Fco. Javier Navarro	94, 98 (DCM)
Blanca Noguera	143, 169 (DCM)
Albert Nogueras	143, 169 (DA)
Eva Pagés	44, 212, 228, 272 (DCM)
Daniel Palacios	81 (DM)
Oriol Paluzie	140, 148, 164, 169, 186, 238 (INS)
Cristina Pedreira	173 (DCA); 234 (DA)
Montserrat Periel	52 (DCM)
Irene Puig	124 (CA)
Albert Puigdellívol	77 (CM); 96, 100, 104 (DCA)
Yéssica Ramajo	96 (DCA)
Ferran Roca	118 (DCA); 180, 238 (DA)
Joan Roca	218 (CM)
Adriana Rodríguez	91 (DA)
Berta Romeo	143, 169 (DA)
Cristina Sáez	218 (DCM)
Álvaro Sainz	52 (BDT); 77, 96, 104 (DCA); 91 (DCM); 135 urb (CS)
Stela Salinas	186 (SIG)
Marina Salvador	132, 198 (DCM)
Maria Sánchez	44 (BDT); 124, 173, 180 (PM); 228 (CM)
Paco Sánchez	50 (BDT); 48 (PM), 60 (CM)
Núria Saura	244 (CS)
Lídia Serrat	186 (SIG)
Mar Sierra	169 (CA)
Luisa Solsona	186 (DCM)
M. À. Soriano-Montagut	50, 57 (DCA)
Gisela Traby	173, 192, 194, 198 (INS)
Daniel Vázquez	212, 228, 272 (DCA)
Carlos Villasur	135 (INS)

PARTICIPATING COMPANIES

AB Paisatgistes	222 (GI)
ABM Consulting	96 (DCA)
AIA Instal·lacions Arquitectòniques	48, 140 (INS)
Ángel Gil Control y Gestión	148 (BDT)
AR47	225, 282 (DCM)
Arau Acustica	132, 186 (ACU)
AT3 Oller-Peña	194 (CM)
Atis Obres i Projectes	246 (BDT)
AVANT	236 (INS)
AYESA	104 (DA)
BAC	77, 91 (CA); 86 (STE)
Baena Casamor Arquitectes BCQ	48 (DCM)
Batlleiroig	40, 266 (DCM)
BBG Estructures	84, 132, 198 (STE)
Bernuz-Fernández Arquitectes	135 lib, 222 (STE)
BEST Costales-Jaén	169 (STE)
BIS structures	228 (STE)
B-lap	282 (GI)
Bosch&Ventayol	52 (GEO)
Brufau Cusó	34 (CM); 275 (BDT)
BT arquitectes	232 (CM)
Calderon-Folch Studio	34 (CM)
Carles Enrich Studio	275 (DCM)
Carles Montobbio i Associats	148 (PM)
Clase	88 (DM)
Col·lectiu Brusi	135 (DCM)
Cómo Design Studio	180 (SIG)
COTCA	140 (STE)
CTP 1999	94, 98 (STE, CA); 260 (DA)
DATAAE	34 (DCM)
Dopec	132 (INS)
DSM Arquitectes	148 (STE)
E3 Solinteg	135 gar (CM)
Ecivil Enginyeria	34 (STE)
Eletresjota	173, 222, 236 (INS); 279 (INS, STE)
Enginyeria Reventós	135 gar (STE)
Eprototips	84 (PTE)
Eskubi Turró Arquitectes	124, 140, 164, 282 (STE)
Factors de Paisatge	246 (GI)
Franc Fernández Arquitectura	246 (DCM)
Fustes Borniquel	48 (STE)
ICA Grupo	124, 143, 164, 241 (INS)
Infraestructures de Muntanya	91 (DCM)
Ingenieros Asociados	225 (HYD)
INTEC, Gestión Integral de Proyectos	173 (STE)
Ivana Rossell Acústica	132, 164 (ACU)
JBP Enginyeria	91 (DCA)
Joan Gonzalez Gou	118, 132, 169, 180, 186 (INS)
JPAM City Makers	194 (DCM)

JSS Efficient Engineering	246 (INS)
JZ Paisatge i Arquitectura	244 (DCM)
MA+SA arquitectura	275 (STE)
Maira Arquitectes	236 (DM)
Manuel Arguijo y asociados	143, 186 (STE)
March-Rius Arquitectes Tècnics	279 (CM)
Martí Cabestany i Puértolas	118, 180 (STE)
Masala Consultors	192, 194 (DCM, STE); 246 (STE)
Meritxell Inaraja Arquitecta	140, 148 (DCM)
MOR arquitectura tècnica	241 (CM)
MOSE Serveis d'Enginyeria	194 (INS)
Mur Arquitectura	124 (INS)
MVA Arquitectura Estructura	236 (STE)
Naturalea	96 (GI)
Naxal Arquitectura	135 lib (BDT)
Oriol Vidal Enginyeria	135 lib (INS)
Otherstructures	91 (DA)
Patrimoni 2.0	140 (COS)
Peris+Toral Arquitectes	173 (DA); 222 (DCM)
PFP, disseny	118, 124, 164 (SIG)
Pi Enginyeria Civil i Urbanisme	52 (STE); 286 (CA)
Proarquitectura	192 (CM)
Proido Consultors	44 (CM); 102 (CA)
Proiectum	212 (SAN)
Santacreu-Moliner	288 (DCM)
SBS Simón i Blanco	40, 266 (INS); 102 (DM); 232 (DCM); 236 (CM, INS)
SCOB Arquitectura i Paisatge	284 (DCM)
Societat Orgànica	143, 186, 234 (SUS)
STATIC Ingeniería	286 (STE)
TECTRAM Enginyers	173 (INS)
Teyle	148 (INS)
TRAM	275 (CM)
UTE CSS Espai Públic	91 (HS)
VVV Proyectos y Servicios con Ingenio	212 (STE); 236 (BDT)
Zeb3consulting	135 lib (SUS)

COLLABORATORS

Eulalia Aran	34 (BDT)
Eva Blanco	44 (CM); 288 (BDT)
Laura Coll	180 (DA)
Josep Cónsola	286 (GI)
Gemma Domingo	186 (DA)
Salva Fàbregas	88 (DM)
Lucía Feu	169 (DA)
Pepe Gil	212 (CM)
Nuno Paiva de Almeida	104 (GI)
Ariadna Perich	279 (DCM)
Jordi Pruna	212 (DA)
Joan Antoni Rodon	140 (BDT)
Crisant Romans	186 (FUR); 241 (DCM)
Lourdes Romeo	244 (INS)
Elisabeth Torregrosa	244 (BDT)
Carmela Torró	244 (STE)
Xavier Vendrell	34 (DM)
Roser Vives	34 (GI)
Gerard Yubero	284 (CM)
Anna Zahonero	135 (GI)

LEGEND

ACU	Acoustics	FUR	Furniture	SAN	Sanitation		
BDT	Budgeting	GEO	Geology	SIG	Signage		
CA	Construction assistance	GI	Green infrastructure	STE	Structural engineering		
CM	Construction management	HS	Health and safety	SUS	Sustainability		
COS	Colour studies	HYD	Hydraulic works				
CS	Construction supervision	INS	Installations	lib	Library		
DA	Design assistance	PM	Project management	roof	Roof		
DCA	Design and construction assistance	PP	Participatory program	gar	Garden		
DCM	Design and construction management	PTE	Prototype engineering	urb	Urbanisation		
DM	Design management	QC	Quality control				

CREDITS

EDITED BY

Barcelona Metropolitan Area (AMB)

EDITORIAL BOARD

Ramon M. Torra, *director AMB*
Albert Gassull, *director of Public Space Services, AMB*

EDITORIAL DIRECTION

Noemí Martínez
Luisa Solsona
Design, Documentation and Communication Section, AMB

Isabel Clos
Editorial Management Office, AMB

CONTENT COORDINATION

Luisa Solsona
Sara Fernandes
Design, Documentation and Communication Section, AMB

INTERVIEWS

Anatxu Zabalbeascoa

ADAPTATION OF PROJECT REPORTS

Isabel Clos

ESSAYS

Ramon M. Torra
Xavier Mariño
Albert Gassull

BLUEPRINT REDRAWING

Sara Fernandes
Katherine Narváez
Design, Documentation and Communication Section, AMB

Mercè Mullerat
Júlia Dubois
Víctor Rufart

EDITORIAL DEVELOPMENT

Ricardo Devesa
Marta Bugés
Actar Publishers

GRAPHIC DESIGN AND LAYOUT

Ramon Prat
Olga Pipnik
Actar Publishers

Àngels Soler

TRANSLATION

Angela Kay Bunning

PROOFREADING

Editorial Management Office, AMB

PRINTING AND BINDING

Arlequin & Pierrot, Barcelona

GRAPHIC MATERIAL

© of the photographs:

Jon Arruti	232-233, 238-240
Borja Ballbé	65
Víctor Bello	97 (top left)
Toni Bernat	201
Benoit Billard	249
Gabriele Bortoluzzi	236-237
Quim Bosch	244-245, 284-285
Josep Cano	95 (top)
Josep Casanova	192-193, 225-227, 282-283
Judith Casas	104-105
Cómo Design Studio	185 (top)
Andrés Flajszer	246-247
Simón García	132-134, 143-147, 169-172, 198-199, 225-227
Adrià Goula	34-39, 84-85, 87 (top), 88-90, 94-95, 98-99, 135-139, 140-142, 148-149, 241-243, 260-265, 275-278
Marcela Grassi	48-49, 118-123, 164-168, 173-179, 180-185
Joan Guillamat	50-51, 97 (top right and bottom), 286-287, 288-289
José Hevia	186-193, 222-224, 279-281
Imma Jansana	23
Benjamin McMahon	107
Gemma Miralda	57-59
Santiago Periel	52-56
Robert Ramos	59, 81-83, 102-103
María José Reyes	60-63
Stela Salinas	30, 72, 114, 131 (top), 158, 191 (top), 256
Jordi Surroca	40-43, 124-131, 194-197
Jordi Surroca i Gael del Río	218-221, 266-271
Jeroen Van Mieghem	44-47, 208, 212-217, 228-231, 272-274
Juan Carlos Vega	151
Xuan Yin	96-97

© of the blueprints: AMB

© of the drawings and illustrations:

Àngels Soler	14-15, 290-291, 296-297, 298-299
DATAAE	36, 37
Antonio Montes	130
Carlos Llinás	119

© of the edition: AMB

© of the texts: their authors

Printed in Europe
Barcelona, April 2023

ACKNOWLEDGMENTS

Master Plan Drafting Service, AMB

Urban Planning Coordination, AMB

General Coordination of Innovation and Infrastructures, AMB

The AMB is especially grateful for the participation of:

Claudi Aguiló Riu
Iñaki Alday
David Chipperfield
Antoni Farrero
Josep Ferrando
Beth Galí
Imma Jansana
Margarita Jover
Paul Lecroart
Carlos Llinás
Cati Montserrat
Javier Ortigosa
Eva Pagés
Oriol Ribera

DISTRIBUTION

Actar D, Inc. New York, Barcelona

New York
440 Park Avenue South, 17th Floor
New York, NY 10016
T +1 212 966 22 07
salesnewyork@actar-d.com

Barcelona
C/ Roca i Batlle, 2-4
08023 Barcelona
T +34 93 328 21 83
eurosales@actar-d.com

Barcelona Metropolitan Area
C/62, 16-18 (Zona Franca)
08040 Barcelona
T +34 93 223 51 51
www.amb.cat

DL: B 4945-2023
ISBN: 978-84-87881-51-0

This book is also available in Catalan and Spanish:

L'espai públic de la Barcelona metropolitana. Intervencions i converses 2018-2022
ISBN: 978-84-87881-49-7

Espacio público en la Barcelona metropolitana. Intervenciones y diálogos 2018-2022
ISBN: 978-84-87881-50-3

FOREST STEWARDSHIP COUNCIL

Paper 100% Recycled
Supported by certifications

This book is printed on
Nautilus Classic paper 120 g/m²